MW00783453

Change Agents

Change Agents

Transforming Schools From the Ground Up

Justin Cohen

FOR INFORMATION:

Corwin
A SAGE Company
2455 Teller Road
Thousand Oaks, California 91320
(800) 233-9936
www.corwin.com

SAGE Publications Ltd.
1 Oliver's Yard
55 City Road
London EC1Y 1SP
United Kingdom

SAGE Publications India Pvt. Ltd.
B 1/I 1 Mohan Cooperative Industrial Area
Mathura Road, New Delhi 110 044
India

SAGE Publications Asia-Pacific Pte. Ltd.
18 Cross Street #10-10/11/12
China Square Central
Singapore 048423

President: Mike Soules
Vice President and
  Editorial Director: Monica Eckman
Program Director and
  Publisher: Dan Alpert
Acquisitions Editor II: Megan Bedell
Senior Content
  Development Editor: Lucas Schleicher
Associate Content
  Development Editor: Mia Rodriguez
Editorial Assistant: Natalie Delpino
Project Editor: Amy Schroller
Copy Editor: Amy Hanquist Harris
Typesetter: C&M Digitals (P) Ltd.
Proofreader: Rae-Ann Goodwin
Indexer: Integra
Cover Designer: Gail Buschman
Marketing Manager: Melissa Duclos

Copyright © 2023 by Corwin Press, Inc.

All rights reserved. Except as permitted by U.S. copyright law, no part of this work may be reproduced or distributed in any form or by any means, or stored in a database or retrieval system, without permission in writing from the publisher.

When forms and sample documents appearing in this work are intended for reproduction, they will be marked as such. Reproduction of their use is authorized for educational use by educators, local school sites, and/or noncommercial or nonprofit entities that have purchased the book.

All third-party trademarks referenced or depicted herein are included solely for the purpose of illustration and are the property of their respective owners. Reference to these trademarks in no way indicates any relationship with, or endorsement by, the trademark owner.

Printed in the United States of America

ISBN 9781071875780

This book is printed on acid-free paper.

22 23 24 25 26 10 9 8 7 6 5 4 3 2 1

DISCLAIMER: This book may direct you to access third-party content via Web links, QR codes, or other scannable technologies, which are provided for your reference by the author(s). Corwin makes no guarantee that such third-party content will be available for your use and encourages you to review the terms and conditions of such third-party content. Corwin takes no responsibility and assumes no liability for your use of any third-party content, nor does Corwin approve, sponsor, endorse, verify, or certify such third-party content.

Contents

Acknowledgments

First things first, thanks to my crew: Cynthia Ho taught me ROCI; Jesse Hineuber shot down my worst ideas and improved my best ones; Brian Edwards orchestrated a transformative feedback process; Carol Whang kept us focused; Sanee Nashashibi indulged my love for words; and Chris Thorn brimmed with an infectious love for inquiry. I am in awe of the whole PSI team, especially Derek Mitchell, who saw the immense transformative potential of this project from the jump and whose thoughtful leadership continues to upend oppressive systems.

I am indebted to the team at Corwin for helping this text flourish at each stage. Dan Alpert is a brilliant, generous editor who knew how and where to push; Megan Bedell helped me make some of the hardest editorial decisions I've ever confronted; and Luke Schleicher brought focus and levity to the process. Thanks to everyone on the production, marketing, and design teams for making the final product shine.

Shout out, also, to the village that supported my growth as a writer and storyteller. Susannah Breslin, Matt Young, and the Carey Institute crew showed me how the pros do it. Kei Williams, RV Dougherty, Sanda Balaban, Chris Stewart, Abby Smith, Paul O'Neill, Anthony Wilson, Chris Gibbons, Chaz Brown, Lea Crusey, Sharhonda Bossier, and many others encouraged even my most eccentric projects. Mon Mohapatra, as usual, was a creative inspiration who turned this book's visuals into art.

Public school teachers are the beating heart behind this book: both the ones who generously shared their stories and those who taught me to think critically. Thanks especially to the late Louis Fuller (ninth grade), who taught me I shared a birthday with John Brown's raid, and to Lori Osler (first grade), who made me write a less vitriolic second draft of an impassioned letter to the editor of *Weekly Reader*.

The most important educator in my life, though, continues to be my mom, Joy, who brings every ounce of her namesake to life. Now that

I'm a parent, my father Alan is more than ever a model of kindness and generosity who astonishes me always. Thanks to my sister Lindsay for being a lifetime bestie; and to the ancestors who are no longer with us— my grandfather Erling's autographed copy of *Savage Inequalities* loomed large on the shelf beside me as I wrote this book.

Finally, thank you to my partner, Sheila, a perfect human, and to our daughter, Azad. Our love has made me strong enough to do the things I've always wanted to do, but couldn't before.

Publisher's Acknowledgments

Corwin gratefully acknowledges the contributions of the following reviewers:

Waldo V. Alvarado
Director of Equity and Diversity
Reading School District
Reading, PA

Patricia Baker
School Board
Culpeper County
    Public Schools
Culpeper, VA

Natalie Bernasconi
Educator
UCSC, Salinas Union HSD
Salinas, CA

D. Allan Bruner
Retired Science/Math Educator
Colton High School
Colton, OR

Rebecca Cohen
School Counselor
Portland Public Schools
Portland, OR

Jayne Ellspermann
CEO and Founder
Jayne Ellspermann, LLC
Ocala, FL

Heidi Guadagni
Learning Specialist
West Linn-Wilsonville
    School District
Wilsonville, OR

Shannon Hobbs-Beckley
Director of Teaching
    and Learning
The American School
    of Sao Paulo
Sao Paulo, Brazil

Scott Hollinger
P–20 Educator
Teachers College Columbia
    University; Capella University;
    Hollinger Education
    Consultants
McAllen, TX

Jessica Johnson
Secondary Principal,
    Adjunct Professor
Dodgeland School District,
    Viterbo University
Juneau, WI

Lynn Macan
Retired Superintendent
    of Schools
Cobleskill-Richmondville CSD
Cobleskill, NY

Debra Paradowski
Associate Principal
Arrowhead Union High School
Hartland, WI

Betty Rivinus
TOSA Special Education
Canby School District
Canby, OR

Lena Marie Rockwood
Assistant Principal, High School
Revere Public Schools
Revere, MA

About the Author

Justin Cohen (he/him/his) is a writer, organizer, activist, and dad. His work explores how education, race, privilege, and public policy intersect. He cofounded Wayfinder Foundation and Neighbors Reimagining Public Safety. He is on the board of Friends of Abolitionist Place, helping to create a heritage center in downtown Brooklyn, committed to preserving radical liberation traditions. Justin has organized with No New Jails NYC, Racial Justice BK, Brooklyn Shows Love, WE ARE Educators for Justice, and others. His writing has appeared in *The New York Times*, *Stanford Social Innovation Review*, *Bklyner*, *Bright*, *Education Week*, *Education Next*, and elsewhere. He has been an organizer in residence at Civic Hall and a writer in residence at the Carey Institute for the Global Good. He served on the education policy committee for Barack Obama's 2008 presidential campaign and has a BA in cognitive science from Yale. This is his first book.

Introduction

by Derek Mitchell

A book about the power of public school teachers and leaders using improvement science to bring about educational equity needs to begin with gratitude.

- If you are a teacher providing excellent instruction, optimism, and love to your students as you fight the tremendous headwinds of the three pandemics—COVID-19, poverty, and racism—thank you.

- If you are a leader striving to meet the needs of students and their families in some of our country's most challenged communities, thank you.

- If you are a district leader buffeted by insufficient investment and heightened expectations on our nation's public schools while trying to manage politics, deliver high-quality support to schools, and sustain your team members, thank you.

- If you are a community member trying to improve schools by tirelessly attending school board meetings and bringing the truth of your lived experience to those often-charged discussions, thank you.

- If you are a parent with concerns about your neighborhood school—but you enroll your child there anyway because you believe in public education—and fight to make the school better, thank you.

This book is a love letter to all of you, to show you that you are seen, your efforts are valued, and your voices are being heard. The COVID-19 pandemic has created a new appreciation of the critical role that our public schools play in all aspects of our society's health and well-being. Many who didn't see it before now understand the important role that our public schools play in shoring up our democracy. At the same time, we are also clear that our public schools have not yet lived up to their tremendous promise.

There are many reasons for this, the biggest being that society keeps moving the goalposts for what we expect from our educators. We ask a great deal from you—now more than anyone ever imagined with COVID-19 still roiling after nearly three years. We look to schools to solve what we often lack the will to properly face in other venues. And we consistently underresource public schools, asking those who work in and around them to take up the slack the best they can. Implementing desegregation efforts, fighting poverty, supporting Americans with disabilities, helping English language learners, fighting gang violence, preventing teen pregnancy, integrating technology, embracing LGBTQIA+ students, and, most recently, accommodating various public health strategies and beliefs during a global pandemic—the list goes on and on. Each of these efforts in the last 80 years to make public schools, and therefore our society, more welcoming and inclusive has required new knowledge, new skills, and new resources for those who work in our schools.

Yet we have never afforded schools sufficient time to master each new expectation before we pile on the next. It is an endless cycle. New, higher expectations are followed by a shortage of resources needed to meet them, leading to a general failure of schools to meet those expectations, followed by blame and castigation.

Just because our public schools are our country's best strategy for producing the healthy, vibrant, and egalitarian democratic society that most of us envision—a lively, loving, learning environment in every single neighborhood in our country—does not mean that schools are the reason for our inability to achieve that ambition.

The never-ending loop of expectations and blame is a trap for teachers and leaders in our most challenged schools. Those of us who have spent decades working in schools know that it doesn't have to be this way. Our work at Partners in School Innovation during the past 30 years proves it.

Partners was founded in 1993 to support Bay Area public schools serving predominantly poor students of color and English language learners in their efforts to achieve educational excellence. Core to our founding principles was an unwavering faith that the communities we serve *can and will* deliver for their families if supported and resourced properly to do so. Now some 30 years later, we still believe in the unique promise of public education to help each of us reach our full potential.

Although a great deal has changed since our founding, unfortunately too much remains stubbornly the same. Students of color from underserved backgrounds remain relegated to the back of the bus of educational opportunity. Teacher turnover is high; the political will to dramatically change the conditions is low. These schools receive less than 70 percent of what is spent on the public schools serving wealthy families, and yet expectations have never been more complex, the prospects of meeting those expectations never more complicated.

Partners has contributed, though, in a small way to one important thing that *has* changed.

We now *know* that chronic underperformance by students in the most challenged schools can be effectively and sustainably addressed. Partners has spent the last 30 years developing, refining, testing, and then expanding the implementation of an improvement science approach that has been shown to move these schools decidedly from the worst performers in their districts to on par with their peers. We've accomplished this in the most challenged urban centers—such as our home communities in the San Francisco Bay Area—and in other contexts far from our home, including the Mississippi Delta, western Michigan, and the home of our nation's founding, Philadelphia, Pennsylvania. More importantly, we accomplished this working within districts' rules, support structures, resource practices, and school models rather than relying upon the more disruptive but typically less lasting and less sustainable "reforms." We got results by pouring into the teachers and leaders already serving in these schools—those showing up every day to deliver for other people's children against sometimes tremendous headwinds.

The foundational learning from spending all that time, effort, energy, and resources has been at once illuminating and obvious: Positive results really come down to investing in people. Everything we did only mattered because of what it *enabled teachers and leaders themselves* to do.

Our experiences remind us that education is a profoundly human enterprise—encompassing relationship-building, motivation, beliefs, and trust. Tragically, these needs are typically given short shrift by policymakers, as if improvement is something done by robots disembodied from the complexity of the communities in which they work.

Yet understanding a school's context and knowing the needs of its students and families have been shown to be key to successful improvement efforts. This is why brilliant thinkers, from Jonathan Kozol to Jeannie Oakes to Rudy Crew to Zaretta Hammond, have cautioned those who support schools to deeply understand the people and places where they work. Partners in School Innovation leans heavily on the writings of these leaders and many others, as you'll see in the following chapters, and this book perhaps contributes a new potentially catalytic insight about the power of improvement science when focused on low-income communities of color.

This brings up a second learning from our decades of self-improvement work: implementing continuous improvement methods without a clear focus on equity simply supercharges and codifies opportunity gaps. We learned that maintaining a focus on equitable outcomes, and not just measurable improvement, requires getting much better at supporting schools in having frank conversations about the impact of racial oppression on their students, systems, and even on themselves. We recognized that our team can't help schools get better at facing this conundrum without having those conversations and challenging one another to face biases within ourselves.

This book is an extension of that challenge, urging educators to own the power of being leaders of change—not protectors of cherished pasts, but forgers of a new more powerful future for us all. To be a change agent requires facing your own personal truths about teaching and leading across lines of difference. This means understanding and embarking on your own equity journey, a process that everyone at Partners undertakes and which every educator featured in this book also has begun to do.

My own equity journey started in middle school on Chicago's west side in one of the city's since-shuttered K–8 schools, Robert Emmet Elementary. Like many of America's schools now, Emmett's student population mirrored the neighborhood, but the staff at the school did not. The students were all Black, like me, and our teachers were almost all white. Aside from occasionally wondering why these folks who obviously didn't live in the neighborhood drove from wherever to teach us, this didn't bother me as a kid because the teachers and leaders at Emmett paid me a lot of attention. I was that kid who tested well, talked a lot, and read the encyclopedia for fun, so I got a lot of positive reinforcement from teachers and especially the principal. The school staff worked extra hard to provide me with opportunities to be "challenged." One such opportunity started me on my path to fighting for equity: an invitation to attend a science fair on the other side of town.

As a middle schooler, I had read somewhere that if we had a nuclear war, nothing but cockroaches would survive. This, for some reason, fascinated me. So I began a series of experiments to determine just what circumstances cockroaches could survive. I won't gross you out with the details, except to say my very thorough experiments came to an abrupt halt when my mother, looking for leftovers to heat up, discovered the Tupperware container filled with my research "subjects" in the freezer. But before my research was abruptly shut down, I gave a class show-and-tell of my findings that was so much fun for my teacher that she and the principal managed to get me an invite to an official science fair at a middle school on Chicago's north side.

This led to my mother and me, one early Saturday morning, taking a bus, a train, and another bus to a part of the city that I had never seen before. My mom dutifully carried my huge posterboard, which had dead roaches pinned above Polaroids and descriptions of my experiments.

As we got closer to the school where the competition was to take place, I was over the moon, seeing impossibly clean neighborhoods lined with trees and parks and beautiful homes braced with flower gardens. I kept asking my mom if we were still in Chicago.

When we arrived at the competition site, I was dumbfounded. We stood on the street looking at a majestic castle of a building surrounded by lawns on all sides, with a large garden on one corner, and additional playing fields out back. I had never seen a school that looked like this. I was expecting a place like Emmet: a factory-looking squarish building with gated windows and a mixture of concrete and tarmac on all sides.

Once inside, my awe continued as we joined others in line and followed the signs to the "science wing" of the school. This school had a science wing. Emmet didn't even have science classrooms. We passed students with their parents carrying everything under the sun as part of their own presentations, and almost all of the students wore lab coats with their schools' names on them. One student was carefully floating a helium balloon model of the space shuttle as his dad followed behind, pushing the tank of helium. Another had a model volcano on a rolling platform and was getting help from several people to maneuver it through double doors. I watched it pass by and looked at the posterboard my mother held and felt a pit open in my stomach.

Once in the lab, my mom checked us in, and we found the spot assigned to us. The huge, high-ceiling classroom had built-in lab stations lining the walls, all with running water, shelves, beakers, bottles filled with various substances, and, to my amazement, working gas burners. I imagined running my experiments there and not in the kitchen while my ma was sleeping. The other kids' experiments left me in a state of wonder: a fully dissected and autopsied pig, an aquarium designed to demonstrate a squid's ink-based protection mechanisms, and live snakes and ants, all of which I contrasted with my posterboard of dead roaches, which seemed pitiful in contrast.

In watching all the students set up their exhibits, it occurred to me suddenly that all of them were white. My mom and I were the only Black people in the room. My young mind started putting it all together then: Why does this school have rolling fields of green grass and Emmet is hemmed in by tarmac? Why do these kids get science lab coats? How does this school get a science wing with well-equipped classrooms when Emmet barely has paper and chalk (which our teachers would regularly buy with their own money midway through the year when initial supplies ran out)?

I looked again at my poster going up—that I was so proud of just a few moments ago—against all of the other exhibits, and I felt . . . well, shame. Which was followed quickly by anger. Burning, roiling, visceral anger.

Even then, I knew that pipes for water and gas didn't grow like vines. Someone decided to build these schools this way, which meant they also decided to build our school without them.

I asked my mom a critical question: "Ma, why do white people get to have gas burners in their science classes, and we don't even get science classrooms?"

My mom had finished setting up my presentation and was looking around at the happy, vibrant, and fun displays as they were going up. I tugged on her sleeve to get her attention, and she looked at me and replied, "I don't know, baby, but that's not what we're supposed to be worried about right now. You're supposed to be here to talk about cockroaches."

That's what I did. And for the young budding scientists, many of whom had never seen roaches up close before, or ever, my presentation was a big hit. But even as I grew more confident as I told and retold my learning story, I also felt somehow lessened by the experience.

On the long ride home, with my honorable-mention certificate, I wondered if the whole thing had been a setup. I wondered how people believed so little in the students at my school and apparently so much in the students on the northside of town. I knew even then it had to do with race, and it seemed deeply unfair to me. "Who decided this," I wondered, "and how do we make them reconsider?"

I returned to Emmet that Monday, and the principal treated me like a returning hero, announcing over the intercom my success and posting the certificate in the office award case for a time. I took the praise a little grudgingly and felt I needed to ask her about my experience.

I described for her what I saw, how I felt, and what I thought it meant. She sat in a chair next to me and took my hands in hers, and before I knew it, I was crying. To this day, I'm not sure why, but the combination of my shame and her comforting me made it all come out. She hugged me as I sobbed for a while, and after a bit, she said through her own tears, "You're right, it isn't fair. I honestly don't know how things got this way, but maybe you'll be the one to fix it."

Looking back some 45 years later, I see that my equity journey began at that moment.

I know from personal experience that inside each of our children are multitudes of powerful positive futures. I know that all children, yes even—maybe particularly—the distracted and angry and unengaged ones, have the potential for brilliance and that our schools are our keys to unlocking that brilliance.

Our public school systems have built-in inequities, much like those in the aforementioned science labs, and the challenge of dismantling those structures is larger than any one teacher, principal, school, or district. But the truth is that teachers and leaders are the most underestimated force for transformational change in our country. They are already everywhere where improvement is needed. They are at the needed scale, equipped with a will to serve, and possess a myriad of competencies that position them to build relationships needed for lasting community transformation.

We have used our school transformation approach—which is illustrated in the stories in this book—to support schools and districts in eight states. The work is powerful, and the results speak for themselves. Our approach is symbolized by the following graphic, and we organized the book by prioritizing the center circle of the graphic, which is the core work that educators conduct with students and their families.

School Transformation Framework

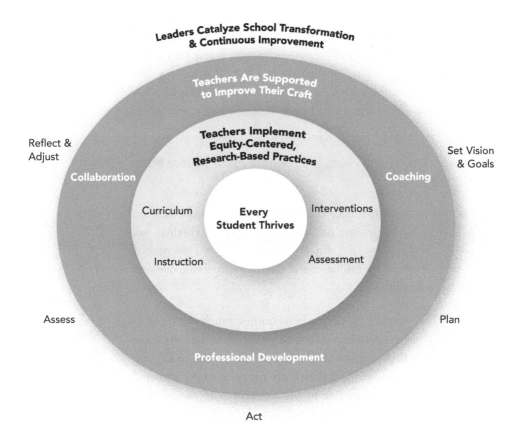

The book begins with equity-centered teaching. Chapters 1 through 4 describe work in the innermost ring, where teachers implement practices that research has shown to be effective with low-income students of color. This is the driving force upon which broader systemic efforts must be based.

In Chapters 5 through 8 you will see school leaders and instructional coaches tackling the work in the next ring, producing a system of professional learning built on collaboration, professional development, and coaching.

The final three chapters, 9 through 11, focus on leaders at the school and district level establishing a continuous improvement method and mindset among their teams, as well as the benefits that arise from doing so.

All of these stories from real people—focusing on real problems within the very real constraints of their varied contexts—hold the ultimate message of this powerful work:

As we wake up from the nightmare of the pandemic, when everything seems to be unraveling and uncertainty is at its highest and hope at its dimmest, we see that the solution to producing schools that meet the needs of each of our children—schools that are lively, loving, learning communities—remains where it has always been. Teachers and leaders who show up every day, even risking their lives and the health of their families to pour into the children of our communities, *are* the solution.

You know that your communities are reeling from the difficulties of the last few years. You know that the political volatility and open hostility have nerves frayed and students, parents, and even your peers on edge. You know that many in your community have lost someone, lost their careers, lost their faith in our institutions, lost their connection to the community itself, or just lost hope.

You don't know what to do or where to start, yet kids are looking to you to help them heal and learn. Read on and you will find that, for our students with the greatest needs, you and your peers *are* the sources of hope you have been looking for.

Derek Mitchell has been the CEO of Partners in School Innovation since 2009. Before taking that position, he earned a PhD in educational psychology from UCLA; served as the director of technology and student achievement for the Oakland Unified School District in California; supported districtwide reform across the country for the Stupski Foundation; and was the executive director of the Opportunity Zone in Prince George's County in Maryland.

Under Derek's leadership of "Partners," the organization has adapted to a dynamic educational landscape and grown to address an expanding need for equity-centered school improvement. Partners has joined with national funders such as the Bill & Melinda Gates Foundation, the W. K. Kellogg Foundation, and the W. Clement & Jessie V. Stone Foundation to help educators build their capacity to serve some of the most challenged communities in the United States. Along the way, Dr. Mitchell has published reflections about Partners' work in a variety of journals and blogs, such as *Phi Delta Kappan,* EdSource, and *Leadership* magazine.

Are You a
Change Agent?

1

CÉSAR CHÁVEZ ELEMENTARY SCHOOL, SAN JOSE, CALIFORNIA

The mood in the teachers' lounge at César Chávez Elementary School was, in a word, skeptical.

And to be honest, kind of exhausted.

The three educators who made up the school's fourth-grade teaching team sat at a small table, eating their respective lunches, while sharing ambivalent glances between bites.

It was rare for teachers to dine together at Chávez, as the school had become a challenging place to work. It was the fall of 2010, and since the late 1990s, state officials in California had labeled this little school in East San Jose as "persistently failing." The school shared this strange label with hundreds of schools in California, not to mention thousands more across the country. Almost all of such schools served children and families whose identities were already marginalized by powerful institutions.

After two decades of government scolding and sanction, the teachers still in the building were either stalwarts or newbies, and almost nothing in between. Teaching at Chávez meant that you were either ruthlessly dedicated to serving the community's children or didn't yet understand the waters into which you were wading.

The reality of this situation sat uneasily on the fourth-grade teachers, who munched on an array of homemade sandwiches and mini carrots

(Continued)

11

(Continued)

and yogurt cups, making nervous chitchat while they waited for a "guest" who was set to arrive any minute now.

The guest for whom they waited was supposed to help them navigate the complexities of school transformation, but if history was any indication, they were bound to be disappointed. Decades of empirical evidence and sociological study indicated that schools like Chávez needed more and different resources to best serve students. Federal and state school improvement policy, on the other hand, tended to ignore and minimize this reality. The fourth-grade team had witnessed, firsthand, many years of lawmaking that eschewed empirical research, while embracing the questionable logic that increasingly draconian sanctions would drive school improvement.

Adding insult to injury, these sorts of sanctions for struggling schools were preceded by decades of disinvestment in the public sector at large, leaving schools to act as the primary locus of public services for families, in lieu of an actual social safety net.

Hence, their skepticism.

These esoteric policy concerns, though, on most days only constituted background noise. While teachers at Chávez and other schools toiled to improve outcomes for children, the message that came through above the noise, often at a fever pitch, was that educators themselves were to blame for these decades of multidimensional institutional failure.

Bad test scores? "Blame the teachers!" Pandemic-induced school closures? "Blame the teachers!"

But what if both test scores and unsafe conditions in public schools are the consequence of centuries of racial segregation, propagated by an unjust housing market and compounded by decades of civic divestment and systemic mismanagement?

"You must not have heard us. BLAME THE TEACHERS!"

The fourth-grade teachers at Chávez had, in fact, heard.

They were used to hearing all of this—and worse—but they patiently, and somewhat dubiously, waited for the person who was scheduled to join them for lunch on this particular day.

The guest for whom they waited for was a former teacher in the district named Meaghen. Meaghen also was anxious about the meeting. She had been brought back to the school, through a partnership with a local nonprofit organization, to serve as a coach. In the preceding weeks, she had attempted to make herself feel at home at Chávez, but because of space constraints, she was working out of a repurposed supply closet that smelled like lunchroom detritus. When she tried to hide the smell by spraying ridiculous quantities of "Paradise Breeze" air freshener, the closet ended up smelling like "Paradise Breeze"-scented trash.

Meaghen had been introduced to the teachers at a faculty meeting the week before by René Sanchez, the principal, who described her as an improvement coach who was "here to help."

(Aside: Nobody will blame you if you just laughed or rolled your eyes.)

Most educators, especially those who have spent time in the crosshairs of school improvement regimes, have encountered a bevy of slick consultants from "the outside." These self-appointed experts show up at schools, often armed with a PowerPoint presentation and "The Answer"—capital T, capital A—for how to improve struggling schools. The teachers at Chávez had heard this song and dance many, many times before, and they were not eager to hear it again.

To the surprise of the fourth-grade team, though, Meaghen was singing a different tune.

She walked into the lounge, the faint smell of "Paradise Breeze" still trailing behind her. She sat down at the table, with obvious humility, and said, "I bet you think I'm going to tell you I have 'The Answer.' I don't. Mostly, I'm here to ask you questions—one question, in particular."

The teachers shared a glance, then gestured for her to continue.

"Has anyone ever asked **you**," Meaghen said, "what **you** think needs to happen to make this school great?"

What if We Told You That You're Not the Problem . . . but That You're the Solution?

Being a classroom educator has never been harder, so if the Chávez teachers' cocktail of anxiety, ambivalence, and hope sounds familiar to you, you're not alone.

Surveys conducted in the last 10 years indicate that teacher job satisfaction is at a quarter-century low, and that was *before* the pandemic. The combination of declining real resources for schools, increased expectations for teachers, greater public scrutiny, and more high-stakes accountability has destabilized the profession, making many educators' lives miserable in the process. COVID-19 only worsened the situation, with acute health and safety concerns layered on top of the uncertainty of toggling between virtual and in-person schooling at a moment's notice.

Plenty of people pay lip service to the notion that the joy has been sucked out of teaching, but few education leaders seem willing to do anything with that information. Teachers, meanwhile, are tasked with solving social problems well outside their spans of control, at the same time as we expect them to help young people thrive against the never-static backdrop of our contemporary world. When teachers *are* invited to the table for policy conversations, it can seem like an afterthought, being asked to opine on decisions that were already made.

In short, educators work against difficult odds, with a fraction of the resources necessary to do the job, all while garnering unconscionably little respect from the populace at large.

And what do teachers do in response?

Show up every . . . single . . . day . . . and rise to the challenge anyway, for as Shirley Chisholm once said, "If they don't invite you to the table, bring in a folding chair."

But wouldn't it be nice if you didn't have to bring a folding chair? What would it actually look like for teachers to be at the center of discussions about school transformation?

This question is more important than ever, as educators everywhere struggle to make sense of the chaos wrought by unprecedented times. Marginalized communities, as usual, experienced the most devastating consequences of the pandemic, but even the most privileged people and institutions can't escape the fallout. Chronic uncertainty is an unfortunate historical reality in communities that experience systemic underresourcing, but the destabilization is a new phenomenon for folks accustomed to privilege.

Fortunately, we have proven models for how to—and how not to—engage educators in driving transformational change against unpredictable headwinds.

Unfortunately, most government-sanctioned "school improvement" work ignores those lessons.

To understand why this happens, a short digression into the recent history of school improvement policy is useful; but if that kind of stuff bores you, please feel free to skip ahead to the section titled, "OK, Cool, Got You, but What Do We Do Now?"

In Which We Digress, Ever so Briefly, to Establish Some Historical Policy Context

For the last 30 years or so, lawmakers have tried to legislate the improvement of schools.

While educators on the ground have worked hard to do this work for literally generations, the contemporary school improvement zeitgeist was birthed from the federal government's decision, at the turn of the 21st century, to hold states and their schools accountable for annual gains on standardized tests. Measuring performance in a transparent way isn't a bad idea, in theory; but for the last generation, "accountability" in education was often oversimplified as "testing," and that dumbing down of important concepts did real harm to the profession.

First and foremost, measuring schools with tests meant that almost all schools identified as "struggling" served high concentrations of children from Black, Latinx, and low-income families. Testing became a proxy for privilege, and not much more. Centuries of institutional racism and underinvestment have created significant and measurable disparities in wealth, income, housing, and health for marginalized folks, so there's no surprise that these factors manifest in public schooling too. Annual testing played a role in making these disparities more obvious to lay people, but identifying problems is most useful when our methods of assessment offer clues for how to solve them.

Testing, as we know, did not do that. While standardized tests, used in narrow ways, can provide broad insights, education policymakers in the last two decades started to use tests in ways for which they were never intended, like teacher evaluation. This heightened focus on testing usually came with few resources for pursuing improvement strategies. Schools that struggled to serve marginalized children were told to get better . . . or else. The scolding rarely came with both resources and support, and sometimes even came with financial consequences, due to federal regulations requiring states to divert funds to private companies.

It's no surprise, then, that the accountability era in education left a graveyard of "*pre-failed educational strategies*" in its wake. A pre-failed strategy is something that was never going to work, like covering up a pothole with construction paper. Pre-failed school improvement approaches were fated to go awry, not just because they were designed to address the wrong underlying problems, but because they rarely incorporated the perspectives of educators like you.

OK, Cool, Got You, but What Do We Do Now?

The era of high-stakes accountability in American schools will end in a protracted whimper and not with a bang. Federal monetary investment in school improvement peaked in the Obama administration, and states continue to roll back strict accountability measures. Since 2020, the systemic response to the COVID-19 pandemic has consumed most of the energy in the public sector, and schools have been no exception, meaning that public attention to testing, and the outcomes they illuminate, is minimal.

But let's not get confused: While test-based accountability, and the draconian improvement strategies that followed, may have fallen out of favor, we still have massive challenges in our schools, particularly those that serve our most marginalized families. Schools should be our country's great equalizers, but instead they often perpetuate—or even exacerbate—our society's biggest inequities.

If this mental struggle sounds familiar, maybe that's why you picked up this book in the first place.

You know that there are issues with how our schools serve the kids who need us the most, but most of the solutions on the table seem disconnected, antiquated, and inadequate. In the midst of all of that, despite lots of speechifying to the contrary, you're pretty sure that the problem is not you but the system itself, which was *never* designed with *all* of our kids—not to mention the realities of the real world—in mind.

And you know what? You're right. You're not the problem.

In fact, you might be the solution.

CÉSAR CHÁVEZ ELEMENTARY SCHOOL, SAN JOSE, CALIFORNIA

René Sanchez, the principal of Chávez Elementary School, was eager for his fourth-grade teachers to disprove the conventional wisdom about "failing schools," a label he despised.

René had started his career as a teacher at Chávez in the 1990s. Even then, the school had an outsized reputation for being a place where chronic underperformance was met with community resistance. In the community organizing text, A *Match on Dry Grass*, Chávez at that time is described as a place where hundreds of parents would show up to community meetings wearing bright yellow t-shirts and stickers that proclaimed "70%"—for the number of eighth graders who couldn't read at grade level.

By the time René came back to be principal in 2009, Chávez was still the lowest-performing elementary school in the Alum Rock Union School District. That district, which is among the poorest in the United States, is located in one of the wealthiest cities in the history of the world: San Jose, California. Nestled on the fringes of Silicon Valley, San Jose is home to more billionaires and millionaires per capita than any other place in America.

In a more equitable country, such an extraordinary concentration of wealth might lead to unparalleled public services. The dystopian disparities of American civic governance, however, mean that while the founders of Facebook and Apple live in the apricot groves of San Jose's western hills, the Alum Rock community is in the flatlands of East San Jose, where most families live in poverty. The district serves over 10,000 students, almost all of whom are Spanish-speaking, and close to 90 percent of whom qualify for free or reduced-price lunch at school, which is a proxy for measuring poverty.

While the community pressure of the 1990s led to modest improvements in the school's appearance, the cosmetic shifts could not hide basic educational facts: Just a small percentage of Alum Rock students would go on to achieve postsecondary academic success,

(Continued)

(Continued)

and the educational outcomes at Chávez were dire enough to land the school on the short list of schools in the country that struggle the most.

René soon discovered that being the principal of such a school didn't leave a person with a lot of wiggle room. He tried making some bold changes during his first year as principal, but the measurable results were disappointing. Before his second year as principal, the district superintendent had a sit-down with René to let him know that the clock was ticking. If the school didn't improve the coming year, the superintendent warned, he might have to invoke "reconstitution," which, under federal regulations, would mean removing half of the staff and assigning them to other schools.

Drastic, to say the least.

René was dead set against reconstitution. He, more than anyone, knew that school was still struggling, but he had only been principal for a year, and having grown up in the community—not to mention having spent his whole career as an educator in Alum Rock—he knew that things could get better.

René was ready to take matters into his own hands, but given the prior year's lackluster results, he conceded that he needed help. To avoid reconstitution, he and the superintendent came to a tentative agreement: René would have one more year to show measurable improvement. To help accelerate progress, he would have to accept some support from an instructional coach who was steeped in the classroom and also trained to lead a new, teacher-centric model for school transformation.

That's how Meaghen ended up in the old supply closet.

Educators Don't Need to Wait for Someone Else to Ignite the Change

While high-stakes testing was disruptive to many schools, the accountability era's overt focus on results introduced two inescapable truths into mainstream conversation about schools.

The first fact is hard to swallow: Many struggling schools show up on the governments' lists every year, meaning that *persistent* underperformance is a reality for a subset of schools. Some schools, *even when compared with schools with comparable demographics*, collapse into cycles of replicating underwhelming outcomes, and after spending enough time in that cycle, it's really hard to escape. The situation is a little like crossing the event horizon of a black hole or being trapped in the Matrix: You have a nagging suspicion that something is wrong, but there's no obvious off-ramp. The persistent struggles of schools like these have caused some policymakers to argue that school improvement is a fruitless endeavor that isn't even worth pursuing. "Bad schools will always be bad," they argue, "so let's not throw good money after bad."

That logic is wrong, and we know this because of the second inescapable fact: The accountability era's relentless emphasis on measurement revealed that *some schools break the cycle.* The existence of schools that don't fit the mold, by beating the odds and shattering the pattern of underperformance, should be a source of enormous hope and celebration. Instead, many policymakers reject the study of those schools and want to dismiss them as "outliers" that we should ignore—a glitch in the Matrix, if you will.

We think that those schools, and the adults who work in them, should be our focus.

Because once you know that transformation is possible, it's hard to look away. And when you look more closely, you start to see success stories everywhere—sharp little glimmers of light and hope dotting a landscape of paper-covered potholes.

Those glimmers of hope inspired this book because they caused us to wonder this: What would happen if we gave educators the tools necessary to change the odds for themselves?

For the last 30 years, the educators at Partners in School Innovation, a San Francisco-based nonprofit organization, have been working shoulder-to-shoulder with educators to accelerate school change, and through pursuing that work, dramatic transformation seems to happen. A lot.

We think it can happen even more.

That's where you come in. We think that you and some other folks at your school need to be in on this action.

Before we go any further, though, it's important to be honest about what it takes to accomplish sustainable transformation in challenging educational environments. The work is hard, and it takes a long time. Think years, not weeks. During those years, some of your peers will be annoyed at you for embracing what they view as unrealistic ambitions, especially at a time when schools are already beset by seemingly endless challenges. You know how Mrs. Howard usually gives Janine's youthful enthusiasm side-eye on *Abbott Elementary*, but then ends up helping out in the end? It'll be sort of like that.

Meanwhile, spoiler alert! There aren't any silver-bullet solutions or shortcuts. You'll experience many setbacks in the process, and you will almost certainly need to make unpopular, counterintuitive decisions in the process.

Does that sound like something you might be interested in taking on?

You're still with me?

Cool.

Because do you know how transformation starts? It's usually when an educator like you decides to do things a different way.

That's how you become a change agent.

Facing Facts . . . and Owning Them

When you're a frontline educator—a teacher, a principal, or an instructional coach who spends every day in school buildings—there are plenty of people outside of schools who want to explain your problems to you: the state, the federal government, the local newspaper, or that one particularly opinionated person at the community meeting (you know who I'm talking about).

When René started his second year as principal at Chávez, he wasn't confused about the results his school was achieving. Nobody knew the data better than he did. The dirty secret in struggling schools is that everyone in the building knows they have issues; they just don't like it when outsiders rub their noses in that fact . . . especially when those outsiders have never set foot in the community.

The farther critics are from the challenges our schools face, the more likely they are to focus on the least nuanced sources of data, which in turn leads to picking the least promising solutions to said challenges. Rating schools based on test scores became the standard during the accountability era—not because those tests were valid, but because they were convenient and easy to explain. Standardized tests are blunt instruments, but everyone understands the concept of a test. Our other mechanisms for assessing school transformation require more explanation, which is a difficult problem when shaping public opinion or policy. As they say in politics, "If you're explaining, you're losing."

One of the first steps to becoming a change agent in your own school, then, is to identify concrete, observable factors that are within your control and figure out how to talk about them. We all know that there's more to a school than a single test score, so educators who want to be change agents need to reclaim the conversation about outcomes in a way that is supportive of educators' efforts and not antagonistic toward them.

If you're not sure where to start, ask yourself the following questions:

Attendance: What does our student attendance look like? How about teacher attendance? Are there different trends at different grade levels?

Discipline & Suspension Rates: How many students get referred to the office every month? Do we have a lot of suspensions and expulsions in our school? Are there racial disparities in how discipline is administered?

Interim Assessments: Do we have interim assessments that let us know whether or not students are reading or doing mathematics at grade level? If so, can those assessments tell us much about the quality and patterns of classroom instruction?

Climate & Belonging: Does our school provide the sort of personal and professional safety necessary for adults and children to take learning risks? Do students feel like they belong here, and what are we doing to increase their sense of psychological well-being?

Long-Term Outcomes: How many of our students eventually graduate from high school on time? Of those that graduate, how many achieve postsecondary success? How do we know? How many get a two- or four-year degree? Are our graduates thriving more generally? Are our former students employed and civically active in their mid-20s?

While some of these questions have taken a back seat to examining test scores, these are perhaps the most important short- and long-term measures to assess when looking at school performance. Schools, after all, should help launch young people into healthy, fulfilling lives. Tests were deployed as an imperfect proxy for a bigger picture.

Once you consider the top-line information, you need to go deeper. Some statisticians will tell you that "the data tell the story," but that's not true. Numbers alone tell an incomplete story. Data and statistics provide useful supporting evidence for a bigger narrative that only you and your colleagues can shape about your school because you know what's actually happening behind classroom doors.

Once you and some peers look at these and other sources of data, it's important to take stock of what you've learned about your current situation. Once in a while, something specific will jump out in the data that's impossible to ignore. For example, you might say, "Whoa, one of our fifth-grade classrooms consistently gets way better math results; what's happening there?"

More often than not, however, the picture is muddier, with just as many ups, downs, and inconsistencies as there are definitive patterns. In schools with chronic issues, just about everything can "look bad on paper."

That's the problem that René and the fourth-grade team at Chávez faced, and that's why figuring out how and where to start is such an important part of the school transformation journey.

CÉSAR CHÁVEZ ELEMENTARY SCHOOL, SAN JOSE, CALIFORNIA

The data, in short, did not look good. René knew it. His boss, the superintendent, knew it. Meaghen knew it, and so did the fourth-grade teachers.

It was not the data itself, though, but rather the promise of doing something different with it this time that had enticed the fourth-grade team into meeting with Meaghen in the first place. The teachers, like René, knew that the prior year had been a disappointment from a student performance standpoint. They weren't entirely sure why, though, and Meaghen had suggested that a hard look at data might open some interesting doors of discovery.

Meaghen prepared for that first meeting with the fourth-grade team by assembling lots of information, disaggregated by grade level, classroom, and student demographics. She also created a comprehensive list of the major academic programs that were happening in the school, including one of the school's signature initiatives, "Response to Intervention."

Response to Intervention is a common framework that schools use to identify and support students who fall behind their peers in learning how to read at grade level. When comparing Chávez's student data to the program's objectives, though, the fourth-grade teachers detected a mismatch. Whereas successful implementation of the Response to Intervention model depends on identifying under 30 percent of a school's students for interventions, the program data at Chávez indicated that well over half of the school was eligible for the program.

Having so many students identified for intervention strategies was overloading the circuits. The fourth-grade teachers supplemented that data with a critical observation: Reading specialists throughout the school were spread thinly, leading to burnout, which further supported the narrative the data was suggesting.

There was another important question lurking in the intervention data, though: Why did so many children in the school need reading interventions in the first place? Was it possible that the school was experiencing a challenge with the baseline quality of classroom instruction?

These questions constituted the first of many uncomfortable realities that Meaghen and the fourth-grade team at Chávez would have to entertain. The middling results were not news to the teachers; the notion that someone would ask them for their opinion as to what to do next was, in fact, unique.

Encouraged by the frankness and openness of that first meeting with Meaghen, the group agreed to meet again the following week. They committed to studying school improvement strategies as a group and agreed that they should be open to doing things differently, even if that required them to change their own personal instructional practices.

For Meaghen, whose training as a coach taught her to listen, ask questions, and identify the most fruitful venues for launching school transformation, the fourth-grade team's combination of frankness, openness to change, and collaborative teamwork was a gold mine.

Follow the Data, Pick a Target, Then . . . Do Stuff

Meaghen's approach to inquiry and transformation was not accidental, but systematic. In the course of a generation characterized by the fits and starts of lackluster school improvement, our field has learned a lot of important lessons about how to, and how not to, pursue systemic change. First among those lessons is that there's no one right way to start improving a school. While policymakers peddle silver bullets and high-priced consultants sell solutions, the reality is that school transformation requires consistent, intentional, relationship-driven implementation of continuous improvement strategies, rooted in equity.

Unfortunately, it would be a terrible idea to put "consistent, intentional, relationship-driven implementation of continuous improvement strategies, rooted in equity" on a bumper sticker. That's more or less the reason we wrote a whole book.

As a school transformation coach, one of the first lessons Meaghen learned was how to put her "shoulder to your wheel." In other words, frontline educators lead, and the coach follows. In the case of Chávez Elementary, the teachers identified the fact that many children were reading below grade level, even relative to demographically similar schools and classrooms. The natural question to ask after unpacking this data was whether there existed challenges with executing grade-level reading instruction in classrooms. While even asking this question was uncomfortable, the alternative explanation—that something was wrong with the children—was untenable.

While grade-level reading instruction seemed like the natural first step at Chávez, "putting a shoulder to your wheel" means following the data, not a playbook. If student attendance is unusually low in a school, it's impossible to move instructional quality because you can't teach a kid who isn't there. A similar problem manifests when high numbers of students are being referred for out-of-school suspension: Learning doesn't happen just because we send a student away.

Sometimes, evaluating data reveals difficult-to-stomach realities about what we prioritize in schools. Many schools experience "within-school opportunity gaps," wherein overall numbers present a very different picture than when the same data is disaggregated by race and socioeconomic status. For example, some high schools offer AP courses but find that very few Latinx students are enrolled in those classes. In other cases, extraordinary proportions of the students who are referred to the administration for disciplinary issues turn out to be Black or Latinx males. While confronting these truths requires deep introspection about the harmful effects of institutionalized racism, ignoring them merely perpetuates inequity.

For better or worse, there is no shortage of issues that require focus in a struggling school, so the hard part about being a change agent is not finding an area of focus, but rather narrowing that focus to something achievable.

Picking a place to start is equal parts art and science, but the following guiding questions can help identify good candidates:

> ***Where does our data exhibit clear room for growth, especially relative to schools with comparable demographic data?*** If your school is a clear outlier, something is wrong. But on the bright side, when you are an outlier, the problem you face probably has a solution, as other educators have gotten different results in comparable environments. Will the things that work elsewhere always work in your school? Of course not. But the odds suggest that there is much you can learn from similar schools.

> ***What instructional tools are equally useful in both virtual and in-person schooling?*** The short-term consequences of COVID-19 on educational systems, and the families served by them, have been devastating. One of the hardest parts of teaching in this era is the unpredictable shifts between in-person learning, which is suboptimal from a safety perspective, and remote virtual learning, which just about everyone agrees is less effective from an instructional standpoint. Which instructional methods and tools seem to work well in both environments? And is it possible to reorganize lesson planning and pacing to accommodate sudden shifts?

> ***Is there a place where we can make fast progress and build momentum?*** A big part of school transformation is persistence, and it's hard to maintain focus without quick wins, particularly in environments that are either rapidly changing or presenting multiple worthy challenges at once. One of many challenges with high-stakes testing is information lag: Standardized test results take many months to process, and once teachers get results, the students who were tested usually have advanced a grade. It's hard to build momentum based on data when you don't get to see that data until your kids are long gone. If there are areas where you can show fast, measurable improvement, go for it. *And by fast, we mean FAST, like in a week.*

Is there a challenge that is best addressed as a team? School transformation requires collaboration at every level. While individual educators can exhibit episodic acts of greatness, sustained excellence at the school level requires teamwork. While the COVID-19 pandemic has caused unprecedented levels of physical isolation, the mainstream use of videoconferencing tools, while not terribly effective for classroom instruction, may simplify group work among teachers. Such group collaboration is essential for transformation. To achieve sustained excellence, collaboration is critical, so picking challenges that lend themselves to virtual work—whether the pandemic is with us or not—can help.

What problem can we solve that doesn't require an infusion of new resources? Not all school improvement strategies are free, but some are. In schools where new money is hard to find, picking opportunities for quick wins that are low cost—or even better, free—is a great way to build momentum.

While this is not an exhaustive list of questions, it's a good place to start. In the process of addressing these issues with your fellow educators, you're bound to come up with even more questions that can drive discussion.

Where you decide to focus, in some ways, is less important than the process you use to identify those areas of focus. In the process of discovery, you'll be exercising many of the important muscles that you'll need to tone in order to carry out the long-term process of school transformation: teamwork, collaboration, adopting an equity lens, honesty, listening, goal-setting, progress monitoring, and real-time data analysis, to name a few.

CÉSAR CHÁVEZ ELEMENTARY SCHOOL, SAN JOSE, CALIFORNIA

After meeting a couple of times, Meaghen and the fourth-grade change agents unearthed a promising idea for how to initiate improvement. The idea was rooted in how their district managed reading instruction.

Years before, the central office adopted a pacing schedule for how to teach reading, rooted in a methodology called "direct instruction."

Using this approach meant that, on any given day in the district, fourth graders across the district would be working on the same content. Teachers worked from "pacing guides" that outlined the topics to be addressed throughout a school year, aligned to what the district suspected would be included on standardized tests. This setup was appealing to some central office folks because it provided built-in mechanisms for assessing implementation fidelity. That said, because all lessons and unit plans were handed down from the district, teachers rarely developed intensive relationships with the content. Teachers were told what to teach and when to teach it. Teachers, as a result, grew accustomed to describing lessons according to the color coding and not the content itself:

"We're teaching green on Tuesday."

"It's Thursday, so you know it's a yellow lesson."

Few educators knew what "green" or "yellow" meant. It was just vague color coding on prepackaged materials.

While the fourth-grade team wasn't sure how they would improve reading instruction, they knew they had to adjust the current approach. First, they decided to get more familiar with the grade-level content standards. Understanding standards at a deeper level seemed like a precursor to helping students reach them. As an instructional coach, Meaghen had received extensive training on standards-based instruction, so she was well-equipped to shepherd this process. She brought the teachers resources, research-based texts, and student work samples to help the learning process.

Second, the teachers agreed to engage in a reciprocal process of observation and feedback. While this sounds like a natural thing to do in schools, for many educators this remains quite unusual and radical. Many teachers treat their classrooms as private territory, and because of how school schedules are organized, it's hard to make time to watch another teacher teach.

Research, however, consistently indicates that collaborative instruction, rooted in observation and a framework for improvement, is a precursor to academic improvement. Meaghen, as a coach, was steeped in that research.

(Continued)

(Continued)

And so, as a team, the fourth-grade change agents agreed to make time to watch each other teach and then provide constructive feedback on that instruction. They worked with physical education and art teachers to do micro scheduling adjustments so that one teacher could be in the metaphorical spotlight at a time when the rest of the team didn't have classroom responsibilities. The goal was not just to watch, but to help each other improve, so their final step at this point was to set measurable goals for the improvement of their practice, on a realistic timeline.

They didn't know it at the time, but in the process of creating and committing to time-limited goals, the fourth-grade team had just engaged in their first ever "ROCI" cycle.

ROCI: The Technical Secret Sauce at the Heart of This Whole Book

At Chávez Elementary, Meaghen acted as a coach, friend, mentor, and facilitator, while the fourth-grade crew identified their first major improvement effort. After picking a target together, they took several additional steps, which together form the basis of what we call "results-oriented cycles of inquiry," or ROCI (pronounced ROW-see).

Spoiler alert: ROCI is the only acronym we will use in this entire book. Seriously. Overusing acronyms is soooo 2010 and gets in the way of deep understanding. But we are going to use this one. A lot. That's how important it is, so you should get used to reading it and saying it aloud.

The ROCI process goes something like this: On a weekly basis, grade-level teams meet to compare lesson plans, identify high-leverage instructional targets for the coming week, look at student work together, and set achievable goals against each of those activities. Meanwhile, school leadership teams monitor progress, establish priorities for schoolwide professional learning, provide resources for achieving those targets, and otherwise support the work of the teachers in the school.

After establishing weekly sets of objectives, educators agree to meet again the following week to reassess and reflect. In doing so, educators create a perpetual motion machine of school improvement. That's the ROCI process. If you spend more than 10 minutes with someone in this book who's engaged in transformation work, you're bound to hear them mention ROCI.

Simple ROCI

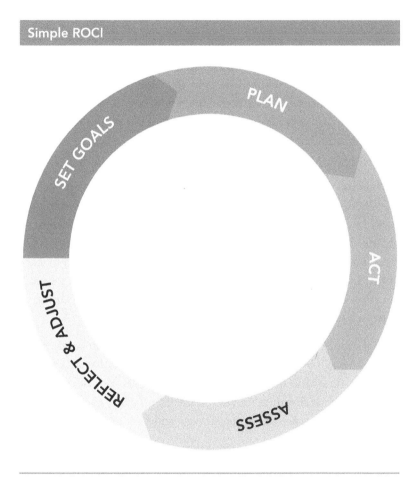

"What's on the agenda for our next ROCI cycle?"

"Did you share the latest ROCI reflections with the principal yet?

"What did we ROCI last month?"

ROCI is shorthand for an improvement process, yes, but it is much more than that. It is an ethos, a way of being, and perhaps most importantly, as it was used in that last example quotation, ROCI is a verb.

The active nature of ROCI is central to the work of school transformation. Improving the quality of teaching and learning in schools is a physical process that requires full participation, all the time.

And while ROCI is a technical process, it is anchored in ancient wisdom. As the old saying goes, "Insanity is doing the *same* thing you've always done and expecting *different* results."

ROCI is just a clever way of making sure you try something *different* this time and then following through to determine if that change in behavior leads to *different* results, ideally a measurable improvement. It's important to remember, though, that nothing goes perfectly the first time you try it. ROCI isn't about trying and jettisoning things in the course of a week. It's about creating regular touch points to refine, improve, and iterate on novel practices, which we otherwise might not see through to their natural conclusions.

While this concept is simple to explain, it's hard to execute in practice. Teachers can sit on a Zoom call, as a team of adults, and come to a calm, rational agreement about what to do once they're delivering a lesson. But every educator knows that the best intentions can go haywire once they're in front of a couple dozen kids. Classroom management headaches, videoconferencing lags, scheduling mishaps, moods, internet outages, and software bugs all get in the way of executing the instructional changes that you and your peers agreed to pursue.

What's more, even if you do manage to shift your practice, there's no guarantee that it will lead to quick results. Sometimes, we pick the right strategy but at the wrong time. Once in a while, the correct strategy seems wrong at first until we build the skills necessary to make it work. Other times, we pick the wrong strategy and have to regroup.

But guess what? That's all a part of that ROCI life because the important part is not to get everything exactly right all of the time. The goal is to create an accountability structure for the creation of good, new habits. Once we know what habits we're trying to build, ROCI helps us commit to practical behavior changes, monitor that commitment, and assess the extent to which we achieve results as a consequence.

If this sounds easy, let's keep in mind that millions of people pay for gym memberships that they never use and that the fad diet business is a multi-billion-dollar industry.

In other words: Building new habits is hard. We ROCI to build new habits.

Are You Ready for This?

So I know what you *may* be thinking at this point: "I didn't become a teacher to be a school transformation expert. I'm also not super confident that I'm a 'change agent,' which is giving big 'overachieving main character' vibes. I have never engaged in continuous improvement before, everyone at my school is in a collective hangover from the last couple of years, and I have no time for this. Also, I have no idea what 'ROCI' is, and, if we're keeping it extremely real, it sounds a little cheesy. Are you sure you want ME to do this?"

The answer is, "Yes. Yes, I do." You kind of have to. Because if you don't, who will?

I make a good point, right?

The whole purpose of this book is to demystify the process of ground-up school transformation for educators like you and your colleagues. If the last two years have taught us anything, it's that the old ways of doing things are inadequate. Educators are being asked to adapt to circumstances unlike any we've seen before, and the top-down approaches to change that characterized public policy until now will never be adaptive or culturally responsive enough for the world in which we live.

Certain schools that have struggled for years—decades even—have always been ripe for ground-up transformation; in a postpandemic world, it seems that all schools are. In the world we're living in, just about everyone feels like a novice teacher again.

This book is based on the real work of frontline educators, using their actual factual names. The stories herein happened between 2010 and 2020, and while we've all lived several lifetimes since then, there's an enormous amount we can learn from how our peers upended norms and broke barriers in their own schools. While all the educators in this book worked closely with Partners in School Innovation, we know that many more people can do this work without consultants, given the right tools.

Speaking of tools, the concept of "improvement science," which informs the technical parts of the ROCI approach, has been all the rage with process-obsessed researchers for decades. That said, there's not much use for a theory that excites academics but eludes educators. Doing the technical part of improvement science—without understanding the ways in which race, privilege, equity, and opportunity intersect in our schools—is a recipe for disaster. That's why the stories and guidance in this book are both anchored in the practical application of improvement science *and* also rooted in a deep structural critique of inequitable systems. You'll notice that "both/and" theme emerging lots of times throughout the book.

More than anything, though, we want you to pick up this book, wherever you are, read a few chapters, and then get to work. To help you do that, we'll tell stories (like the ones about the educators at Chávez Elementary) and then describe the skills and mindsets educators adopted in those stories. As such, we're using a narrative structure that switches back and forth between storytelling and explanatory writing. Lots of people enjoy that style, but some find the alternation distracting. If you're finding it hard to follow, don't sweat it. Try reading all of the shaded vignettes in a chapter first, then read the other parts after. To make it easier to act on what you've learned, we'll end every chapter with a checklist summary, reminding you of the concrete steps taken on the path to transformation.

This first chapter was all about *getting started*. School transformation isn't a linear process, so it's hard to identify a clear starting point for this work. That said, because school transformation is, at its core, about personal transformation, we're starting in the most natural place: *wherever you are*.

So what do you think? Are you ready to be one of the change agents your school needs?

Because if you are, you're going to need some comrades in the struggle. It's impossible to do this work alone. Fear not, though. We have some ideas about where you can find them, and that's what the next chapter is all about.

THE GETTING STARTED CHECKLIST

- **Embrace your role as a change agent.** We don't need to wait for outsiders' permission to do things differently. If you suspect your school could be doing something better, say so. The admission can be liberating, and you might find out that there are some other educators who have been thinking the exact same thing.

- **Keep your eye open for other change agents in your school.** In this chapter, the fourth-grade team and the school principal were natural allies in starting school transformation. That doesn't need to be the case. Your ragtag group of change agents might include an instructional coach, a paraprofessional, or a crossing guard. Find whoever else is relentlessly committed to change and start a conversation.

- **Acknowledge your challenges and commit to addressing them.**
  Even the highest-performing schools have challenges that need
  addressing, especially in an era of pandemic-induced instructional
  shifts. Wherever your school is on the performance continuum,
  there is something that would benefit from rapid improvement
  and progress monitoring. In the case of underresourced schools
  in marginalized communities, the hard part won't be finding a
  challenge to address but figuring out where to start. Sit down with
  an instructional coach, other teachers, an assistant principal, or any
  trusted colleague to begin the conversation.

- **Look at data together and talk about what you see.** *While data
  don't* tell the whole story, qualitative and quantitative information
  can help to start an objective conversation. When you sit down with
  your colleagues, use a few critical data points as a starting point. And
  remember, when we say "data," we don't just mean "test scores."
  Data is so much more than high-stakes testing, and if we only look at
  scores, we'll miss huge opportunities to make measurable changes
  on a shorter timeline. If data is "not your thing," that's okay. You're
  having these conversations to get more comfortable with using data
  in your practice.

- **Pick a starting point and commit to trying something both new
  and measurable.** The first step is not to change *everything*, but to
  change *something*. After you and your colleagues look at the data,
  you'll have a better idea of what elements of your instructional
  practice need to shift, so don't skip the data! Once you pick
  something you want to try, figure out how you'll know if it's going
  well or not. Maybe you'll engage in group classroom observations.
  Maybe you'll develop a short "check for understanding" that
  you can administer to your classroom after a week. Whatever
  you decide to do, make sure you can make the adjustment in the
  following week, and then commit to meeting again with your team
  to talk about how it went!

- **Reflect on what you learn and adjust accordingly.** Changing
  practice without reflection ignores one of the most powerful parts
  of ROCI: the inquiry and learning component. It's rare that an
  adjustment is perfect and leads to immediate success. Without
  adequate reflection, we don't refine our practice and might continue
  down unproductive paths.

(Continued)

(Continued)

- **Lather, rinse, repeat.** This is where the rubber meets the road. The next time you step in front of your classroom, you're going to do something new—maybe even something you've never done before as an educator. Are you nervous? Good, you should be! Change is hard! Scary, even! But here's a little secret: You know how they always say "failure is not an option"? That's complete BS. Failure is absolutely an option. If we're not failing once in a while, we're not taking enough risks. The goal is not to avoid failure, but to learn from the process of trying something new, even if it doesn't work the first time.

CHAPTER 1: DISCUSSION QUESTIONS

1. Have you ever felt included in the decision-making at your school? How did that feel, and what was the outcome? On the flipside, have you ever felt excluded? What was that like?

2. Is there anything about your school you think needs improving? Do people talk about those issues? Does your school invite difficult conversations or discourage them?

3. Have you ever been able to add a new habit to your routine, either personal or professional? Or have you ever removed a bad habit? What worked and what didn't in that process?

Assembling Your Crew

2

Several months passed, and Meaghen recruited another coach, Tiara, to join the crew in formation in the old supply closet.

While their cycles of inquiry work—aka ROCI—had started to gain more traction, their attempts to deodorize the room had been less successful. The Paradise Breeze air freshener had worked a bit too well. After repeated attempts to cover the smell of trash, the room smelled so intensely of the cheap aerosol that they began referring to the makeshift office as, simply, "Paradise Breeze."

The snarky nickname created enticing recruitment opportunities. "Meet me after school at Paradise Breeze" became shorthand for "We'll be discussing standards-aligned instructional practices in a windowless room that you might still think is janitorial storage."

In other words: Come for the cool, misleading name; stay for the relentless focus on results.

Meaghen was excited to have Tiara's help at Chávez. Tiara, a former elementary school teacher in the next town over, had developed a knack for distilling content standards to their essence in a way that was accessible to both students and teachers. That experience, coupled with her local knowledge, meant that she knew both Chávez's contextual challenges and the state-mandated instructional goals like second nature.

Together, Meaghen and Tiara formed a formidable duo.

(Continued)

(Continued)

And yet, most days, they found themselves alone, gazing outward from the doorway of Paradise Breeze, trying to entice other educators to join their crew.

They had hoped their success with the fourth-grade team would generate enough cred to branch out to other grade levels. By the spring, the fourth-grade teachers had formalized their ROCI cycles. They were meeting as a grade-level team on a weekly basis, with Meaghen and Tiara's support. Every meeting included a preplanned agenda, hard examinations of real data, discussions about whether or not they had achieved the prior week's objectives, and goal setting for the following week.

This was textbook ROCI, and within just a few months, the fourth-grade team at Chavez had become a self-contained engine of academic improvement. Unlike other kinds of school reform that depended upon waiting for test scores, the ROCI approach led to small, immediate, measurable improvements. While changes didn't occur every day, the fourth-grade teachers began to see incremental shifts in their practice within weeks. Through making time to observe and provide feedback on each others' teaching, they learned to adopt additional shifts from their peers.

The process wasn't magic, but it felt new and exciting. And, not for nothing, it was nice to be a part of a group whose energy challenged the malaise that had dogged the school culture for years.

Therein, however, was the rub. The "little-fourth-grade-team-that-could" might chug along and get results, but without a mechanism for taking their work beyond the calming shores of Paradise Breeze, that work, however potent, would struggle to expand.

On the one hand, there was something liberating about trying something new without the added pressure of scrutiny and scale. On the other hand, this newly formed revolutionary cell of change agents had something to offer the broader system, and if they were on to something, it was educational malpractice not to share.

System change, though, seemed like a stretch, as they kicked ideas around the old supply closet.

Becoming a Ground-Up Change Agent in a Top-Down World

When honeybees need to find new nesting grounds, no one single bee is responsible for picking the new spot. In a single hive, which might include tens of thousands of bees, several hundred will strike out as a group and investigate alternative future sites. After exploring a handful of promising alternatives, the colony debates the merits of the various choices through a complex process of inter-bee dialogue and disagreement, a little bit like the last scene in an episode of *House Hunters*. When the process is complete, the hive migrates to the new site.

In executing this kind of complex group thinking, bees possess, in the words of MIT data scientist Dr. Sandy Pentland, a "collective intelligence that is independent from, and greater than" their individual capacity to solve problems.

In this regard, humans have much in common with bees. When we come together to solve problems as a group, the results are almost always stronger and more durable than when handed down from on high. Research from Dr. Pentland and others demonstrates that the most powerful ideas and innovations spread through humanity—not by brute force or compulsion, but through the activation of social networks, built on interpersonal relationships.

Unfortunately, since at least the 1990s much school improvement policy has ignored these dynamics, favoring the top-down, splashy, and dramatic instead of the bottom-up, dynamic, incremental, and sustainable. National decision-making is not always a bad thing, as the idea of exclusive hyperlocality makes little sense in the 21st century; consider, for example, the response to the COVID-19 pandemic, where school officials were forced to make independent decisions about matters of global safety.

Concentrating power at the top, however, has led to the real and perceived marginalization of educators' voice in the process of school improvement. While there is nothing about standards-based instruction, or the application of data to improve classroom practice, that is inherently "top-down," the way these reforms have been administered often treats educator buy-in and feedback as an afterthought.

That's why becoming a change agent at your own school is such a revolutionary, paradigm-shifting concept. In acting more like bees and less like bureaucrats, we can find, assess, build, and deploy smarter solutions to complex problems. Unfortunately, after decades of adapting to top-down reform approaches, many of our schools and systems lack the muscle memory and connective tissue necessary to propagate and expand ground–up solutions.

That's why we're dedicating this whole second chapter to one of the most important factors in stitching together the social fabric that allows good ideas to spread: good, old-fashioned relationship building.

Relationships are a foundational ingredient in driving, sustaining, and accelerating ground–up change. As such, the ability to forge new relationships is one of a handful of essential skills that change agents must hone. While we sometimes describe relationship building as a "soft skill," there are a whole range of concrete, learnable competencies that drive relational work, including respecting community, sharing leadership, giving feedback, receiving feedback, creating high-performing teams, and two-way communication.

All of those elements are critical, but one big skill we think about a lot is the ability to identify early adopters and collaborators.

The concept of the "early adopter" is central to the literature and research around the cultural dissemination of new ideas and technologies, and the notion offers powerful insights when considering change agency within public school systems. Changing behavior is hard, scary, unusual, and uncomfortable. While it's possible in theory—if not desirable—to force people to do something differently, there's no guarantee they'll do it well.

That's why early adopters are so crucial to the process of social change in schools.

Early adopters often have greater tolerance for risk and, therefore, are willing to get a little uncomfortable trying new approaches to old problems. In the case of the fourth-grade team at Chávez, their role as early adopters had them doing three things differently right away: They met as a team to discuss the subsequent week's lesson planning, used data to inform those plans, and departed from the district's strict pacing guides in order to make some professional judgments about how to link classroom instruction to standards.

Being a Successful Crew

SOME POTENTIAL QUESTIONS TO ADDRESS . . .	
Purpose and Goals	– Why do we exist as a team? – What specific outcomes are we aiming to achieve?
Membership	– Whose voices do we need on the team? Who is missing? – How do we ensure we are being inclusive? – Do we collectively possess all the skill sets we need to achieve our goals?
Roles and Responsibilities	– What unique strengths, skills, and knowledge do we each bring to the table? – What are our potential blindspots? – Who does what, and when?
Ways of Working	– How do our intersecting identities affect the work we are doing together? – What are our norms and agreements around communication? – How will we make decisions and hold each other accountable?

It's important to remember that all change, no matter how small, can be scary. While none of the shifts previously described came anywhere near what one would consider "life or death," each adjustment necessitated a modest risk calculus—a tiptoe out on a limb versus a nosedive into the abyss. In taking on those risks, early adopters show others that trying new things can create great outcomes, making it easier for the next group of change agents to give it a try.

That last part is critical: Not all change agents are early adopters! Even if you aren't the first person to the party, you can still be a leader for change. Some of the most powerful proponents for transformation emerge in the messy middle of an effort, which we discuss in later chapters.

Beyond that, sometimes the first people at the transformation party form a new clique that reinforces old, tired norms about who gets to be included in the change process. Personal identity markers like race, class, and gender can play a harmful role in determining whose voices are prioritized in a school, and it's important to make sure that bad old habits don't infect new transformation efforts. Reach out to people across lines of difference and keep in mind that the "first followers" are just as important as the "first movers" in spreading new ideas.

The idea isn't to form a new, exclusive clique. Transformation work means abolishing artificial divisions that prevent us from working together.

That's why it's so important for the early adopters to sharpen relational skills.

You've gotta assemble a bigger, more formidable crew.

CÉSAR CHÁVEZ ELEMENTARY SCHOOL, SAN JOSE, CALIFORNIA

After several months of prioritizing ROCI, the fourth-grade crew was in a groove. Practices that had once seemed novel began to feel more like habits. Things that once caused spikes in anxiety, like looking at unflattering student data, became easier because that information wasn't used as a "gotcha," but as a tool for reflection.

This was a sign to Meaghen and Tiara that it was time to branch out.

There were several challenges with branching out at Chavez, though. The first was the absence of concrete channels for sharing new practices. Because so much of the curriculum was scripted, teachers were not accustomed to using schoolwide professional development as a collaborative learning space. When teachers got together for meetings, they were more likely to receive canned presentations about compliance.

Absent formal channels for sharing stuff, the next place to look was the informal ones, but those were strained too. Chávez wasn't a toxic place, but it wasn't necessarily collegial either. Teachers tended to keep their heads down and mind their own business, showing the sort of learned social avoidance that comes from years of having been told that you're The Problem. Programmatic churn, layer upon layer of reform, and frequent teacher turnover meant that there were two major groups of teachers in the school:

1. The Survivors: folks who had been there forever, seen everything, learned to avoid controversy, and were justifiably skeptical of new ideas; and

2. The Newbies: novice teachers with very little experience, placed in the school through little choice of their own, and therefore with few outstanding relationships on the ground

The fourth-grade team knew that making inroads would be an uphill battle with both groups, so the team started devising a plan. Because the school day was packed with instructional responsibilities and few breaks, union representatives were disciplined about monitoring extra minutes getting tacked onto the school day. Teachers were known to stand up and walk out at 4:00 p.m., even if a scheduled meeting hadn't ended yet, so relationship building had to happen during school hours. Figuring out how to do that in a context where most time is spent in a classroom was tricky, to say the least.

Meaghen and Tiara decided to be "strategically opportunistic." When enticing the fourth-grade team into meeting for the first time, Meaghen had observed teacher behaviors throughout the school, with an eye toward finding creative ways to strike up conversation. She realized that there were only a few places in the school where casual convo seemed to happen: on the playground during lunch duty, in the faculty lounge during free periods, and outside the principal's office when people were on their way to and from meetings.

Armed with this information, Meaghen and Tiara started spending their spare moments lingering in these liminal spaces. They volunteered for playground duty and joined the circle of teachers that tended to congregate near the swings. They asked René, the principal, to share his meeting schedule so that they knew when people might be coming from, or going to, group meetings.

While this approach might give off modest stalker vibes, it was effective—so much so that the team started cheekily calling their ideas "Meaghen's traps."

The motivations behind the traps were pure, though. All the team wanted to do, after all, was get more teachers involved in ROCI.

Over time, more and more teachers were willing to have a conversation. After a few weeks, a third-grade teacher expressed interest, leading to a ROCI meeting. Fifth grade followed several weeks later.

And by the end of the spring semester, all but one grade-level team was engaged in transformation work.

They Told Two Friends, and Then They Told Two Friends . . .

"Meaghen's traps" were a creative way to initiate and build new relationships in a context where trust is low, suspicions are high, and spirits are exhausted from unfulfilled promises. Even in the most trusting of environments, though, there is an art and a science to building productive relationships. In many organizations, especially schools, there exists a formal hierarchy that dictates who talks to whom; there are also informal channels that privilege some voices over others, which can reinforce unequal—and unethical—power dynamics rooted in race, class, gender, and privilege.

Real, authentic relationship building disrupts old ways of doing things through creating new interpersonal dynamics that can facilitate radical change.

One fruitful place to look for guidance in this arena is the domain of community organizing, where trust is earned, hierarchy is rare, and consensus building is the norm. Community organizers routinely seek to facilitate ground–up change among historically marginalized people, and the skills developed by organizers over the course of generations are useful when assembling a crew to tackle a big local challenge.

Skill #1: Listening

One of those skills is listening. As we mentioned in Chapter 1, listening is a critical precursor to forming relationships that lead to transformation. Great listeners quickly find common ground with their peers, identify promising venues for collaboration, and build consensus. Meaghen and Tiara had extensive training in, and experience with, listening to their peers and colleagues in order to understand the root causes of challenges. Their willingness and ability to listen—with an ear toward eliciting otherwise unspoken truths—is a competency essential to the work of building relationships and, therefore, also to the work of improving schools.

The toughest truths about a school's challenges rarely emerge during a few minutes of small talk, so you have to practice getting to the bottom of things. One way to practice is to conduct "deep listening exercises" with a colleague.

Practice Deep Listening

1. First, sit face-to-face with a partner, ideally someone in your school whom you don't know well.

2. Pick a question that requires intense thought and introspection.

3. Take turns listening to each other answer that question for a predetermined length of time. Ten minutes each is a good start.

4. When it's your turn to be the "listener," don't interject with your opinions or ideas; just listen until your partner is done talking. When they've said everything they want to say and if there's still time left on the clock, ask a question to deepen your understanding. Keep going like this for a full 10 minutes. Resist the urge to end the exercise early, even if the other person stops sharing. As the listener, embrace the discomfort of silence, continue to listen, and work on your ability to frame probing follow-up questions.

5. Don't forget to spend a full 10 minutes as the listener!

6. When you're done with your turn as listener, switch roles, and the other person becomes the listener for a full 10 minutes while you reflect and answer their questions.

Another way to improve listening skills is to exercise "stepping back" during a meeting, particularly if you're accustomed to talking a lot in group settings. While it might sound counterintuitive, the process of "saying less" can have a transformative positive effect on the quality and quantity of your contributions. One practical way to "step back" is to "hold your comment" when you think you have something critical to add. Let at least two more people speak before sharing your idea and see where the conversation goes. Your ideas are bound to be sharpened by the contributions of others. (*Side note*: The corollary practice to "stepping back" is "stepping up." If you are someone who is reluctant to share during group settings, practice "stepping up" instead!)

Skill #2: Trust

Trust takes time to earn. The trust-building process, however, can be accelerated through taking meaningful steps, and sometimes risks, together as a community. Calculated communal risk-taking one of the core design features of ROCI: Through participating in incremental, confidence-building inquiry cycles, educators ramp up their ability to do things together as a group, which can be leveraged to exert more creativity, take increasingly complicated risks, and drive additional trust-building activities on a broader, schoolwide scale. When it's "safe to fail" at the early stages, you set the stage for bigger, bolder work later.

In books like *Crucial Conversations* and *The Speed of Trust,* management consultants and self-help experts discuss other behaviors that can drive or derail the trust-building process. Transparency is a common theme, as hiding critical information is the antithesis of creating a trusting environment. In contemporary workplaces and schools, information is often held in "silos," which can isolate individuals from the data and context necessary to make decisions as a group.

One quick way to enhance transparency in a school is to regularly discuss schoolwide achievement, attendance, disciplinary, and assessment data. Part of the reason these data points can be so anxiety producing for educators is because we tend not to discuss them on a regular basis. If schools and the teams within them build data transparency into their regular practices, the emotional weight of that sharing is lessened.

Skill #3: Giving and Receiving Feedback

Another big factor in building meaningful professional relationships is giving and receiving honest feedback in real time. Great feedback is best given—and received—in appropriate doses. Teams that tackle big challenges together will encounter roadblocks, make mistakes, and experience hardships. The ability to talk openly and honestly about the most difficult things, even if that means sharing something uncomfortable about a teammate's behavior, is essential to moving forward together.

The first rule of giving feedback—whether positive, negative, neutral, or constructive—is that the guidance must be specific and actionable.

"Hey, Tiara, that presentation was great!" might be nice to hear, but there is no specific or actionable information in the praise.

A more useful piece of positive feedback might be something like, "Meaghen, I really liked the way you disaggregated our school's disciplinary data by racial identity in that presentation. I'm not used to seeing the information presented so pointedly, and the way it was described made me reflect differently on our students' experiences."

Research across sectors also indicates that adults best incorporate constructive feedback if they receive five positive comments to every one negative comment. This is a rule of thumb, and you don't have to keep a running tally of every interaction you have with colleagues. That said, it's important to keep this "golden ratio" of feedback in mind because when the scales tilt too far in the other direction it gets harder and harder for someone to hear and incorporate constructive comments into their practice. Consider what it's like to hear criticism when you're agitated or angry—in one ear, out the other.

Creating durable relationships among a crew of like-minded change agents requires communicating, listening, trusting each other, and taking incremental steps as a group. While each of these skills is adjacent to core educational competencies like pedagogy and instructional leadership, these skills are not necessarily emphasized on ed schools' syllabi. That is neither a knock on ed schools nor a dismissal of these skills; it's just a statement of fact. In some ways, these skills are more native to other domains, like the aforementioned grassroots organizing or social work, where decentralized decision-making, ground–up power, and trust-building are foundational elements.

That said, when you're an early adopter change agent in a school that needs improvement, you are, in many ways, a community organizer. You're starting from the ground up, in a specific context, to achieve definable wins that can drive the whole community forward.

You're also confronting and managing power dynamics that can alternately help or hinder the process. That's why building relationships with your peers, while essential, is just a part of the puzzle.

You have to think up, and out, as well.

CÉSAR CHÁVEZ ELEMENTARY SCHOOL, SAN JOSE, CALIFORNIA

René Sanchez, the Chávez principal, was pleased that the grade-level teams were starting to gel. He stayed abreast of their work through Meaghen, who acted as connective tissue between the classroom teachers and school administration. He watched with optimistic curiosity, providing cover with the district as necessary, while early adopters on the faculty navigated new continuous improvement processes together.

He even learned and embraced the ROCI lingo.

While the proverbial clock was ticking on his transformation strategy, René knew better than anyone that transforming his school would require not just time but also the broader community. He had grown up in the neighborhood, whose most famous citizen—César Chávez—was also the namesake of the school he helmed. Chávez (the person), along

(Continued)

(Continued)

with his partner Dolores Huerta, organized farm workers throughout California under the motto "Sí se puede," a testament to the possibility inherent in collective community power.

By the time René became a teacher, though, that famous tagline—in English, "Yes, we can"—had been reappropriated by locals as "Leave, if you can" (or "Sal, si puedes") to reflect the increasingly dire civic situation. The schools, like many of the city's public services, had fallen into disrepair. PACT, a community-based organization under the banner of the PICO network, had been organizing parents for years to demand more progressive education policies from the Alum Rock school board. The activists' complaints about Chávez (the school) were straightforward: a lack of basic educational materials, crumbling hallways, and unsanitary bathroom conditions.

PACT publicized the physical conditions at Chávez, which galvanized families. René was hired to transform the school after a more transformation-oriented board was elected in the early 2000s. At that point, the basic physical conditions had improved, and relentless community organizing meant that the district could no longer get away with denying the school its basic needs.

Chávez's next growth spurt, however, would be just as complicated as the first. While René inherited a school with toilet paper and cleaner hallways, student achievement results, disciplinary data, and longitudinal districtwide student success rates were as low as ever.

As such, embracing the ROCI process was just one component of René's role in transformation. He also had to play ambassador back to the superintendent and other district leaders, who were counting on René and him team to deliver concrete results. In taking a teacher-led, ground–up approach to school improvement, René was bucking multiple national trends at once. He knew the teachers needed space to work and deliver, and he intended to provide the room they needed to grow, even though the superintendent had made it clear that time was a finite resource.

The other major diplomatic role René had to play was with the community at large. Although he will be the first to tell you that he's not a "touchy-feely guy," René's heart and family were all in East San Jose. The local history was his own, and he intended for the collective future to be even brighter for the children he now served. He attended community meetings, met with local stakeholders, and comforted families, all of whom were anxious to know whether his plan for improvement would lead to better results than the broken promises of the past.

In short, René viewed the whole city as part of the transformation crew, and he treated them as such.

Making Friends Everywhere: Garnering Community and Family Support

School transformation requires the improvement of teaching and learning. Period. That's why we started this book—and our chronicling of the transformation journey with classroom teachers. Top-down approaches to school reform are limited, in part because policy changes take too long to manifest in classrooms and, as such, are difficult to link to actual student achievement.

On the flip side, though, bottom-up reforms are vulnerable to a related, opposite problem: Classroom-level changes can remain so far below the radar of policymakers that good ideas nurtured on the ground may never get the chance to expand and flourish.

In other words, it's possible to enact a "systemic reform plan" without ever affecting the quality of teaching and learning . . . but it's also possible to change the quality of instruction in classrooms without achieving a systemwide effect. The fourth-grade crew at Chávez could meet for years, avoiding the limelight, and nobody on the outside would necessarily know what was happening.

That's why building relationships with families and the broader community is essential to every school transformation initiative. Building relationships outside of the school is hard work, though, especially for educators operating in politicized contexts. It's possible to read the vignette detailing the experience of Chávez and PACT and think that community engagement is synonymous with tension. But the other way to understand that story is that families and communities have deep, inherent power that must be understood, acknowledged, and respected.

When the community organizers at PACT were holding rallies about Chávez, it's safe to say that the relationship between the school and the community had taken on an adversarial character. Sometimes, that sort of pressure is necessary. As Dr. Martin Luther King Jr. noted in his *Letter From a Birmingham Jail,* there is a difference between "a negative peace which is the absence of tension to a positive peace which is the presence of justice."

While hastening justice can involve short-term strife, it is hard to run a successful school amidst constant tension. That's why educators engaged in school transformation must enlist various stakeholders around the transformation process, even when relationships with the public have become sour. The strength to persevere will come from the power of community, even if the community and the school haven't been on the same side lately.

One group of stakeholders to engage is, of course, children and their families. Unfortunately, too many schools, especially those serving marginalized communities, treat families as an afterthought—or worse, an obstacle to school transformation. Parents, guardians, aunts, uncles, grandmas, and cousins can be your biggest cheerleaders during the process of transformation, but they have to be engaged early and often.

There are numerous benefits to having strong, clear communications with families, and it is critical to mitigate the obstacles that threaten authentic relationship building. Language barriers—both literal and metaphorical—are real and complex. Most parents don't know the jargon we learned in ed school, so it's important to practice discussing pedagogical strategy in plain language. If families at your school speak languages other than English at home, educators and front-office staff should be able to speak fluently in families' native languages. Nothing says "you're not welcome here" like a school secretary speaking increasingly louder English to a grandparent who was born in another country. The written word matters too: Make sure that the fliers you send home are in languages that families can read.

Another barrier to communication with families is power dynamics, which exist among education professionals and marginalized communities. Many parents who send their children to struggling schools may have negative associations with schooling; perhaps they also attended a school that didn't serve them well, or maybe they've tried to get attention for their children in the past, only to have educators and administrators ignore them. Whatever the reason for the broken trust, it's important to revisit the skills we discussed in the prior section to build transparency with families who may not be predisposed to trusting educational institutions.

One additional barrier to establishing great relationships with families is time and place. Sometimes, schools schedule community meetings at 4:00 p.m. on a Wednesday and wonder why attendance is low. Guardians and parents, particularly those who work hourly jobs, do not have the luxury of attending meetings during work hours without experiencing financial penalties. "Attend this parent–teacher conference at the risk of losing your job" is not a productive way to entice participation. Schools in the process of transformation must consider how to "meet parents where they are" to achieve strong, lasting relationships. Consider weekend meetings or town halls later in the evening. Texting and phone calls can be effective when meetings are impossible to coordinate. Because of COVID-19, more and more families are comfortable with videoconferencing technology, which may create additional opportunities for interactions that don't require physical attendance.

Another critical place to seek outside relationships is with community-based organizations. In the vignette that started this section, local community organizers were so frustrated with the school that they mounted an adversarial organizing campaign. Antagonistic relationships with local organizations do not, however, need to be the norm. Proactive outreach among schools and community organizations can create lasting trust and great outcomes for children.

Beyond visibility and activism, some community organizations offer concrete services, which can be a boost for schools with fewer resources. Those services might include family counseling, mental health support, college admissions help, or after-school programs. As with any relationship, the best work happens when schools and communities are transparent about their needs and hopes for a partnership. If a school already is struggling to juggle relationships with a handful of after-school providers, it's okay to say "no, thank you" when the next group approaches. While this might sound counterintuitive, the most successful school transformation projects tend to involve fewer, stronger partnerships and not just a long list of organizations on a flier.

One way to make that process easier is for schools to conduct a "needs assessment" to proactively identify what service gaps exist for their children and families. That assessment can be a survey that families fill out at the next parent–teacher night, an online form, a series of focus groups, or all of these. However a school decides to assess, understanding what services children and families need is an important antecedent to enlisting outside partners in filling those gaps.

Philanthropies and the local business community constitute another place to look when identifying resources that can help drive improvement. As is the case with community organizations, transparency and trust are critical here. Private interests have a history of imposing their will on schools, through leveraging their power and money, causing some educators to turn their backs on potential collaborations with foundations and companies. While a healthy dose of skepticism can be helpful, there are countless parties outside of the school building who can bring resources. It's important to create a context where those folks can be helpful, especially when their motives and values are aligned with yours.

Different private entities can offer different kinds of support. Sometimes, resources are available as grant dollars that your school can put toward critical pieces of a transformation agenda. Other times, resources come as "in-kind" support, which can be any number of things: an executive on loan to help with strategy, free trips to visit other schools that have already transformed, or needed supplies. This is another place where having conducted some sort of "needs assessment" is critical. When funders or companies ask you how they can be helpful, it's important to be prepared with concrete answers, rooted in data.

As you're building relationships inside and outside of the school, heed the advice of Jim Collins from his classic book on transformation, *Good to Great*: It's not enough to "get people on the bus"; you also have to get them in the "right seats." Remain vigilant for partnership opportunities and flexible enough to figure out how to enlist partners in the right ways.

CÉSAR CHÁVEZ ELEMENTARY, SAN JOSE, CALIFORNIA

René, Meaghen, Tiara, and the teachers at Chávez were driving toward something big.

As Tiara had anticipated, using standards-based instruction as the centerpiece of grade-level team meetings was a perfect way to engage teachers in collaborative practice. By the end of the second semester of the 2010–2011 school year, most grade-level teams were meeting for weekly ROCI cycles.

The process was far from perfect. Sometimes, team leaders forgot to prepare agendas for meetings. Other times, teachers abandoned agreed-upon changes once they got in front of their classrooms because they blanked on what they had decided to do in the first place. None of these mistakes, it turned out, was detrimental to the change process. Because every week, the grade-level teams would meet again and recommit to improving together.

The work was just starting, though. Now that the team at Chávez had crewed up, they needed to think about next steps and how to start building momentum for schoolwide, and maybe even systemwide, change.

René was concerned about accelerating the work, though. The superintendent had agreed to let René and the team run with the transformation initiative, and he was pleased by the early progress, which he monitored through regular meetings with René, Meaghen, Tiara, and other members of the crew. René played a primary role in communicating back to the district, ensuring that there were "no surprises."

But there were, in fact, some surprises, as is the case with all transformation efforts.

Through engaging classroom teachers in standards-based instructional design, the Chávez crew had realized that the district's pacing guides were a potential obstacle. Try as they might, it simply was not possible to use the district's scripted pacing while also ensuring that teachers became masters of their content.

This created a conundrum for René. Some principals revel in butting heads with central offices, living for the thrill of paying bureaucratic jiu jitsu. René was not one of those principals, as he saw tension with his colleagues in the central office as a major distraction from constructive work. He knew that minimizing unnecessary tension was critical to sustaining collective willpower—inside and outside of his school—for the transformation work.

Could he pick a fight when he needed to? Sure. But in his judgment, this early in the game simply was not the right time.

(Continued)

(Continued)

In light of that, the Chávez crew, with Rene's blessing, agreed to minimize tension until the end of the school year. They would err on the side of asking forgiveness later and not raise the issue of the pacing guides with the central office. Grade-level teams continued to meet and engage in ROCI cycles. René and his instructional leadership team held space for monthly goal setting, and the district seemed excited about the progress.

As the school year approached its end, though, and the team began planning for the following school year, they knew that the status quo wouldn't last forever.

The second—not to mention third and fourth—years of change management would require a level of honesty with the central office for which they still needed to prepare.

School Transformation Is a Marathon, Not a Sprint

The complicated relationship between a school and its central office is the stuff of legend among educators. The importance of managing this relationship in a positive direction is so profound that we've dedicated an entire chapter later in this book (Chapter 9) to navigating the opportunities, challenges, and struggles that arise when transformation is afoot.

For the sake of this chapter, though, we thought it was important to close with an important reminder: Some of the most critical relationships you need to cultivate are with the people who work at your district's central office. The relative strength or weakness of those relationships can be the difference between a transformation process that is hard, but manageable versus one that feels like a series of poorly anesthetized root canals.

In the best-case scenario, the central office is full of confidants, cheerleaders, and collaborators, ready to put *their* shoulder to *your* wheel of transformation.

In the worst situations, the central office is the "party of no," committed to shutting down every creative idea that emerges from you and your crew.

The reality, as is the case with most relationships, is usually somewhere in the middle—hopefully, somewhere closer to marital bliss. Because school transformation doesn't happen overnight, you need to think of your work as a marathon, with the central office playing a role that alternates between support crew and referee. When you need administrative backing, whether in the form of resources or permissions, you're going to need them to be there. And when you and the crew screw up, the relationship needs to be strong enough that you don't disqualify yourself from the rest of the race.

Despite the fact that a relationship between a school and a central office might be hierarchical or supervisory, it's still a relationship that requires cultivating. In the previous vignette, René was careful to keep his superintendent abreast of the work, in part because he knew that he would need more explicit support later when harder challenges cropped up.

Because remember, we're just getting started. If your work attracts too much negative energy and attention in its early days, it will be hard to get the long-term gears of transformation in motion.

But on the flip side, if you can get some quick wins and use those to build additional trust, the later months and years of your journey will be just a bit easier. Success breeds success, and an object in motion is harder to stop than one standing still.

That is why, in the next chapter, we'll head a few miles north of San Jose to San Francisco to talk about how to move those gears, build momentum, and find bright spots to build upon.

THE RELATIONSHIPS CHECKLIST

- **Understand your role as an early adopter.** You were willing to take the risk of becoming a change agent before others. That's why you're reading this book! Not all of your colleagues will have the same risk tolerance. That doesn't mean they aren't change agents—just that their role in the process of change hasn't become obvious . . . yet. Part of your role as an early adopter is to help your peers find their roles and voices.

- **Build relationships like a community organizer.** The skills and competencies that you need to drive change are not exclusively

(Continued)

(Continued)

pedagogical in nature. Whatever your role is in a school, when you're building momentum for ground–up change, you're also a community organizer. And remember, how you define "community" should be expansive enough to include anyone who wants to be a part of your transformation crew.

- **Make time to practice the skills that lead to strong relationships.** Listening, transparency, and trust are all essential to forging lasting relationships. While these qualities may seem abstract, like anything else in your life, doing them well requires explicit attention. Make time with your crew to practice these core skills, using the activities we shared in this chapter. You can also try these skills at home, if your partners, roommates, and families are patient enough!

- **Remember the 5:1 golden ratio of feedback.** Giving and receiving quality feedback is a form of love. If we cannot tell the truth about our relationships to each other, how can we be truthful with the children we teach? Hone your feedback skills with your crew. The more feedback you give and receive, the easier the process becomes.

- **Look inside and outside of the school building for critical relationships.** School transformation requires internal and external support. Whether that support comes in the form of resources, talent, in-kind help, or the sustenance of community political will, it is very hard to sustain long-term transformation without public backing. Conduct needs assessments to determine what supports your school needs and map the assets in your community to determine what individuals or organizations might fill some of those needs.

- **Cultivate your relationship with the central office.** Your colleagues in the district office can be huge allies in advancing the cause of transformation. Whatever the starting context for your relationship with those colleagues, you should aspire to making the people who work there part of your crew.

CHAPTER 2: DISCUSSION QUESTIONS

1. When was the last time you tried to solve a complicated problem, working with a group? How did that work compare to solving problems alone?

2. Are there barriers that exist in your school when it comes to building relationships with peers, parents, and members of the community? Which of those barriers can you challenge? Which require administrative support?

3. Who are your biggest allies in the school? What steps would you need to take to enlist them in the work of continuous improvement?

4. Who are your biggest allies outside of the school? Who can help you to enlist those allies in this work?

Finding Bright Spots and Building Momentum

3

For Tamitrice Rice Mitchell, becoming a principal in San Francisco's Bayview was more than a job; it was a homecoming.

The Bayview—and neighboring Hunters Point—together compose a corner of the Bay Area that James Baldwin once called "the San Francisco Americans pretend does not exist." Tamitrice calls it home. She remembers running the streets there as a child, reveling in the sense of pride and protection that comes from knowing that your best friend's aunt will both have your back and set you straight if anything ever goes wrong.

It was this unique combination of family, community, and togetherness that drove Tamitrice to become an educator. She started her career as a teacher, and by the late 1990s she was ready for the next challenge. One of the Bayview's hidden-gem elementary schools, the Dr. Susan McKinney-Steward Academy, or just "Steward" for short, had recently started an innovative early education program for three-, four-, and five-year-olds. When the program's founder stepped down, Tamitrice stepped up.

Tamitrice grew to understand the school as intimately as she understood the surrounding community. She excelled in the role, and in 2004, when local superintendent Arlene Ackerman chose Steward to be a part of the city's "Dream Schools" initiative, Tamitrice was the obvious candidate to lead the charge.

(Continued)

(Continued)

The Dream Schools represented an innovative approach to school improvement that relied on steering additional resources to schools in historically underserved communities. Through her leadership of the early education program, Tamitrice had honed two distinct skills that were essential to doing that sort of work in San Francisco: first, the instructional prowess needed to teach all children against the headwinds of systematic, multigenerational disinvestment; and second, the bureaucratic know-how required to drive more resources to the Bayview amidst competing demands from San Francisco's white liberal communities, who generally take a more skeptical view of resource equity once that discussion involves the migration of real dollars from places with greater wealth to places with greater needs.

Through her work with the Dream Schools, Tamitrice developed a reputation as a doer, and when the long-serving principal of Steward retired several years later, Tamitrice applied for and got the job.

She inherited, though, a school in the midst of an identity crisis. In the 1980s, Dr. Susan McKinney-Steward Academy had been a beacon of educational excellence for the Bayview, with legendary principal Leslie Jones acting as, in Tamitrice's memory, "a walking billboard for educational excellence by any means necessary."

But the decades since the school's heyday had coincided with a period of turbulent social change throughout San Francisco, a place where tech headquarters and tent cities often came to share the same city block. While unchecked gentrification fueled massive social displacement everywhere in The Golden City, nowhere was this more damaging to the social fabric than in the Bayview. A *San Francisco Magazine* article from 2008 described the neighborhood as a place "where just about every resident had lost a loved one at some point to bullets or drugs."

This was the milieu in which Tamitrice became principal.

While Tamitrice was under no illusion about the social context in which her school existed, where some folks saw negative narratives, she saw history and promise.

Leading in this context, though, required threading a whole bunch of needles. Tamitrice had to manage conflicting ideas about the school and the students she served—not just from members of the community, but inside her own brain. On the one hand, she knew that her neighborhood was far from perfect; on the other hand, she knew that the negative narratives were central drivers of bad education policy that treated her school as dispensable. She knew that many of Steward's challenges were beyond her control, yet she also resisted the notion that she and her faculty were nothing but victims of circumstance.

Fueling her sense of promise was Tamitrice's long memory. All she had to do was look back 20 years to summon images of a school that was doing much, much better for the community's kids; she could even remember her own childhood in the 1960s, when local civil rights leaders flirted with the dream of social equality and the local schools were a beacon of that hope.

Things in the Bayview were far from perfect even then, but that never got in the way of seeing beauty alongside the challenges. Tamitrice viewed herself and her crew as shepherds in a multigenerational tale of community thriving.

For if the kids at Steward represented the dream, she and her crew had a responsibility to be the dreamkeepers.

How We Talk About Schools Affects How We Think About Schools

If you listen to folks talk about underresourced schools long enough, you might end up with some seriously messed-up ideas about our children's families and communities. These misconceptions permeate our collective consciousness through every conceivable media channel: local news that prioritizes sensationalism over storytelling, filmmaking that relies on tired tropes about inner cities, politicians looking to score cheap points, and teacher preparation programs that cater to missionary impulses.

Policymaking can make matters worse. In the last generation of education legislation, lawmakers relied on a host of infantilizing terms and ideas, many of which reinforced paternalistic relationships between marginalized communities and political power structures. Elected officials, philanthropists, commentators, and writers of all backgrounds used words like "failing" with little obvious concern for how that sort of thinking manifests in the treatment of children, families, and educators.

Words matter.

How we describe social challenges has significant ramifications for the mechanisms we use to address them. Consider the terminology of the "war on drugs." The policies related to that pursuit have had no impact on drug usage or distribution but in the process have caused the disproportionate criminalization and incarceration of Black and Latinx men. The casual use of conflict language has resulted in the adoption of tactics that inflict further violence.

Such is the case with deficit-based approaches to describing our public schools.

Using language that pathologizes children and their communities makes it harder for us to solve actual educational problems. It's impossible to treat children as future leaders when we approach them as problems to be solved, and the pursuit of improving schools is futile if we assume that the institutions themselves are inherent liabilities. Even the schools beset by the most intransigent generational challenges brim with hope, inspiration, and vision.

That's why we're dedicating this chapter to the idea of building momentum through finding and leveraging bright spots.

The identification of bright spots isn't just an exercise in making ourselves feel better, although it can have that effect. The search for bright spots is a fundamental rewiring of the way we think about, discuss, and process our understanding of the children and communities we hope to serve. Dr. Gloria Ladson-Billings studies educators who are successful in teaching students from marginalized backgrounds, which she describes as only possible through "a deep connection to the students' culture and the school community." By reorienting our hearts and minds toward a school's and community's assets, we open ourselves to the immense possibilities of authentic transformation.

Consider the story of Dr. Susan McKinney-Steward Academy. Tamitrice demonstrates what it looks like to bring an assets-based lens to the challenges of her school, even when the community's vital signs seem to be pointing in a troubling direction. It's important to note that adopting such a glass-half-full mentality doesn't mean ignoring reality. As someone who grew up in the community, Tamitrice is aware of the various social challenges that manifest as a consequence of generational poverty. She just doesn't choose to dwell on them and is studious about not allowing preconceptions and stereotypes to infect her language and thinking.

Transformation crews need to follow that example.

One way to start is to monitor the rhetoric you use to discuss children, adults, and communities. Like the golden ratio of positive to constructive feedback we discussed in Chapter 2, note whether or not you're achieving similar ratios in your meditations on children and their families. Constructs like "disadvantaged" and "at-risk" might describe real-world circumstances, but too often, those terms end up connoting innate human characteristics rather than their contextual social circumstances. Likewise, when you describe a school as "failing," consider what that designation says about a parent who attended that school and now sends their own children there.

To that point, finding bright spots while leveraging an assets-based mindset requires understanding the unique circumstances that led to our current time and place in history. You need to know a school and its community well enough to see the soft curves where everyone else just sees sharp edges. Every school, no matter how much it struggles, has a whole litany of existing assets that play an outsized role in creating the academic and social culture of the institution, ranging from the physical to the personal to the ephemeral. A newly renovated school gym can be a source of pride, and so can a school's motto. The veteran crossing guard, who knows every child's grandma's name, is an absolute gem, as is the garden outside the second-grade teacher's window.

The crews you've met in the first few chapters of this book, as you might have guessed, are bright spots too.

But remember, adopting an assets-based approach doesn't mean being unrealistic. Sanitized versions of a school's history are an inadequate foundation for building toward the future.

As the aforementioned James Baldwin once wrote, "An invented past can never be used; it cracks and crumbles under the pressures of life like clay in a season of drought."

That's why you must learn a school's *real* history and not the version outsiders have adopted as shorthand.

DR. SUSAN MCKINNEY-STEWARD ACADEMY, SAN FRANCISCO, CALIFORNIA

The Great Migration of the early- to mid-1900s witnessed an extraordinary shift of America's Black population from the Jim Crow South to the ostensibly free North. In San Francisco alone, the Black population expanded so rapidly from the 1940s to the 1970s that Isabel Wilkerson, in her book *The Warmth of Other Suns*, describes the Bay Area in the 1950s as a "satellite of colored Louisiana."

The draw of the North was as much pragmatic as sociocultural. San Francisco, like other northern enclaves, offered southern families the promise of land, liberation, and labor. Tamitrice's grandparents moved from Texas to the Bayview during this wave to take advantage of job opportunities at the Hunters Point shipyard.

By the 1960s, though, that promise already seemed like a dream deferred.

The influx of new Black residents to the Bay Area triggered an equal and opposite reaction from the city's white power brokers. City planners, developers, and banks rated neighborhoods based on their demographics and adjusted their lending practices to keep blocks segregated. This practice, which is now called "redlining," had the effect of concentrating Black families in residential enclaves where property values were artificially depressed. White property owners, real-estate brokerages, and mortgage lenders colluded to prevent Black families from owning homes and accumulating generational wealth.

Because the modern Bayview was created through redlining, it shares a series of characteristics with other neighborhoods shaped through that practice: racial housing segregation, public schools with high concentrations of low-income families, and the explicit suppression of opportunities for Black wealth accumulation.

Redlining continued into the 1980s, when it was officially banned, but other practices replaced the old approach to racial segregation. San Francisco adopted draconian residential zoning restrictions in the late 20th century, which ended up having a similar effect. Curtailing upward physical development in dense communities, like the Bayview, caused housing costs to explode by almost 400 percent during the period between 1986 to 2009. The predictable result of this unbridled escalation was that many low- and middle-income families could no longer afford to live in places where their parents and grandparents settled.

The Bayview, which had once offered so much promise, was on the path to becoming yet another bastion of unaffordable privilege.

The effect of rapid gentrification on schools was dramatic. Many parents whose professions allowed for mobility moved to more affordable suburbs; families that could not manage to move got pushed into increasingly predatory rental arrangements. California's statutory cap on real-estate taxation made the situation more tenuous; when housing prices skyrocketed, the law prevented schools and other public services from raising new revenue commensurate with the price appreciation of the surrounding real estate. Whereas high-priced suburban homes in America tend to come with admission to well-funded schools, California's regressive "Proposition 13" ensures that this fails to happen in the state's fast-gentrifying cities. Unchecked price increases, coupled with real-dollar declines in local tax revenues, beget crippled public services.

Tamitrice became principal of Steward during these peak years of gentrification-fueled displacement. The community's socioeconomic shifts meant that, by the time Tamitrice was a school leader, the neighborhood had changed from a place where multigenerational Black families could create homes to a place where very few people could afford to live at all. Most of the folks who owned homes in the community either acted as landlords or sent their kids to private schools.

Leading a school in this context meant being an instructional leader, systems thinker, public spokesperson, and diplomatic liaison. She needed to both cultivate an environment of excellence among educators in the school, while identifying public and private sources of support that might ameliorate generations of disinvestment out of her control.

If that sounds like a big job, that's literally what principals in many American cities are asked to do.

Fortunately, Tamitrice had some wind at her back in the form of local bright spots. Since the 1960s, a network of like-minded school administrators had been at the forefront of the Bayview civil rights community. This crew's support was essential to building Tamitrice's

(Continued)

(Continued)

capacity and confidence. She also had a group of teachers and administrators in the schools who shared her values and were "ready to go." While some of the teachers were newer and less experienced, they had raw talent, enthusiasm, and an understanding of how racial equity intersected with educational opportunity at Steward. With some professional development, mentorship, and structured collaboration, Tamitrice knew that they could become real pros in no time.

She even had the ear and support of a new assistant superintendent, Guadalupe Guerrero, who had been an educator in the Mission, the next neighborhood over. His charge was to accelerate school transformation efforts across the city, which attracted him to the efforts at Steward.

That work, however, was turning out to be harder than Tamitrice expected. Early in her first semester as principal, Guadalupe stopped by the school to conduct an assessment of the school's readiness for improvement. He sat with the instructional-leadership team, walked the hallways, and reviewed documents. He spent the most time, though, observing instruction across the school, lingering long enough in classrooms to get a real taste for what was happening.

After several hours, Guadalupe sat with Tamitrice and her instructional-leadership team in the front office and shared what he saw, in a matter-of-fact, almost clinical fashion. He noticed a lot of gaps, and he was not shy about identifying them.

Instruction was good in some classrooms but inconsistent, he said. Collaboration was happening at some grade levels but wasn't systematic, he added. There was no clear evidence that all teachers were using data to drive instruction, he observed, and when he did notice things going well, bright spots if you will, it was hard to connect those individual highlights back to a schoolwide approach.

In short, if there was a problem to be found at Steward that fall, Guadalupe saw it, noted it, and commented on it.

And although his critique was tough, it was also, unfortunately, fair. He left Steward to make another school visit, and the instructional-leadership team at Steward sat staring at each other in the front office, somewhat stunned.

"He just slashed me," Tamitrice said to her team, looking around to see their reactions. "And you know what? He was right."

There's Gold in Them There Hills

Bright spots are most valuable to us when they are visible and when we can find concrete ways to build upon them.

While Tamitrice makes no bones about how tough Guadalupe was in his initial assessment, his unvarnished perspective was an important factor in driving improvement. Guadalupe had been a principal in a similar context, so Tamitrice respected his opinion; as we discussed in Chapter 2, the ability to give and receive actionable feedback is an important antecedent to school transformation. In offering that feedback, Guadalupe was supporting her work in several ways. First and foremost, he wanted to ensure that Tamitrice was seeing the same things he was seeing. Finding bright spots is critical, but they cannot protect us from acknowledging reality. Second, he wanted to validate her urgency as a school leader; being a change agent can ruffle feathers, so it can be helpful to have a friend in high places who is willing to deliver tough messages in front of your team.

Finally, and perhaps most importantly, he was helping to widen the school's aperture, from the bright spots to the bigger picture. Building momentum for school transformation requires not just finding things to celebrate but also using those positive elements as leverage for pushing further. In his feedback, Guadalupe was clear that he saw positive elements but that few of them rose to the level of systematic.

That's why every school on the brink of transformation needs to conduct a *school transformation review*.

A school transformation review, when conducted thoroughly, is like sifting through an enormous sandbox to unearth all of the treasure—not to mention the not-so-awesome stuff—buried within. Instead of looking for precious gems or dinosaur bones, though, the school transformation review is designed to uncover the ingredients necessary for driving sustained improvement.

The good news is that every school has *some* of the ingredients already. You just have to be disciplined about finding them. It's one thing to identify an anecdotal bright spot; it's a whole other thing to unearth them in a comprehensive way. Whereas deficit-based approaches to school improvement dwell on the absence of personnel and resources, ground-up change rooted in continuous improvement only works when we generate momentum from ingredients that already are present in a community.

When coupled with the community asset map that we described in Chapter 2, the results of a school transformation review provide a detailed snapshot of your school, like the "X" on a map that says "You Are Here."

You can't get somewhere else without first knowing where you are.

There are dozens of school improvement rubrics that examine hundreds of dimensions of school operation, from the speed of school lunch service to the colorfulness of bulletin boards in a fifth-grade hallway. While there are countless things a crew can examine as part of the school transformation review, there are a few big categories that seem to provide the biggest lift in the early stages of a process.

Results-Oriented School Leadership

The first area in a comprehensive review looks for *school leadership that is oriented around results*. While the role of a principal is central, examining school leadership is broader than assessing the capabilities of a single person. Looking for results-oriented leadership in a school means finding out if the school has a coherent vision, examining the depth of school–family partnerships, analyzing communications challenges, and interrogating the extent to which school decisions are driven by real student information and data. Finding evidence of results-oriented leadership in a school means asking questions like these:

- How does the school leadership team articulate annual goals for improving instruction?
- What is the extent of the school's commitment to culturally responsive teaching?
- How do school leaders adjust and adapt their own practices and behaviors based on evidence and outcomes?

Professional Learning Systems

Identifying *systems for professional learning* is the second major area in a school transformation review. While just about every study of school improvement indicates that collaborative professional learning is one of the single, biggest predictors of sustained success in a school, few schools build and monitor the extent, quality, and caliber of professional learning. While most educators have experienced "professional development" delivered perfunctorily in a lunchroom for 40 minutes on a Friday afternoon, real professional learning is embedded in everyday practice and happens through the deep examination of one's own capabilities. Finding the bright spots in a school's approach to professional learning means asking questions like these:

- How does the school create time for teacher collaboration on an ongoing basis?

- When teachers receive professional development, what mechanisms are present that allow them to translate the learning into action?

- How does the school cultivate professional learning communities that create the context for learning on an everyday basis?

Core Instruction

The final area for investigation in a school transformation review is the ***core instructional program***. While the curriculum is a part of the instructional core of A school, the presence of strong curricula alone is an insufficient condition for translating momentum into academic success. A great curriculum poorly implemented doesn't get you very far, while mediocre instructional materials in the hands of a master educator can lead to surprising levels of student understanding. Unearthing the strengths of a school's instructional program means asking, among other things, these questions:

- What are the processes for aligning daily instruction to core learning standards?

- How does our curriculum respond to the cultural identities of our students, and how do we affirm those identities as assets?

- How do we systematically develop student vocabulary across subject areas?

- How do we assess student progress, and what methods do we use to disaggregate that information in meaningful and useful ways?

There are dozens of aspects of a school that you and your crew should examine in a school transformation review. While it's useful to agree on the most critical elements, you don't need to recreate the wheel and spend weeks designing questions. (We've included some sample review rubrics and frameworks in the web-based resources that accompany this book.) As with everything else related to your newfound ROCI lifestyle, a school transformation review is best conducted with a crew so that you're building social norms around schoolwide observation.

And remember, "observation" is the operative word here. The school transformation review should not be an evaluative tool; otherwise, its magic will dissipate. For myriad reasons, some rooted in rational suspicion, there are educators who become skeptical and defensive once folks start marching around the school building holding clipboards with rubrics. If teachers suspect that you're trying to identify weaknesses, or play "gotcha," it will be hard to build the trust, camaraderie, momentum, and community-wide care that is essential to execute cycles of inquiry over time.

Which brings us to one final point about the school transformation review: Notice that in the categories and questions previously mentioned, we did not discuss individual actions, but rather concrete evidence for the existence of systems. That's intentional. A school transformation review is not about assessing individual teaching performance or leadership capacity, and it certainly is not a tool for educator evaluation. A school transformation review does, though, seek to identify concrete evidence of systemic factors that drive school transformation. That includes describing observable adult behaviors, while collecting artifacts that support those behaviors, including curricula, assessments, professional learning plans, and documentation about the school's vision.

In conducting a comprehensive school transformation review, your goal is not to blame and shame educators, which too often happens in schools that have been underresourced. Your goal is to paint a precise and accurate picture of your school's starting point while unearthing existing assets and bright spots that can be built upon. Only then can you identify interventions that are likely to work in your unique context.

Once you do all that, you start to build momentum.

DR. SUSAN MCKINNEY-STEWARD ACADEMY, SAN FRANCISCO, CALIFORNIA

Tamitrice liked to say that there was a strong history at Steward, but they just had to bring it out of the rubble and ashes. After Guadalupe's tough but fair initial visit, Tamitrice knew that her work was cut out for her. Perhaps most importantly, Guadalupe had made clear that he was deeply vested in her success and was eager to support her in cutting red tape to hasten the kinds of supports they needed to make progress.

Guadalupe wasn't the only person in her corner. Tamitrice's crew included a seasoned instructional-leadership team, transformation coaches from the district central office, and an outside expert or two. She also ran with a tight-knit network of strong school leaders throughout the Bayview who understood exactly the kind of uphill battle that she was facing. (A group of sympathetic peers—who are ready to spend a long night doing karaoke after a particularly tricky week—is an oft underappreciated ingredient in the ROCI process.)

That extended Steward crew came together to conduct a comprehensive school transformation review, which put a finer point on many of the challenges that Guadalupe observed.

The challenges, though, were complemented by a host of assets, both within the school and in the surrounding community, that could be built upon: The leadership possessed loads of talent and represented the broader diversity of the Bayview community; there were local churches and community centers that were willing to lend time, energy, and resources to the transformation process; and the school already used a strong battery of interim assessments that provided useful insights into student progress, especially in math.

In short, Tamitrice knew where her assets were, and she was ready to act. To build momentum, though, they needed a plan. Tamitrice relied heavily on Tim, the school's dedicated transformation coach, whose skills were, in many ways, a perfect complement to hers. He was a data geek who had spent much of his career helping teachers understand and grapple with numbers and statistics. He knew how to map global systems thinking into concrete strategies, and he was a whiz with student information.

Tim, Tamitrice, and the instructional-leadership team put their heads together and collaborated to figure out where to focus. Everyone in the crew had seen school improvement plans in large binders on front-office shelves, collecting dust. They did not intend to waste their time that way. The group was committed to a communal, generative process of ideation, which they knew would unearth more good ideas than any one of them could ever find sitting in a room alone.

(Continued)

(Continued)

Beyond building a plan that considered the perspectives of the whole leadership team, Tamitrice and Tim knew that the right plan would strike an important balance between ambition and achievability. Tamitrice was motivated to fix everything—right now!—but she knew that Tim's linear approach to problem-solving could sharpen her tactics through strategic sequencing.

This process—one of translating the bright spots they unearthed in the transformation review into a longer, more substantive plan—involved a lot of whiteboarding.

Tamitrice and Tim spent hours at a time in the principal's office, over the course of many days, squeezing every last bit of ink out of tired felt-tipped dry-erase markers. They made matrices, drew diagrams, and fumbled through flowcharts.

There was a method to the madness, though, because they were looking for two significant things. First, they were trying to find some quick wins rooted in the school's existing assets. If they could find quick wins, Tim reasoned, it would create excitement and allow them to build momentum toward longer-term goals. Tim liked to call this process "finding the small wheel," which could in turn be used to turn the "big wheel," which represented the overall goal of schoolwide transformation.

Finding the "small wheel that can turn the big wheel" became a mantra for the crew—a pithy statement capturing the logic of systemic momentum building.

They identified the improvement of math instruction as a promising candidate for the "small wheel." There was a crew of teachers already working together on math teaching with the support of a content specialist from the district. According to their reliable interim assessments, only about a third of the kids in the school were testing at grade level on math assessments; that said, the school transformation review had revealed some instructional bright spots in math teaching among the school's novice teachers.

The instructional-leadership team decided to lean into math improvements. Tamitrice encouraged the teachers to meet as grade-level teams, creating collaborative time in the school's schedule wherever she could. Meanwhile, Tim provided both technical and moral support. He prepared agendas for meetings, held workshops in how to conduct classroom-level data analysis, and generated visualizations based on student information.

The second thing they were trying to find was a little more elusive. While the expression "the small wheels turn the big wheel" is easy enough to say, the mechanism by which that happens in practice is more complicated. Even if they encouraged grade-level conversations about math instruction *and* provided leadership support for that endeavor *and* analyzed data as a leadership team, those things could all happen without manifesting as schoolwide gains.

The second big thing that Tamitrice, Tim, and the crew were looking for was a hypothesis. They needed a description of how the small wheel's revolutions would lead to moving that big wheel—the connective tissues between highlighting the school's bright spots and driving sustainable change.

They needed, in other words, a theory of action.

Theory of Action: A Concrete Way to Translate Small Wins Into Big Ones

Momentum, in the sense of classical Newtonian mechanics, describes how objects move once they're already in motion.

Children and communities are, of course, not simple machines, but the complex social dynamics that manifest in schools have a lot in common with physics. Running a good school depends on myriad successful interactions every day, and when things are going well, success breeds success. Lots of good microinteractions among students and educators fuel a positive vibe, translating into ever more positive momentum. The better things go over long stretches of time, the easier the momentum is to sustain.

When things are going poorly in a school, though, long sequences of negative interactions have the opposite effect. Negativity feeds on itself, driving animus, suspicion, and an overall bad vibe. People stop coordinating and trying, creating a feeling of free fall.

The hard thing about momentum is that it's equally strong in both positive and negative directions. If you're in a rocket soaring toward the nearest planet, momentum will keep you moving through the cosmos; but if you're in a barrel plummeting down a hill, momentum also will make sure you don't stop until you land at the bottom of a canyon.

Unfortunately, some struggling schools feel like being in the tumbling barrel, and if *you* try to stop the barrel—*alone*—you're bound to get flattened.

That's why ROCI-ing, as part of a crew, is so critical to changing the vibes in a school. Building positive momentum over time, especially in schools with lots of challenges, requires orchestrating small successes with intention. ROCI, when you really commit to it, is a systematic way to generate a steady stream of quick wins that build on each other. Change agents learn how to highlight these wins—no matter how small they are—through celebration. They amplify good news, reinforce the great work of other change agents, point out moments of joy, and encourage the sort of risk-taking that leads to achieving more and more wins.

Eventually, enough wins accumulate to reverse the momentum. Instead of one brave but misguided person diving in front of the barrel, the crew acts in concert, with a series of wheels and pullies that, when cobbled together, can stop the barrel's descent.

The challenge, however, is to institutionalize those virtuous cycles of inquiry in a way that connects the small wins to a broader systemic agenda that can lead to sustainable transformation.

Which brings us back to Tamitrice and Tim's "whiteboarding," which like ROCI, is kind of fun to use as a verb.

The goal of their creative fervor was to find a coherent pathway between quick wins and sustained success. Their quest was for something that was equal parts treasure map, decoder ring, and origin story. The framework they sought needed to include an honest reckoning of the current condition of the school, a vision for the future, and a logical description of the process of moving from the starting place to the aspirational place.

Enter the ***theory of action***.

In its purest form, a theory of action is a series of if/then statements about expectations for the change, improvement, or transformation of a system. For example, one *if/then statement* might be "if we use collaborative planning time to discuss how we teach the adding of fractions, then our collective instructional abilities in that domain will improve, and student performance in adding fractions will get better." The statement is strong because it has an actionable antecedent (the "if" part), measurable outputs and outcomes (the "then"), and the connection between the two components is rooted in empirical data (research indicates that collaboration leads to improved instructional capabilities among educators).

If you put together multiple if/then statements that collectively describe a process of schoolwide transformation, then you can create a theory of action.

The if/then statements that make up theories of action are simple to repeat, yet they are challenging to craft and execute. Many schools do not have them at all, making it hard to connect daily instructional activities to long-term goals. Some schools have theories of action on paper but fall short of actualizing them in practice. Other times, educators craft if/then statements, but the logic of the statement isn't rooted in empirical research, so it's not helpful for driving practice. For example, an if/then statement that says, "If we give all children laptops, then they will learn math," is unhelpful because there is no research connecting the antecedent to the outcome.

While there is no single template that all schools should use for a theory of action, there are some common ingredients in a particularly strong one.

First, a theory of action should fit on one page, in a simple graphic, and be written in jargon-free language. A theory of action that goes on for 10 pages and contains lots of "educator-ese" will be hard to remember and even harder to explain to people who don't have a PhD in pedagogy. You should be able to explain the theory of action to everyone in your school community, from the grandpas to the lunch ladies to the special-education paraprofessionals.

Second, the theory of action should include a handful of research-based, data-informed if/then statements. One statement is too few, and 10 is too many. Your statements should be connected to your school goals, and you shouldn't have any goals that aren't supported by appropriate if/then statements. An objective without an if/then statement is just a wish, or as W. Edward Deming, a pioneer in the field of improvement science, liked to say, "A goal without a method is nonsense."

Third, your theory of action should include a statement of your crew's values. Here is the place to articulate in explicit terms the ideals, motivations, mantras, and beliefs that drive your technical practice. This is where you talk about things like love, equity, community, and empowerment, concepts that motivate us to show up every day to achieve our tactical goals. Our values help to steer us when we have to choose among competing priorities, which is a daily struggle in schools that need systemic transformation.

Finally, strong theories of action should include the list of community and school assets that will help propel us toward the change we seek. While some change agents can look at a one-page document and immediately see their place in the transformation process, other folks benefit from seeing a more explicit description of what their role might be. Parents, gym teachers, community-based organizations, faith leaders, and everyone in between needs to be able to find themselves in the theory of action. Being explicit about how they might support a plan, through putting them on that one-pager, can help generate buy-in and enthusiasm for your work.

The one-two punch of the school transformation review and the theory of action is quite powerful. The review process helps a school to identify its current state ("You are *here*"), and theory of action describes the process of moving from the current state to a future vision ("*If* you do these things, *then* you will get *there*").

While these steps sound linear and straightforward, the process of getting there is messy and fraught. Some of your if/then statements may be wrong, which is why they are hypotheses and not gospel. How you execute in your particular context will matter just as much as the research basis behind the hypotheses. Meanwhile, smart people can and will disagree on what they see in a school transformation review; the process of coming to consensus will reveal disagreement and tension, which is important to manage as a crew.

The goal isn't to construct a perfect roadmap from which you never deviate. Rather, your aspiration should be to use the analytical tool of the school transformation review, coupled with the development of the theory of action, as opportunities to build schoolwide consensus about where you're starting, what your bright spots are, and how you're going to use them to get where you're going.

Or as President Dwight Eisenhower once famously said, "Plans are worthless, but planning is everything."

DR. SUSAN MCKINNEY-STEWARD ACADEMY, SAN FRANCISCO, CALIFORNIA

At the beginning of Tamitrice's second school year as principal, Guadalupe Guerrero's tough first visit was a distant memory.

For the most part.

Instead of scarring Tamitrice and her crew, the critical diagnosis and feedback had been equal parts motivating and liberating, like someone stepping to them and saying, "Game on."

With a year as principal under her belt, Tamitrice was beginning to see how she could connect the dots between her early wins and a long-term transformation plan. Through designing a theory of action and conducting a comprehensive school transformation review, the instructional-leadership team had narrowed its focus to a few major areas, all of which required significant collaboration.

The instructional-leadership team itself had been a bright spot from the jump. That team, which included not just assistant principals at the school but also coaches from the central office and partner organizations, operated like a team of educational architects. The school transformation review gave them a diagrammatic view of their current floor plan, and the theory of action provided a description for how to renovate toward their future vision.

The team met regularly. Just as grade-level teams rely on data to drive their cycles of inquiry, so did the instructional-leadership team at Steward. Instead of establishing weekly ROCI cycles, though, the leadership team adopted monthly cycles, which allowed them to gain broader visibility into the work happening within grade-level crews.

Second, these monthlong inquiry cycles adopted by the leadership team gave the grade-level teams adequate time for weekly experimentation: trial, error, doing new things in response to conditions in classrooms, recovery from mistakes, reflection, and dissecting their actions after the fact. Cultivating the collaboration capacity of these grade-level teams was central to Tamitrice's vision. If the instructional-leadership team acted as architects, the grade-level teams were the

(Continued)

(Continued)

builders who turned vision to reality. Teachers assembled regularly in grade-level teams to discuss instructional practice and engage in ROCI cycles.

The final major area of focus for the school was driving discussions about race and equity. While Tamitrice had spent a lifetime navigating these waters as a Black woman, she realized that she needed to be much more intentional about building her whole faculty's capacity to have conversations about race. Whereas the role of race in the distribution of resources and educational opportunity had been an implicit theme at Steward and in the Bayview for decades, Tamitrice and her crew knew that lasting transformation would require making those conversations explicit.

"Anyone who's ready and willing can teach here," Tamitrice told her team, "but you can't be a successful teacher in this building if you can't have a serious conversation about the way race and racism intersect with our children's lives."

To begin building the faculty's understanding of these issues, Tamitrice encouraged her crew to look inside and outside of the school. Teachers examined data, which demonstrated racial disproportionality in student suspensions. Examining that data led to frank conversations about how the racial demographics of the teachers didn't match those of the student population, which in turn allowed many of the teachers to acknowledge that they lacked significant grounding in the community's culture and institutions. A lot of Steward's educators drove in and out of the community each day without seeing much beyond the school, so Tamitrice rented a bus during one professional learning week. Everyone from the school got on the bus to visit local churches and community centers, further broadening the frame through which teachers could build relationships with students and their families.

The focus on instructional leadership, grade-level inquiry cycles, and racial equity delivered dividends.

Guadalupe came back that fall to get a handle on the school's progress. Accompanied by Tamitrice, he walked the school again, observing classrooms, asking a lot of hard questions, and having challenging conversations with educators.

He was, in a word, floored. "Something special is happening here," he said, "and it's obvious throughout the school. Changes are palpable, and that is evident in more consistent practices from classroom to classroom."

While Steward was far from perfect, the changes were notable at a schoolwide level. He saw the theory of action on paper, but it was clear that the faculty was living the transformation work, and that's something you can never find in the documents themselves. Guadalupe was even more effusive in his subsequent visits, noting that the school was instrumental in building momentum for broader systemic strategies that were just beginning to play out throughout the city.

The small wheels were turning, and the big wheel was beginning to budge.

The End of the Beginning

One year into a school transformation process, things were starting to improve in a visible way at Dr. Susan McKinney-Steward Academy. But while early gains are exciting, the goal of transformation isn't change for change's sake. The goal is sustained excellence for all children, which takes far longer than a single school year.

When we started talking about school transformation in Chapter 1, we mentioned that ROCI was more than a process—that it was something closer to a lifestyle. At this point in the book, we hope you're starting to understand what we mean when we say that.

Consider the routines of continuous improvement present at Steward after just one year of school transformation work. The teachers were meeting weekly, in grade-level teams, conducting their own cycles of data-informed inquiry about classroom instruction. That core classroom work was being supported by an instructional-leadership team. The team of instructional leaders themselves were participating in a different ROCI cycle, on a monthly timeline, which examined the impact of schoolwide interventions on classroom instructional practice.

ROCI: All the Time, at All Levels

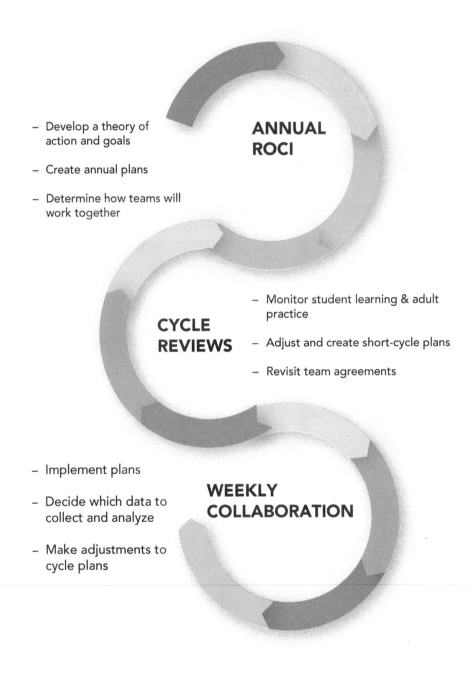

- Develop a theory of action and goals

- Create annual plans

- Determine how teams will work together

ANNUAL ROCI

CYCLE REVIEWS

- Monitor student learning & adult practice

- Adjust and create short-cycle plans

- Revisit team agreements

- Implement plans

- Decide which data to collect and analyze

- Make adjustments to cycle plans

WEEKLY COLLABORATION

ROCI, on top of ROCI, on top of ROCI . . . the small wheels turning, all the while beginning to spin the larger ones.

The replication of ROCI across a school is much, much easier if you have a crew that achieves quick wins and builds momentum. Once you've established some momentum and are ROCI-ing schoolwide, that's when the real stuff starts to happen. Instead of building skills and trust in isolation, that work is happening as a schoolwide team. When an individual teacher discovers something new about their own practice, there are habits and mechanisms present to amplify and institutionalize those shifts. Norms start to change, and hopefully, the mood of the school starts to adapt accordingly.

But when all of that happens, it means you're just getting started.

Schools that struggle for decades need more than a few semesters of living the ROCI life to achieve sustained excellence for all children. Not to mention, inquiry cycles alone are necessary, but insufficient, to sustain the technical and cultural change needed to realize breakthrough successes.

As the stories of the Bayview illuminate, an equally important component of addressing lasting change in schools is a commitment to equity. Working to ensure equity in schools means understanding the cultural and systemic factors—rooted in race, class, identity, and public policy—that create disparate opportunities and outcomes for children in historically marginalized communities.

While some approaches to school improvement ignore these factors—or worse, argue that individual effort and "grit" are sufficient to overcome centuries of institutional racism—real school transformation requires deep reckoning with these realities. Grappling with educational inequity in communities like the Bayview requires understanding the sociocultural factors that create generations of resource disparities and disinvestment.

We cannot improve educational opportunities for children while ignoring the world in which they live, but these multigenerational systemic factors are not destiny. We also cannot allow the existence of these systemic problems to cause institutional paralysis. There are schools and districts that defy these realities every day, through sustaining a focus on results, as well as building relationships and systems to drive those outcomes over time.

More schools could be engaging in that kind of transformational leadership, but the work is hard. The only way to maintain focus, over the course of many years and against the headwinds of historical systemic disparities, is to establish extraordinary discipline in the art and science of getting things done.

This very practical and painstaking sort of implementation is what we'll dissect in Chapter 4.

THE BRIGHT SPOTS AND MOMENTUM CHECKLIST

- **Cultivate an assets-based mindset.** Decades of negative rhetoric about schools and the families they serve have fostered counterproductive, deficit-oriented frames that frustrate the work of transformation. Because you're a change agent, you know that a different world is possible. One of the most important shifts you can make in your role is modeling the sort of assets-based analysis that will foster a growth mindset across your school.

- **Learn and understand your community's history.** No matter how much you already know about the place where you live and work, there is always more cultural wealth to discover. Schools exist within a community context, and whether you grew up in that community or showed up for the first time when you started teaching, the stories of the past can help unlock the pathway to the future. Schools in need of significant transformation often are situated in communities with a history of racism, displacement, segregation, and systematic disinvestment. These histories are important to know, even though historical oppression need not imply perpetual, fruitless struggle.

- **Find bright spots, get some quick wins, and celebrate the heck out of them!** Building momentum for social change is equal parts art and science, but one proven way to accelerate the process is to look for quick wins. No win is too small to celebrate! If you build a habit of pointing out and making a big fuss out of incremental progress, more and more of your peers will become vested in the long-term process of transformation.

- **Conduct a school transformation review.** While it's helpful to identify assets in your school on an anecdotal basis—particularly in the service of finding quick wins—at some point you have to undertake a more systematic unearthing of strengths in your school. A school transformation review, rooted in an objective, qualitative rubric, will give your team a deep sense of where the biggest opportunities exist to drive change—not to mention, the process will help to create a shared language and sense of purpose among your peers.

- **Develop a "theory of action."** School transformation is a process of moving from one place to another. Once you know where you've been and where you want to go, your school's theory of action is the framework for making smart decisions about how to get there. A good theory of action includes if/then statements about inputs and outcomes, a set of values that undergird those process statements, and a series of goals that let us know what it would look like to achieve that overall vision.

- **Always. Be. ROCI-ing!** ROCI isn't something you learn, do, and then forget . . . it is a new part of your life as an educator that acts as the practical foundation for long-term, sustainable transformation. ROCI cycles for teachers should be weekly, and schoolwide leadership ROCI cycles are most effective in monthly or quarterly increments. As with any habit, ROCI is challenging to start and much, much easier to do if you make the practice habitual.

CHAPTER 3: DISCUSSION QUESTIONS

1. What kind of language do you use to describe the school you work in? How does your rhetoric emphasize bright spots, and when do your words gravitate toward the negative? How about your peers? How do they describe the school and its children?

2. What does professional learning look like in your school? When is it systematic, and in what cases is it episodic? When is it event driven versus when is it embedded in everyday practice? Who sets the agenda for professional learning, and who has input in that process?

3. Practice writing an if/then statement about your own classroom or school! Don't worry about perfect wording—just give it a try.

Focus, Follow Through, See

4

The Art and Science of Implementation

If you walk west from Dr. Susan McKinney-Steward Academy, through the outskirts of the Bayview, after about a half a mile you hit Highway 101. Middle schoolers from around the community walk under this six-lane Bayshore Freeway to get to the Amos Freeman Middle School, which while technically located in the Portola neighborhood, is one of but two traditional public middle schools serving the Bayview.

Visitors to "Freeman" are greeted by a grand painting on the school's Girard Street entrance, depicting, at its center, Dr. Martin Luther King Jr. The portrait of Dr. King is flanked on either side by other international heroes of freedom and liberation: Aun Sang Suu Kyi, Susan B. Anthony, César Chávez, and Ghandi.

On a crisp fall day in 2014, Michael Essien, the assistant principal of Freeman, and Hansa Kaipa, an instructional coach, were walking through the hallways of the school, doing their best to project positivity, as they made their way to a scheduled administrative-team meeting. The crew at Freeman was in the early months of learning the habits of ROCI. Michael and Hansa had worked with the faculty to build structures for inquiry cycles, and some of the emergent strategies were starting to stick.

(Continued)

(Continued)

Around every corner, though, something conspired to shake their collective confidence in the process. Students cluttered the hallways while classes were in session, and few of the stragglers seemed eager to find their seats. The situation behind closed doors wasn't much better, as teachers often struggled to connect with disengaged students. Just a week before, Hansa had observed a classroom where a teacher was sitting, teaching only three students, while everyone else played on their phones.

Hansa held her breath as they turned into the seventh-grade hallway. She had grown accustomed to encountering scuffles during her walk-throughs.

Michael sensed her tension. "It's okay, you can say it," he said, turning to face her. "This school is chaotic."

The chaos, though, had been a draw for Michael. Earlier that fall, he had been appointed assistant principal of Freeman, and he was motivated to jump-start a school transformation process, inspired by the progress under Tamitrice's leadership at nearby Steward.

But whereas by the time of Michael's appointment Tamitrice and her crew were a few years into flipping the script, the crew at Freeman had just begun.

When Michael started as an administrator, Freeman had the highest rate of suspensions in the district, and almost all of the students who were disciplined were Black boys. Freeman's teachers awarded more "D" and "F" grades than almost any other school in San Francisco, and of 23 content teachers, 14 were new, hired at the beginning of the current school year.

In short, according to just about every metric, Freeman was on the opposite end of what you want to see in a school: high suspensions, low academic performance, high teacher turnover, and sagging morale.

Michael had become an educator, though, to do justice work. As a Black man, he knew that he had to confront a whole closet full of his own demons about public education to best serve the students at Freeman. For generations, San Francisco had cultivated disciplinary systems that relied on punishment first and positive reinforcement as an afterthought. Breaking that cycle of punishment and disengagement would mean not just pushing against the entrenched attitudes and biases of the teachers in the school but also interrogating the extent to which he had absorbed some of those prejudices himself.

Michael was not alone in confronting his biases. Hansa, as a school improvement coach, had worked across a handful of schools in San Francisco. She and her colleagues had worked at Steward and other nearby schools, but the challenges at Freeman seemed more daunting than at the local elementary schools. The basic tenets of child development were throwing wrenches into their transformation plans; the manifestations of adolescent rebellion are more pronounced than the playful mischief of elementary schoolers. The middle grades are when a lot of child misbehavior stops being clothed in cuteness.

Michael and Hansa saw a lot of not-so-cute behavior on their way to the administrative-team meeting, which was being held in the school's less-than-private front office. The administrative team was part of a series of teams that Michael had already built, which were essential to their work of continuous improvement: an instructional-leadership team of teacher team leads, a "Culture Club" of teachers who were elected by their peers to be a voice for school change, and the administrative team, which met weekly to handle operational issues.

Hansa aspired to use the team structures to cut through the chaos of the school and make it easier for teachers to do their jobs. At her best, she was a choreographer of adult behavior. She designed and facilitated educator interactions in such a way that teased out everyone's best contributions, and she was adept at figuring out how to link commitments to behaviors. She could see the interconnections among grade-level collaboration, schoolwide communication, ROCI cycles, and results; she knew that building momentum and staying on track would require everyone to play their parts.

Chaos, however, is the enemy of elegant choreography. While Hansa had done her best to coax the administrative team into patterns of constructive collaboration, on most days the team seemed more interested in venting frustrations.

(Continued)

(Continued)

While Hansa knew that providing space for the occasional gripe session was part of the process, she was eager to move past the negativity in service of moving a transformation agenda. The team had talked extensively about what their priorities ought to be, and there was consensus that the school culture had to shift. Finding a new approach to student discipline would be essential to that project. There always seemed to be a student behavior crisis brewing somewhere in the school, and firefighting these incidents got in the way of thoughtful execution.

Compounding the problem, the school's primary response to the chaos—suspending and punishing students—was not working and was feeding a downward cultural spiral.

Michael and Hansa arrived at the office and tried their best to set the tone. They had worked together to choreograph this day differently, with an eye toward aligning the school's professional development plan with the instructional-leadership team's stated goals. The administrative team crowded around the tiny conference table at the back of the front office, holding stacks of papers and clipboards, many a head of hair in disarray. They wedged themselves into seats next to the copy machine. Because the conference area had no door, the din of the hallways rang through the room.

Trying to block out the hallway noise, Hansa sat down and passed out an agenda, eager to have a solid 30 minutes of distraction-free conversation. If they could spend that much time connecting the dots between the strategies articulated in their theory of action and what they were all observing in classrooms, that would constitute a win.

Within five minutes of starting the meeting, though, Hansa's hopes collapsed. A middle schooler ran to the back of the office—there was no door, after all—and yelled to the team about a problem she was having with another student.

The administrators, thrown into rapid response, barked into their walkie-talkies and scattered to respond.

Hansa was left alone at the table, agendas and chairs in a state of disarray. With that, her careful choreography collapsed. Again.

The Art of Execution—aka
Hard Things Are Hard

If you've stuck with this book this long, and you and your crew are ROCI-ing, immersed in the work of implementing transformation strategies in your own school, I don't need to tell you that *talking about* this work is radically different from *doing* this work.

Transformation requires you and your crew to do new things, every day, in coordination. You're adopting new strategies all of the time, and so you're also sort of nervous while you're experimenting in a way that you haven't experienced since you yourself were a student. To add insult to injury, all of this anxious experimentation takes place in front of, wait for it, children . . . those notoriously sophisticated and unforgiving critics of even the most error-free adult behavior.

The flip side to the messiness is that, if you've made it this far, you've got some momentum on your side. As we learned in Chapter 3, getting the metaphorical wheels turning is critical to sustaining support and enthusiasm for your efforts. We also learned that planning and strategizing are essential, even if the plans themselves are ever-changing documents, subject to all sorts of shifts once they confront the daily reality of execution in the human-centered environment of a school.

Hence, Hansa's frustration in the previous vignette, where she's trying to implement an adult-learning agenda against the backdrop of a school in a constant state of crisis.

Doing great work on a regular basis, even without constant distractions, is hard. Doing transformational work within the context of a struggling school, where distractions are the norm, is even harder. While our culture tends to valorize visionaries and people who articulate grand strategies, visions only get as far as a fancy PowerPoint presentation unless a whole bunch of folks have the patience, energy, and technical capabilities to do the work on the ground.

There is a difference, in other words, between "talking about it" and "being about it."

Implementation is the day-to-day practice of being about that transformation life. Throughout this chapter, we're going to discuss a variety of tools and tactics that educators use to drive focus, professional learning, and consistent execution. At its core, this work is about connecting the dots between the theory of action you wrote on a whiteboard—to the work that you and your peers must do every day, on the ground, in the trenches of schools.

In other words, we're going to talk about doing the darn thing.

We're not going to mince words: Doing the thing is hard. Management consultants, life coaches, and spiritual gurus have made fortunes pontificating on the ephemeral art of implementation. One of the most successful business books of all time is called, simply, *Execution* and is dedicated to describing, in excruciating detail, how to, you know . . . do stuff.

But why is doing stuff so hard?

One useful way to think about the complexities of execution is to envision the process of cultivating a garden. To make your garden beautiful and life-sustaining, there are a few big things that you have to do infrequently, maybe just once every year: turn over the soil, plant shade trees that you hope will flourish in years to come, and assess what you planted in prior years that didn't thrive.

Beyond the momentous yearly things, there are other activities you do somewhat more often, perhaps once per season: add fertilizer to garden boxes, trim large bushes, and plant perennials.

The annual and seasonal activities are critical, sometimes exciting, and create immediate visual evidence of progress. In the scope of yours and your garden's life, though, those annual and seasonal things happen with remarkable infrequency.

There are other things, though, that you need to do all the time—like, literally every single day: water the plants and weed the garden. Watering and weeding never seem to stop.

Water the plants and weed the garden. Water the plants and weed the garden. Water the plants. Weed. The. Garden.

The garden metaphor makes it obvious why we sometimes describe the nitty-gritty implementation of a thing as "getting in the weeds." That's because implementation is thankless, grueling, repetitive, and, quite frankly, messy. There's no way to love every single day of implementation. Some stretches will be outright brutal, and there will be dirt under your fingernails if you do it right.

One significant way to make implementation more manageable is with structure. Despite the frustrations evident in the vignette at the beginning of the chapter, there's evidence of structure there. Freeman had an administrative team that was meeting on a regular basis. That's a start, even if the meetings weren't perfect. The school also had an instructional-leadership team, composed of teachers who wanted to take on more significant roles in the creation of instructional priorities. In addition to those two teams, there was also a "Culture Club" elected by the faculty, which provided focus and energy for the school's transformation objectives.

Once you have some team structures in place, it's important to protect time for collaboration. Educators who drive successful transformation initiatives describe collaborative planning time as "sacred." If walkie-talkies are wailing and students can enter a meeting at will, the sanctity of collaborative time is disturbed. Do what's necessary to ensure that your crew has the time and space to focus on your goals. Pick a room for professional learning that is out of the way from the main bustle of the school. Create rules around the use of electronic devices in those meetings. Some teams go so far as to have attendees place their phones in a basket at the front of the room at the beginning of collaborative time. That might sound like an extreme measure, but if everyone is checking texts and emails during a serious conversation, you're not really conducting deep work together.

Finally, implementation requires focus. One of the mantras we use when in the messy middle implementation part of school transformation is "*Focus, follow through, and see.*" The ROCI process creates well-defined inquiry cycles for trying new things. Picking short-cycle goals allows us to *focus* on a limited number of new things; establishing the time frame for an improvement cycle creates the container in which we *follow through*. And then, we *see* what happens.

Sometimes, the result is a flourishing bed of tiger lilies, and other times, a groundhog eats our tulip bulbs.

The key to seeing what's happening in a school is openness and transparency. As we discussed in Chapter 2, transparency around goals and activities is a huge part of building trust with your fellow change agents. One way to see whether or not our work is taking root is through watching each other teach. Peer observation, without an evaluative component, is central to implementation. Seeing how educator practice manifests in classrooms, while drawing concrete linkages between those practices and the established priorities in a theory of action, is the only way to know whether you are, in fact, doing the thing.

Remember, though, all of this is easier said than done because sometimes "the thing" you need to "do" is so deep rooted and systemic that it requires cooperation across large numbers of adults for a sustained period of time.

And that's when you really need to get in the weeds.

AMOS FREEMAN MIDDLE SCHOOL, SAN FRANCISCO, CALIFORNIA

The constant sense of chaos at Freeman was a barrier to making progress. Michael knew, though, that the surface manifestations of disorder were just indicators of a deeper set of systemic issues.

In particular, Michael was troubled, at a soul level, by the way students were treated at his school. Even when compared to other struggling schools, Freeman's disproportionate use of harsh discipline stood out. The problem was so egregious that the *San Francisco Chronicle* noted that there were over 2,000 office referrals at the school in Michael's first year as assistant principal. That's the equivalent of four trips to the office for every student.

Part of Michael's existential crisis over the disciplinary situation was that he saw himself in the children at the school. As a young person, he had been labeled a "bad kid." Young Michael had a sharp mouth, a biting sense of humor, and a little chip on his shoulder about being told what to do by adults who didn't understand him. That label, not to mention decades of cultural influences that reinforce messages problematizing Black men, had left him with some significant personal baggage.

Unpacking that personal baggage was essential to Michael's leadership journey. In the course of improving his practice as an educator, Michael had come to realize that he himself harbored a boatload of implicit biases about children that looked like him. Internalizing these caustic messages had caused him to view student discipline not through a lens of care, but through a prism of crime and punishment.

"When I was a less experienced administrator, a young person would come to my office, and I would just rain fire and brimstone," Michael says. "But I eventually came to realize that my reaction was exacerbating the conflict. Sometimes, giving a kid a glass of water and a granola bar is the right response."

Michael suspected that the strict disciplinarians in his own past might roll their eyes at his newfound realizations about youth development, but the scientific research was on his side. Suspensions, expulsions, and zero-tolerance punishment policies do not have strong empirical relationships to curbing student misbehavior, let alone improving student achievement. Moreover, those sorts of punitive responses, which tend to overuse the removal of students from classrooms, lead to less instructional time, fewer opportunities for academic enrichment, and an overall weakening of school culture.

The data and research provided a technical lens through which to view the problem, but Michael knew that addressing deeper cultural issues was just as important to his journey. While Black students make up just 16 percent of schoolchildren in America, they account for close to half all suspensions nationally. As a Black man himself, Michael knew that the underlying reasons for this disproportionality were structural and that his own internalized biases played a role in worsening the problem.

He observed many of those same attitudes and prejudices manifest across his faculty. Most of his teachers, though, were not Black and lacked personal grounding in the phenomena that was driving the problem.

To accelerate systemic change on this issue, Michael would have to both lead the adoption of new technical solutions while simultaneously creating a context in which his teachers could do deeper, interpersonal work to understand the systemic manifestations of racial inequality in their own school.

As hard as that work sounded, Michael, Hansa, and the crew agreed that it was the right work to prioritize. The disorder in the school was taking a toll on everybody, and it was clear that the current approach was not working. If they could get a handle on the culture through changing their approach to discipline, maybe they could also cut down on the sort of interruptions that were making it impossible to collaborate in the first place.

This central component of their theory of action, then, was quite clear: If we reduce the use of punitive behavioral measures, then we will capture more learning time and improve the culture of the school.

Doing Stuff Together Means Learning Stuff Together

The educators at Freeman wanted to shift from a system that used draconian punishment measures to one that was more aligned with driving school culture through reinforcing positive behavioral norms. The foundations for driving schoolwide change were in place. They had multiple crews working on the issues. Those teams had crafted some coherent if/then statements that drew linkages among these inputs and academic research on school improvement, so they were confident that this particular emphasis could demonstrably improve the school. ROCI cycles were already a part of regular practice, and educators were looking at data together on a regular basis as a part of ongoing grade-level collaborative teams.

Changing a school's disciplinary system, however, unlike issues that can be dealt with within a grade-level team, is a systemic challenge that requires coordination across an entire school. Students need to understand how consequences are going to change as the result of these shifts. Teachers have to practice dealing with modest interruptions at the classroom level, and administrators need to build muscle memory around supporting teachers.

In other words, everyone in the school needs to learn, together, how to do something differently than they've ever done it before.

While most schools have episodic professional development opportunities, transformation requires a systematic approach to adult learning. Schools that undertake significant improvement efforts need to create a culture of professional learning that is aligned with transformation efforts. That might sound obvious in theory, but consider how rare that alignment is in practice.

Let's take a hot second to be honest about our experiences with professional development in schools. How often have you walked into the Friday-afternoon workshop knowing that you were going to get absolutely nothing out of it? If the standard agenda is 90 minutes long, maybe it starts 15 minutes late because of dismissal issues. Then, the first half hour is just a series of compliance announcements, and nobody is even pretending to care. When the time finally comes for the "professional development" part of the afternoon, it's a slide presentation delivered in a dry monotone by a retired principal.

Lots of things might happen in those kinds of sessions, but authentic learning is not usually one of them.

Real professional learning that drives transformation is different. That kind of learning is aligned to priorities, targeted in a way that changes adult practice, and connected to ongoing work that will happen after a group session is over. To return to the implementation mantra, transformational professional learning creates explicit opportunities to *focus*, *follow through*, and *see*.

When it comes to *focus*, a professional learning agenda must connect to the theory of action. In the case of Freeman, Michael and his crew needed to shift disciplinary practices to be less punitive. Professional learning, therefore, needed to include tools, tactics, and strategies for creating a positive school culture outside of punishment. All staff at the school, for example, received training in de-escalating potentially explosive confrontations. Teachers learned how their words, expressions, and body language can affect triggered students, and they practiced using language and gestures that mitigate outbursts.

After learning new skills together, a crew in pursuit of transformation must build mechanisms for ensuring that everyone *follows through* on what they learned. Because so much of follow-through in a school happens behind closed doors, peer-to-peer accountability matters a great deal. Grade-level teams should create time for collaborative discussions of the schoolwide-learning agenda. During those sessions, educators should discuss their experience with follow-through and unpack challenges. Continuing with the example of de-escalation training, some teachers may not remember the skills learned in the training and need to refresh those skills with their peers. Maybe someone froze when they needed to deploy their new skills and is realizing they need more role-playing time, or "practice," to ensure that new behaviors are easier to deploy in the heat of the moment when emotions are high. Student confrontations can trigger our own fear and safety responses, making it hard to react in a rational manner.

There are other tricks you can use to increase the likelihood of follow-through. For example, try sending a text message to the group chat when you use a new skill to see if that makes the process more fun. Some schools create short, nonevaluative rubrics to assess follow-through, which you can use to assess your own progress: Give yourself a "1" if you haven't even started trying the new thing yet, and a "4" if you're knocking it out of the park.

Finally, crews that want to improve together must start to *see* changes. Peer observation is one concrete way to accomplish that goal. Teachers can commit to observing each other, either as a group or individually, and then provide real-time feedback on the deployment of new skills. It's important to remember that you don't have to be perfect yourself in order to provide peer feedback. You can be in the midst of learning a new skill and still have the wherewithal to identify areas for growth in a coworker's deployment of said skill. As always, it is important to disentangle regular feedback from the sometimes toxic process of teacher evaluation. The vast majority of observation time should be constructive and growth-oriented: no clipboards, no checklists, and fix your face. Oh—and no scowling from the back of the classroom, especially if your colleague makes a mistake!

It's hard to be good at a new thing the first time you try it, and seeing your peers in the back of the room can raise the stakes even further. You and your crew are going to make a lot of mistakes in the school transformation process. A significant part of doing the thing is committing to the thing and then sticking to the thing, even when the thing seems hard and you don't particularly like doing the thing.

Like trying a new unfamiliar food, you might not like the thing on the first bite.

That doesn't mean, though, that you should abandon ship at the first sign of resistance. Growing pains are inevitable in the transformation process, and things take time to work.

Time itself, though, can be a significant part of the implementation challenge. Many of us lack the time to do the things we already know how to do, let alone new things. Schools in need of improvement are notorious black holes when it comes to time. How can we be expected to find time, especially when there doesn't seem to be any to spare?

AMOS FREEMAN MIDDLE SCHOOL, SAN FRANCISCO, CALIFORNIA

Hansa brought snacks because she knew it was going to be a long meeting.

Fortunately, a few subtle shifts in scenery had made it possible to curb the interruptions that had plagued collaborative-meeting time. First, the administrative team created a "mute your walkie-talkie" rule during group meetings. Administrators at Freeman were used to coordinating crisis response on the fly, and lowering the volume during sacred planning time was crucial to creating a culture of calmness.

Second, they found a new location for their collaborative sessions. The doorless front-office space, which also was the copy room, was not ideal for collaboration. On the second floor of the building, though, tucked at the end of a hallway, was a seventh-grade classroom nobody was using. There were four, long lab tables on wheels that could be rearranged as needed and copious wall space for generative group work.

Perhaps most importantly, the room had a door, and that door had a lock.

The spare seventh-grade science room became the school's dedicated adult-learning space, and they used the room as an annex for creativity. Within weeks, the walls were covered. On one wall was a giant graphic organizer titled "What We Want for Our Students When They Leave." That organic space became a place where teachers added more and more colorful sticky notes over time, describing their growing aspirations for youth. On another wall was a poster titled "Who I Want to Be as an Educator," where teachers, administrators, paraprofessionals, and aides could all share their personal aspirations for professional growth.

The irony of working behind a literal "closed door" was that it created a lot more transparency about what adults in the building were doing at any given time. Whereas some teachers had started as ROCI skeptics, many more came along once they started popping into the dedicated professional learning space. With the curtain pulled back, they could see that ROCI involved very little private scheming and a whole lot of connecting the dots between theories of academic growth and observations about instructional practice.

On this particular day, Hansa started the administrative-team meeting with an icebreaker, as she almost always did. The crew used personal questions like "Who was your own favorite teacher and why?" or sometimes cheekier prompts like "Fall is the greatest season: true or false, and defend your premise." The goal was not to engage in rigorous debate, but rather to get to know each other better through lighthearted sharing.

After the icebreaker, they discussed the Culture Club's recommendations for schoolwide professional learning. The school was already beginning to execute changes to the disciplinary system, and as part of adjusting other elements of the school culture, Michael had asked the elected group of teachers to provide a list of

(Continued)

(Continued)

recommendations to the administrators so that the school's learning agenda would be built on teacher input. Armed with the Culture Club's ideas, the administrative team scheduled six weeks of professional learning focused on the priorities that the teachers identified.

To make those priorities transparent, Hansa wrote each one on a sticky note and put it on the least messy of the classroom's walls. The wall quickly became just as cluttered as the rest:

1. Develop instructional bright spots.

2. Ensure that every staff member is 100% clear on their next steps after collaborative planning time.

3. Reduce office referrals through implementing de-escalation skills.

4. Cultivate a spirit of continuous learning through using the instructional-leadership team as a pilot.

5. Build professional development focused on relationships and relevance.

6. More rigor!

7. More critical thinking skills in content classrooms!

8. Create classroom time for structured student-to-student interactions around content.

Once all of the sticky notes were on the wall, the team looked in silence at the priorities. Somehow, the magnitude of their work together seemed even more daunting once each priority was written in Sharpie.

"Wow," Michael said, saying aloud what the rest of the group was thinking. "We need to do a lot of stuff."

There's Never Time to Do Everything, but There's Always Time to Do Some Things

We started this book on the premise that there are no secret elixirs, silver bullets, or magic wands in the process of school transformation. There are tips, tricks, and best practices, but most things that appear to be shortcuts just lead to bigger problems later, and research indicates that educators get better at their practice when they collaborate and learn from each other, which takes—you guessed it—*time*.

Finding time to collaborate is surprisingly hard. Every decision you make as a transformation crew is a verdict on how you plan to use time. If you add something new to the docket, that initiative will take time. Moreover, every *explicit* affirmative decision your crew makes about how to use time ends up being an *implicit* decision about how *not* to use time. Whether or not you articulate those trade-offs in your planning, the outcome is the same: You spend time on some things and not on other things.

Time might be a construct, but it also is our most limited and precious resource when engaging in the work of transformation.

Consider your average school day. You start at some point between 8:00 and 9:00 a.m., and the school day ends at around 3:00 p.m. If you're a teacher, in the intervening six hours, give or take, you might have four hours with children, 40 minutes for prep with your peers (if you're lucky), 20 minutes of gossip (because we should be honest), and another hour of lunch/recess/other duties.

When, precisely, are you going to collaborate in pursuit of transformation?

It's hard enough to be the best educator you already know how to be within that kind of grueling schedule. School transformation work expects us to do all of that, while simultaneously shifting our practice and mindsets about what's possible in a school through deep change management work with our colleagues.

Finding the time to make these shifts is not just a part of the work—it *is* the work.

Many educators who read this book will see familiar themes in the struggle of the Freeman educators to find time. Often, the thing that overwhelms us most in school transformation is the unspoken notion that we do not have time to do all things that we know are important. A little voice pipes up from the back of our heads during these meetings saying, "Ya'll are clear there is no way we have time to do all of this stuff, right?"

Well, let me tell you a little secret: The voice in your head is correct.

The reason transformation work requires prioritization and focus is because there is too little time in which to do everything we want to do. As counterintuitive as this may sound, when your school seems to have a million problems, your best bet, usually, is to *do less*.

That means stopping doing things.

It's hard to stop doing things, but it can be liberating. Some of our commitments feel good but have little impact on student learning. Sometimes, we commit to an extracurricular activity, knowing that a loyal school partner has made that work a priority. And yet, every new commitment takes time, even if it's just an hour every week. Agree to five new things, and that adds a whole other day of work to your schedule each week. The easiest things to stop doing are self-imposed and disconnected from your crew's focus. It's harder to stop doing things that are mandated by your district or required by law.

Beyond eliminating stuff from your schedule, there are other ways to find more time. One way is through the strategic deployment of coaches, resource teachers, and administrators to manage classrooms while grade-level teams meet. This is cheaper than paying for substitute teachers, but it also requires significant coordination among adults who may not be used to tagging into classroom instruction. If you don't have enough on-site educators to execute this strategy, perhaps your district has instructional coaches who can adopt classrooms for an hour once every couple of weeks.

Schools can also use substitutes to create common release time. While some schools continue to experience staffing shortages, leadership teams can decide to use their substitute teacher budgets more systematically, to create predictable time for grade-level teams in service of collaborative time.

Beyond finding other adults to act as classroom teachers, another strategy for finding time involves rethinking the school schedule. Schools that have art, music, and physical education teachers can rearrange their electives to create common planning time. While this requires coordination across grade levels and with administrators, the result can be a no-cost realization of more planning time for teacher teams.

One final place to look for time is those preexisting, unsatisfying professional development sessions we talked about earlier. Whenever your school holds mandatory professional development, you can carve out some of that time for grade-level collaboration. Using time in this way creates consistency, drives expectations for coordinated professional learning across grade-level teams, and takes some of the guesswork out of the question "When are we going to have time to meet again?"

If time is the container for your collaborative professional learning, a variety of activities will fill that container. One consistent thing is, you guessed it, ROCI. Grade-level collaboration should always include regular reflection on your short-cycle goals for inquiry, and it's a good habit to always discuss those goals during the first few minutes of a meeting. As we discussed earlier in this chapter, monitoring the adoption of new technical skills also is a good use of collaborative time. The teachers at Freeman had adopted de-escalation as a technique for behavioral intervention, and they used collaborative time to practice and rehearse those skills.

As many educators have learned, though, it is not just the technical skills of pedagogy that require time to develop. Adaptive changes, which require the interrogation of fundamental beliefs and mindsets, also require time.

Nowhere is that sort of adaptive work more important than in dealing with the racial inequities that often undergird the way students are treated in our schools.

AMOS FREEMAN MIDDLE SCHOOL, SAN FRANCISCO, CALIFORNIA

The conversations weren't going to be easy, but Michael knew they had to happen.

The faculty had already completed de-escalation training, but that was just one part of the puzzle of solving the school's disciplinary problems. Beyond that work, there were other shifts that the educators at Freeman needed to adopt: the use of a cooldown room in lieu of office referrals or suspensions, strategies for reintegrating students into classrooms after behavioral referrals, and training modules that explain linkages between youth trauma and the manifestations of disruptive behavior.

The technical work, though, seemed to be the easy part. Michael understood that long-term change would require everyone in the school to confront their long-standing biases about how Black children ought to be treated in classrooms. The crew realized there was no way to do that well without having serious, open, deeply personal conversations about race.

Having discussions on topics so charged requires careful preparation. Michael, Hansa, and a small crew collaborated to figure out how to

(Continued)

(Continued)

facilitate the journey in a way that provoked personal breakthroughs and not emotional collapse. Many of the teachers in the school were white and unaccustomed to talking openly about race. Given the faculty demographics, the crew knew that the framing would be critical because, while honesty and vulnerability were necessary, the crew wanted to provide accessible on-ramps for people without skills and experience discussing race.

In keeping with their approach to transformation, the crew decided to focus on data, and they started the discussions in the various leadership teams. At one of their initial meetings, Michael broke down national data on incarceration and policing, calling attention to the fact that Black men are wildly overrepresented in jails and prisons, relative to their proportion of the broader U.S. population. From there, he shared national educational data, not just for Black and Brown students, but also for students with other historically marginalized identities, like LGBTQIA students and students with learning disabilities. Like the national policing and prison data, marginalized students were severely overrepresented in suspensions, expulsions, and extreme punishment.

After examining the national data, they moved to their own school data, to see whether Freeman was evincing similar patterns.

The school was.

Michael, Hansa, and their small crew realized that presenting this data, couched in a discussion around race to a group of predominantly white educators, could feel confrontational. "I want people to face the truth," Michael said, "but I can't just tell my newly hired teacher, who hasn't yet realized that her own privilege is manifesting in the school, that the whole situation is wrong. I had to discover my own implicit biases over time, and it's no different for anyone else."

To create the most constructive conversations possible, the crew started the conversation about racial equity within the administrative team. Then, they shifted to the instructional-leadership team and Culture Club. In these smaller-group conversations, teachers and administrators talked about how their own personal beliefs and biases might manifest in interactions with kids.

Michael broke the ice in every meeting by sharing his own story. He talked about being a Black child in a school like Freeman and how the way he was treated caused him, as a young educator, to rehash cycles of trauma and punishment on other children. His vulnerability created a context in which other educators could be honest about their own personal backgrounds without fear of being shamed.

To bring the point even closer to home, Michael asked students at Freeman to share their own experiences. Rather than pose these questions in a classroom setting, where the students might feel uneasy with the power dynamics, the crew decided to hold a "panel discussion," like they had all seen at professional conferences.

This time, though, the expert panel was composed of middle schoolers from Freeman.

At the next schoolwide faculty meeting, all of the adults in the school sat in chairs, arranged in audience rows in the school's large, airy, sunlit library. At the front of the room, three Freeman middle schoolers sat at a table, ready to present their expertise to the crowd.

The panel discussion started with some awkwardness, as the students weren't accustomed to speaking without interruption for long stretches of time while the school's teachers listened. But they quickly got the hang of it. They shared some of their most challenging experiences as young people. They described families impacted by the criminal justice system, dangerous encounters with local police, and moments when their own teachers treated them as part of the problem.

Many of the stories carried overtones of racial discrimination and bias.

The teachers were rapt, the students felt empowered, and Michael's crew was encouraged.

Because that day in the library, the kids themselves had broken the ice on some of the hardest topics that anyone in the school would ever need to confront.

Equity Work = The Work

As we close our meditation on the complexity of implementation, we should keep in mind the values that drove us to pursue not just education as a profession, but transformation as a mission.

While debates rage about the politics of schooling, just about everyone agrees that great public schools should be ladders to opportunity for young people, while serving as the centerpieces of thriving communities.

Unfortunately, our public schools have a long way to go before they can keep that promise. As we discussed in Chapters 1 and 3, racist policymaking throughout the 20th and 21st centuries created a profoundly unequal educational system, whose roots are linked to segregated housing. Those policies exacerbate existing wealth disparities while reinforcing racial separation and prejudice.

Beyond these systemic issues at the intersection of schooling, housing, and wealth, disproportionate levels of adult and child poverty create high concentrations of untreated trauma, which can manifest as misbehavior in schools. Many children and adolescents do not yet have the social, cognitive, and linguistic skills to tell us that their behavior is rooted in trauma and frustration. It's our job as educators to figure that out. If we address only the manifestations of those inequities without considering the underlying social conditions that led to their creation, we abdicate our responsibilities as professionals.

Or put more simply: Punishing students and throwing them out of school for expressing their trauma in the only way they know how is unfair, unjust, and cruel.

Discussing equity, working through our own personal demons, and building the capacity to have difficult conversations about the intersections of race, class, and privilege is not ancillary to the work of school transformation; it *is* the work of school transformation.

Developing Your Equity Lens: Multiple Pathways

Adopting and sharpening your equity lens is a lifelong process. Each of these pathways is an entry point to that work, all of which will open additional doors for discovery.

ADOPTING AN EQUITY LENS REQUIRES CHANGE AGENTS TO:	DOING THIS WORK CAN LOOK LIKE:
Commit to self-reflection and personal growth	— Reflecting on one's own identity and privilege — Understanding one's own biases — Demonstrating growth by making changes to behavior
Shift equity conversations from theory to practice	— Pursuing improvement goals with equity at the center — Interrupting racist behaviors
Understand how the history of systemic oppression connects to outcomes today	— Learning hidden histories — Taking stock of whose voices and perspectives are not included in mainstream narratives — Drawing explicit connections between policy and outcomes
Demonstrate deep respect for students, families, and community	— Planning and facilitating community roundtable discussions — Engaging in home visits — Building relationships with community organizations
Build cultural bridges with individuals from different racial and cultural backgrounds while acting in solidarity with historically oppressed people	— Following the lead of affected children and families — Advocating for equitable policies and practices

Focusing on that work does not mean ignoring the technical aspects of school improvement, and anyone who insists that it does is obfuscating reality in pursuit of a political agenda, not an educational one. Teaching our students means understanding them, the families they come from, and the communities that they call home.

If we cannot see our kids fully, how can we ever teach them?

Long-standing structural racism, rooted in generations of policymaking and prejudice, are just some of the myriad barriers we face when we try to transform schools. Change agents and their crews must confront these biases, in addition to old habits, inertia, exhaustion, institutional intransigence, resource hoarding, and countless other barriers that get in the way of school change.

If we've said it once, we've said it a thousand times: Nobody ever said that this change agent work was going to be easy.

That's why the next chapter looks at some of these barriers to change and some of the other common factors that can derail a transformation project.

THE IMPLEMENTATION CHECKLIST

- **Get in the weeds.** Don't just talk about it—*be* about it. Most of school transformation is the hard, day-in-day-out work that nobody will acknowledge or thank you for. That doesn't make it any less important, and if you work with a crew, it can be extremely fun and gratifying. Find ways to celebrate the little wins with your crew, building habits and mantras that mitigate the grind.

- **Structure is your friend.** Build structures that you need and abandon the ones that aren't helping. Create teams that work together and ensure that there is a coherent agenda for their work. Build sustainable processes that connect the dots between your stated theory of action and the work in classrooms. Document that work and create as much transparency as possible about why you're creating structures in the first place.

- **Focus, follow through, and see.** Once you pick priorities for transformation, it's essential that you build habits that allow you and your crew to not just follow through on those priorities, but also to identify tangible evidence that folks are trying new things in their classrooms. If you need to move things around in your schedule to create opportunities to see those changes, do it. If change isn't visible as shifts in teacher practice, adjustments in student behavior, or measurable outcomes, it's probably not meaningful enough to keep doing. That said, don't abandon something just because it's too hard or not working immediately. When you're doing something new, you can't expect to be good at it right away.

- **Build a professional learning agenda.** Professional learning should be mapped to your stated priorities as a school. Start by planning for the month ahead and then try doing a full semester at a time. Also, it's critical to think of all collaborative time and professional development as serving your broader learning agenda. The more stuff you do that's disconnected from the broader agenda, the more disjointed transformation will be.

- **Stop doing some stuff.** Most struggling schools have a litany of projects and programs that look good on paper but aren't moving the needle in real life. Focus requires the paring down what some people call the "Christmas tree" of initiatives, where every ornament is a shiny new thing to try.

- **Make time for the stuff that matters.** As a corollary to "stop doing some stuff," when you start doing new stuff you must make time for it. Time is a limited resource, so figuring out how to find new time requires scheduling ingenuity, flexibility, and sometimes financial resources.

- **Have the hard conversations. That's the work too.** Challenging conversations about race, equity, privilege, and identity take time, and that's okay. You need to make time for the things that matter, and these conversations matter. A lot. Having courageous conversations in a way that creates the context for personal and institutional change is an art and science unto itself. Invest the time and energy necessary to facilitate these discussions in a way that provokes change while not causing people to further retreat.

CHAPTER 4: DISCUSSION QUESTIONS

1. What kinds of distractions can get in the way of your work as a change agent? Are there things you can do to minimize them? What's in your control versus what is outside of your sphere influence?

2. What does your school "make time" for, and what does that prioritization tell you about what the school considers to be important? What would it take to make time for ROCI and continuous improvement work?

3. Do you and your peers talk about race, equity, and concomitant social challenges in your school? Is that discussion treated as outside the scope of your job or central to it?

Who Said Change Was Gonna Be Easy?

5

It was the first day of school at Polk Elementary in greater Grand Rapids, Michigan, and Sarah Hundt was appreciating the reading nook that she had created for her second-grade classroom. A small bench formed the centerpiece of the sacred little space. The comfy seat was piled high with poofy pillows, which were nestled atop a cushion upholstered with a black and white zigzag pattern, all of which Sarah had made herself from bolts of fabric she procured at a local craft store. On a bookcase behind the bench sat large metal block letters, arranged to say "SHH & READ."

This cozy little corner was "Reading Nook Version 2.0." Sarah had arrived at the improved incarnation through trial and error. The year before had been her first as a classroom teacher, and that year's iteration was admittedly more makeshift: There was no bench, and the prototype pillows were covered with a rainbow-print vinyl tablecloth. Her second graders had been ruthless critics: On the first day of school that prior year, her very first as a teacher, a group of students had ripped the vinyl covers to shreds while she was monitoring the hallway for dismissal.

The unceremonious shredding had been one of many slights—some micro, some macro, some real, some perceived—that Sarah had endured during her debut teaching year. She was determined to do everything in her power to make sure that year two was different.

(Continued)

(Continued)

That first year, though, had taken Sarah by surprise. She had credentials from one of the largest, oldest, and most prestigious universities in the state. Her coursework there, at least on paper, was designed to prepare her for the rigors and exigencies of classroom teaching in the state's second-largest—and, by many measures, most culturally diverse—city.

It didn't.

That cultural diversity had been a welcome, if at times shocking, shift for Sarah. She grew up and attended public school in a town on the northern outskirts of Lansing, a place she describes as, among other things, "extremely white"—a whole 95 percent white to be exact, according to census data.

While Sarah cherished her childhood, she knew that the rest of the world looked different than her hometown. She hoped to bring the best memories of her youth to her new home near Grand Rapids, while learning to navigate a place whose cultural dynamics were a dramatic shift from her limited, monochromatic upbringing.

Second-year Sarah knew that the decor of her classroom was no substitute for preparation, but that didn't stop her from going hard. In addition to the reading nook, she adorned her bulletin boards with seasonally appropriate borders and backsplashes. Every bookshelf in the room contained bins, which organized books by both genre and level; a handful of her more intrepid second graders had helped her do the sorting.

She complemented the decor with competence. On the first day of school, second-year Sarah welcomed her kiddos by name when they arrived in her classroom. Unlike the first year, when she skimped on establishing routines—believing that systems would get in the way of relationships—she established rigorous classroom management structures. The payoff was immediate: Her classroom was more orderly, but no less vibrant or caring. Within just a few days, her preparation, experience, and humility seemed to pay educational dividends.

And then, the unexpected struck yet again.

On a Tuesday afternoon, just 17 days into the school year, the principal pulled Sarah into the hallway after a staff meeting

"I have bad news," the principal said, as Sarah tensed up. "We just lost one of our fourth-grade teachers, and I need to move you to that team. In two days."

"Can I at least get the weekend to move my stuff?" Sarah asked.

"No," the principal replied, "I'm sorry."

Second-year Sarah walked back to her classroom, stunned.

The next afternoon, she organized her students into a reading circle, and they read Dr. Seuss's *Oh, the Places You'll Go* together, in the nook.

Then, they talked as a group about the meaning of the book, before Sarah explained to the second graders that she would be leaving their classroom.

A handful of kids burst into tears, as Sarah struggled, somewhat successfully, to hold hers back.

Hello, Expectations . . . I'd Like to Introduce You to My Dear Friend: Reality

Elementary science teachers tell students about the concept of a "vacuum" as a proxy for describing an idealized state of nature. Objects inside of a vacuum behave as they are predicted to behave "on paper" in a frictionless environment devoid of outside intervention. The vacuum is unspoilt, an experimental Garden of Eden.

When some experts discuss public schooling, it can seem as if their ideas were invented in a vacuum. The metaphorical vacuum of education policy is devoid of children, parents, extended families, snow days, tantrums, recess scuffles, loud lunchrooms, and nosy coworkers. Inside of the vacuum, there is elegant talk about pedagogy, praxis, and theory, while nowhere to be found is any discussion of how, in fact, what gets discussed inside of the vacuum applies to the reality of teaching . . . particularly in communities that serve large numbers of marginalized young people.

Every crew working in the trenches of school transformation discovers, quickly, that changing how things work in schools does not occur inside of a vacuum. Quite the opposite. One of the only predictable things about teaching in a transformative environment is that the unpredictable is bound to happen.

Or put more bluntly, if you make some cutesy pillow covers for your first day of school, you can pretty much expect them to be in shreds before recess.

Preparing one's heart and mind for the unexpected and chaotic might sound like too pessimistic a way to approach teaching, but this attitude is rooted in pragmatism. Management guru Jim Collins describes this practice as confronting "the brutal facts of one's reality." His and other change management experts' research indicates that such a disposition is a necessary precursor to transformational change.

Mindsets and technical skills reinforce one another. The first four chapters of this book covered the technical facets of ROCI, a cyclical inquiry process designed for school-based implementation. Mastering the mechanics of improvement is hard in any context, but against the backdrop of American public schooling, it can feel impossible. Any attempt to change schools will encounter friction, and this chapter is about identifying and mitigating the most common sources of that friction.

Easier said than done.

Figuring out where to expend your energy is a big part of your battle, as some obstacles are outside of our everyday control, like generational wealth gaps and segregation. While those external factors remain most consequential in schools that serve marginalized children, the COVID-19 pandemic affected everyone, awakening many formerly insulated families to the institutional disparities that cause educational instability.

While addressing these global, political, and cultural challenges is both urgent and important, all of that is outside of our direct control on a daily basis—not to mention beyond the scope of this book—and school transformation is possible without touching those things. There are a bunch of other challenges within your sphere of influence, though, and that's what this chapter is all about. We'll discuss where to expect resistance when you try to change things and what strategies you can use to mitigate that resistance. While some of the obstacles to change are obvious (like vocal naysayers), the unspoken challenges, some of which are buried within the depths of our own psyches, are harder to detect yet critical to confront.

Which brings us back to Sarah's turbulent early years of teaching. Her experiences, while frustrating, are not unusual for novice teachers High teacher turnover and staffing unpredictability are more the rule than exceptions these days, and systemic staffing challenges manifest as uncertainty for teachers. Having strong grade-level teams, a strategy we discussed in Chapter 2, helps to mitigate such attrition while making it easier for new team members to gel.

Fortunately, that's what Sarah encountered when she joined the fourth-grade crew at Polk.

She found among the fourth-grade teachers a crew that was already having difficult conversations, confronting sources of friction that Sarah had, at times in her life, been afraid to even mention.

POLK ELEMENTARY SCHOOL, GRAND RAPIDS, MICHIGAN

Sarah was frustrated to switch grade levels so early in the school year, but one unexpected upside of moving was that the fourth-grade teachers at Polk were something like a "Dream Team."

That crew—which included veterans Randa and Birgitte—was working with a transformation coach named Palak, who supported ROCI cycles while holding space for complicated conversations about the social dynamics in the school.

Sarah was intrigued that they were talking about doing things "a different way."

Sarah was ready for anything different, as her teaching experience to date had been a comedy of errors. That said, the crew's conversations were a bit scary. A custodian had once joked to her that she probably expected her teaching experience to be "fluffy clouds and rainbows," but what she encountered around Grand Rapids was more complicated. Her university offered no full courses in classroom management, and any hints she got on the topic were predicated on the idea that two or three kids in each class would present with significant behavioral challenges; her first classroom had seven. A graduate course in English language instruction glossed over literacy instruction for students who come from non-English-speaking homes; 70 percent of the kids at Polk fit that description.

But perhaps the most striking thing that Sarah noticed at Polk was who got sent to the office. Most of the students in the school were native-Spanish speakers from Central and South American families, but the school also

(Continued)

(Continued)

had a sizable group of Black children. The vast majority of the students who were sent to the office, suspended, or expelled were Black.

"How," Sarah wondered, "in a school full of different groups of children, does one particular group get blamed for so much disruption?"

Sarah raised this exact question during one of her first meetings with the new crew. She was afraid to admit her ignorance, but her upbringing, preparation, family life, and racial identity had left her with significant blind spots relative to the topic of race, and she was frustrated without concrete information.

Whereas many of Sarah's peers and superiors were uninterested in addressing these questions, the fourth-grade crew was ready to have a serious conversation. Palak had experience facilitating conversations about how race intersects with teaching and learning, and she encouraged the fourth-grade crew to embrace the complexity of the conversation. They talked about national disparities in student discipline and how the patterns represented at a macro level were manifesting at Polk. They talked about what behaviors triggered office visits and whether the teachers were administering such referrals in an inequitable manner when it came to Black children.

The discussions weren't easy, but Palak was motivated by the crew's progress. If this small group could have a constructive conversation, she surmised, so could the rest of the school. Sarah was a great case in point. She was a newer teacher, and like the vast majority of the teachers in the city, she was white. Her vulnerability could provide an entry point for other white teachers to discuss their experiences.

Excited about the potential to drive interpersonal transformation, after a few weeks of intensive conversations about race and equity with the fourth-grade crew Palak told the administrative team about the work. She knew that more conversations like these would be central to the broader project of school improvement, and she was eager to expand.

The response, unfortunately, was not warm. The rest of the administrative team seemed confused about why they would try anything of the sort.

"I don't know why we would do this," one assistant principal said, staring blankly at Palak. "After all, aren't we supposed to be color-blind?"

If We Can't See Our Students, How Can We Teach Them?

In the book *Why Are All the Black Kids Sitting Together in the Cafeteria?*, Dr. Beverly Tatum strives to answer the direct yet complicated question she poses in the title. In framing the issue with such unadulterated curiosity, Dr. Tatum invites dialogue. Many educators—particularly those who are white—find themselves asking this exact question in their early years of teaching.

The answer, as it turns out, has much to do with the psychology of child development. The adolescent years involve periods of intense identity reckoning for all children, irrespective of their racial backgrounds. For children who are Black or Brown, particularly in America, this usually includes explicit discussion of racial identity. Most children of color will encounter some form of overt racism during their childhood, and even if they do not, families justifiably feel compelled to prepare kids for that eventuality, through unvarnished, age-appropriate explanation—aka "the talk."

Most white children, on the other hand, do not have discussions about race at an early age, and if they do, those discussions tend to focus on the racial identities of others and not themselves—hence, wondering why the Black children sit together instead of posing the corollary but equally revealing question, "Why are all the *white* children sitting together?"

Failing to grapple with their own racial identity leaves large swaths of white children believing that the concept of race does not apply to them. As a consequence, most of the white population ends up entering adulthood without a significant understanding of how their own racial identities affect their approach to the world. While some white folks end up coming to terms with their racial identity as adults, many remain in a state of permanent, ignorant preadolescent stasis with respect to these topics.

This stasis is enabled, more than anything else, by "color blindness."

There's no easy way to put this, so I'm just gonna come out and say it: Color blindness is BS. It has no intellectual merit as an ideology and constitutes an enormous impediment not just to school transformation, but to social progress writ large.

Color blindness emerged as an approach to discussing—or more accurately, *not* discussing—race at the end of the 20th century. The idea was rooted in the notion that, if we acted as if we lived in a world in which race was not a factor in life outcomes, then we might accelerate the coming of such a world. Most children raised in the 1980s and 1990s consumed the rhetoric of color blindness in schools and media, but the hypocrisy of the idea was always self-evident to anyone who wasn't white.

Might we "dream" of a world where race doesn't matter? Absolutely.

Is that the world we live in, though? Obviously, no.

Color blindness, though, was appealing to folks with power and privilege. White people in particular were able to use this ideology to position racism as a relic of the past—and not a persistent problem in the present.

Unfortunately, the personal, emotional, and psychological attachments to color blindness are difficult to penetrate. Dr. Tatum, in her aforementioned book, describes a phenomenon wherein white children learn that their experience is "normal" and that everything else is somehow an aberration. When white folks make it to adulthood without having their sense of "normalcy" questioned, doing so at a later age can take a toll on the sense of self. That's why creating barriers to childhood discussions about race are so dangerous: The risks of carrying invented fantasies into adulthood are disastrous and violent.

Color blindness still manifests in our schools in myriad ways: curricula designed with the white experience at the center; white cultural norms in assessment batteries; and as was the case at Polk, San Francisco's Freeman, and so many other schools, massive disproportionality in the administration of punishment. Scores of educators complete bachelor's and master's degrees in education without ever having serious conversations about these disparities, just like Sarah did.

Sarah and Palak discovered that color blindness trumped other critical values at Polk, including historical truth and the quest for educational results. The resistance to discussing race wasn't confined to the school administration. When the crew attempted to discuss race with their peers, a polite decline was the most common response. Discussing race and racism just wasn't something that "nice" people do.

While the deployment of fake comity to avoid difficult topics is by no means unique to Grand Rapids, this disposition toward evasive cordiality is so ingrained there that they even have an expression for it:

"West Michigan Nice."

Unfortunately, "West Michigan Nice"—and its other incarnations—is a "cultural loophole" that prevents a community from telling the truth about both its present and its past.

POLK ELEMENTARY SCHOOL, GRAND RAPIDS, MICHIGAN

The angles and curves of the American home and office were created by designers and manufacturers in and around Grand Rapids. Herman Miller designed the world's first cubicle, Steelcase invented the ubiquitous four-drawer filing cabinet, and dozens of other companies in "Furniture City" shaped and crafted the aesthetic that came to dominate mid-century catalog shopping and, much later, Instagram. Through much of the 20th century, one in every three jobs in Grand Rapids was in a furniture factory.

And, it is important to note, the furniture industry excluded Black workers for most of its history.

While Grand Rapids was predominantly Dutch until the early 20th century, the city experienced major cultural shifts between 1910 and 1940 during the Great Migration, when the Black population of the small city quintupled. The subsequent reaction of the white community is a microcosm of how racism functions in the American North because, while giant metropolises tend to dominate our stories of racial strife, the majority of migrating Black families settled in midsized cities, not places like Chicago and Detroit.

The conservative power structure of Grand Rapids confronted that influx of new Black residents, making the city fertile ground for what historian Todd E. Robinson calls "managerial racism." In his book *A City Within a City*, Robinson details the ways in which the city's growing Black population tested long-standing boundaries set by white officials and how the white populace reacted. Grand Rapids hosted multiple regional conferences of the Ku Klux Klan throughout the 1920s, drawing tens of thousands of white hoods to the city's streets. Local businesses maintained policies forbidding Black patronage, including the downtown B. F. Keith Theater, which had separate sections for white and Black patrons until 1925. Black workers were prevented from working in the furniture industry through the 1930s, and by 1940, only *one* of the thousand-plus employees of the school system was Black.

The situation was tantamount to, in Robinson's words, "fighting for non-existent work positions, social mobility, and respectability in a white man's hell."

(Continued)

(Continued)

Despite white resistance, in the 1940s and 1950s the city's Black community blossomed. Churches, community organizations, advocacy groups, and small businesses flourished. The Third Ward, in the city's southeast quadrant, became a hotbed of Black empowerment. Some schools in this "Black Belt" went from having just a handful of Black students to a white minority in a 20-year period.

The most striking transformation happened at South High School, the prestigious Third-Ward academy that had groomed the region's most famous resident, Gerald R. Ford. By the 1960s—when Ford was the top Republican in Congress and well on his way to becoming United States President—South High was majority Black, even though the school had sponsored a "Junior Ku Klux Klan Club" through the 1950s, which included the years when the white future POTUS attended.

South High's transformation triggered fear in the white community. Responding to racially motivated concerns about "gang violence," in 1966 a local superintendent asked the strict disciplinarian principal of South to use harsh measures to enforce the district's dress codes. A feature article in *Jet Magazine* later that autumn related the subsequent struggle over the infamous "mustache ban," which led to student walkouts, protests, and citywide disruption. The consuming debate foreshadowed the many ways in which disparate administration of hair and grooming standards has been used to suspend and expel Black children throughout America.

After the strife of the 1960s and the mustache ban, the city followed a pattern of suburbanization that is familiar throughout the North. South High School closed in 1968 as part of a half-baked school integration plan that further divided the community. Black families continued to assert their rights to equality in civic services, while white families fled to the new, segregated suburbs, depriving the civic center of resources and tax revenue.

The city population reached its nadir in the 1980s, then rebounded at the century's end in part through massive civic investments by private interests, like the family foundation of future U.S. Secretary of Education Betsy DeVos. Municipal revival in the downtown, however, tended to exclude the interests of the Black community, for as residential real estate and civic infrastructure in the city's center flourished, Black families were further concentrated in the southeastern Third Ward. Beginning in the late 1990s and early 2000s, large groups of Spanish-speaking families from Central and South America, many of whom came to the city for the promise of seasonal farm work, congregated in the southwest corridor, just across the highway.

Polk Elementary School, where Sarah came to teach, sits at the intersection of these two communities. Despite growing up in a community that was mostly white, Sarah was surprised to find that all of her peers at the school were white as well. She had expected at least some diversity on the staff, but some of western Michigan's oldest demons remained unexercised.

Palak, who had grown up as an Indian American kid in the Detroit metro area, was also thrown by the homogeneity of the western Michigan teaching force. In Detroit, both the students and the teachers in public schools reflected substantial racial diversity; around Grand Rapids, the student population was diverse, but the teaching force was not.

These demographic realities complicated the process of confronting issues of racial bias, which showed up every day.

Overt stuff was easy to identify, if somewhat harder to call out: During one leadership-team meeting, a teacher declared that many kids would never perform at high levels because they were "from the hood" and poor; another white teacher, frustrated by a conversation about cultural nuances within the African diaspora, wondered aloud if she could identify as "Afro White" if she started wearing braids.

The subtler stuff, though, was even more pernicious. If those were the things people said out loud, what remained unsaid?

Unfortunately, "West Michigan Nice" gave teachers permission to avoid discussing racial bias in the interest of preserving professional politeness. Building a learning agenda that could penetrate these dual defenses of niceness and color blindness was an enormous challenge, which is why many schools never even try.

Palak, Sarah, and the crew, however, were determined. They sought the support of Ebony English, a coach from another local school, to help. They knew the work wouldn't be perfect, but they had to start somewhere.

Let's Talk About It:
Most Teachers Are White

The National Center on Education Statistics collects millions of data points relative to the characteristics of American schools. According to the most recent survey data, almost 80 percent of all U.S. school teachers are white, while more than 50 percent of all public school children are not. Only 7 percent of Black students attend a school district where the proportion of Black teachers matches that of the student body, and the concomitant data for Latinx students are even more striking: just 3.5 percent.

International research confirms the positive effect of students having teachers who look like them, especially for children from historically marginalized backgrounds. Having a single Black teacher in elementary school has a dramatic effect on Black students' sense of self, likelihood of graduating from high school, academic performance, and long-term life outcomes. Everything from literacy to suspension rates to college matriculation moves in the positive direction for students when the teaching force is diversified.

The reasons for the striking homogeneity of the educator labor force are complicated and historical. Many of the same racist trends that drove segregation in the Michigan furniture industry affected employment in public schooling well into the 20th century. Schools of education, as gatekeepers for the profession, played a role, as did professional associations. The way desegregation was attempted, especially in the South, led to the termination of thousands of Black teachers, exacerbating the problem rather than ameliorating it.

The aim here is not to point fingers, but rather to create context for conversation. Just as we cannot discuss student literacy or disparities in office referrals without a realistic understanding of our current data, neither can we discuss the racial dynamics of teaching and learning without understanding the demographics of our educators themselves.

In Chapters 3 and 4, we discussed the complexity of leading adult learning on the topics of race and equity. Whatever the racial demographics of a school faculty, those conversations will not be easy. Multicultural teams will struggle, as white teachers often seek to "learn" from their Black and Brown peers; these dynamics put teachers of color in the position of doing free labor to enhance their more privileged peers' understanding, recreating cycles of trauma in the process.

Faculties that are mostly white—like the team at Polk—face other challenges, such as finding adequate entry points for the conversation. If a culture valorizes color blindness, introducing the topic of race can cause deflection, evasion, blame, or even ridicule, as we saw in the earlier vignette. From the standpoint of racial identity development, discussing race with a white faculty is likely to trigger negative backlash due to folks' own senses of self being called into question; there's a reason that one of the most popular books on race published in the last decade is called *White Fragility*.

The fear of provoking white tears, though, cannot prevent schools from having honest conversations about identity. The comfort of white people in America has always been prioritized at the expense of Black liberation, and many of our schools are complicit in perpetuating that false choice. Faculties with lots of white teachers do not get a pass on this topic because of their homogeneity; quite the contrary, these are the places that require the most intensive reckoning.

That's what needed to happen at Polk, which is why Palak and her peers explored as many routes as possible to initiate the learning process.

POLK ELEMENTARY SCHOOL, GRAND RAPIDS, MICHIGAN

The racial imbalances at Polk were, unfortunately, not unique. Palak and Ebony, as instructional coaches who moved through multiple schools, saw similar patterns manifesting around western Michigan. Historical data indicated that the local student population was becoming more diverse over time, while the teacher labor force was becoming even more white.

This divergence presented a challenge—not just for students who might go through years of public schooling without seeing a single teacher who looked like them but also for the adults themselves. Ebony and Palak suspected that initiating a systemic conversation would require both technical and adaptive approaches.

To start, they created reading groups, using books like Zaretta Hammond's *Culturally Responsive Teaching and the Brain*. Several grade-level teams read the book, which anchors responsive teaching practices in the neurobiology of child development, providing an entry point for teachers who respond to hard scientific research.

They also introduced the topic of equity during whole-school professional development. Ebony and Palak curated video clips, including a TED Talk from Harlem-based educator Geoffrey Canada, who described the intersecting challenges of racism and public policy

(Continued)

(Continued)

in his community. They used current events to stimulate discussion as well, as more video evidence of police violence against Black children seemed to crop up each day.

Conversation about text and media alone, though, was insufficient; to really break through, they would need to get more personal. To do that, they reached out to educators from around the school district to collect stories of how race showed up in their work. The stories were plentiful, but one in particular seemed like a fruitful place to spark conversation. A coach from a nearby school described a parent—a woman of color— who felt disrespected by a teacher. The parent had confronted the principal, saying she was treated badly because of her race.

Palak knew that similar things had happened at Polk, but she thought that introducing a scenario from another school might lower the temperature of the discussion. To build guardrails, Palak and the crew decided to deploy a role-playing protocol. They used a tool called "The Fishbowl," named for the fact that the activity asks educators to act out roles in a scenario, while others watch, discuss, and offer feedback from a circle of chairs, arranged outside the metaphorical fishbowl.

In this particular case, one person would play the teacher who was rude to the parent, and another teacher would play the principal, who was charged with giving constructive feedback to the teacher. The activity was set up in the gym, late on a Friday afternoon, against the backdrop of a rainbow-colored mural, a grinning Harry Potter at the center.

Things became tense, quickly. The "teacher" told the "principal" she didn't like being called "racist." The "principal" pointed out that she didn't say the word "racist"; she just said the parent felt that race was a factor in her treatment. After several minutes of escalating tension, the educator playing the "principal" asked for help from the audience because she was flailing. The most vocal members of the faculty expressed sympathy with the "teacher" in the scenario, who they felt was being attacked unfairly. Everyone else held their comments and squirmed.

Palak looked around at Ebony and her fellow coaches, who had joined from other schools. Ebony signaled to her to "cut" the activity, which she did, but not before folks began to raise voices.

And then, the bell rang and the day was over. The faculty left the gym and headed home. Ebony and Palak stayed back to debrief.

"Was that worth it?" Palak wondered aloud. "I feel like we barely addressed the elephant in the room."

"We have to start somewhere," Ebony responded. "We're in western Michigan. Any conversation we have about race is going to have people up in arms. If we just keep doing the surface stuff, nothing is going to change."

Spoiler Alert: There's No Completely Comfortable Way to Talk About Hard Things

Hard stuff is hard.

The Fishbowl activity in the previous vignette ended with more questions than answers, and even the skilled facilitators involved learned lessons about how to start the conversations next time. The goal of modeling hard conversations, though, isn't to control the situation to achieve a neat outcome, but rather to embrace the inevitability of messiness when tough topics are at hand. The Fishbowl approach is helpful because it allows for serious conversation while de-escalating the risk of introducing the most personal elements of real-world scenarios.

To ensure that role-playing activities like The Fishbowl are constructive, crews in transformation mode should work with facilitators. The ability to navigate these sorts of conversations takes a lot of practice, and having someone who knows the metaphorical ropes is a huge advantage, although not a guarantee that things won't get spicy. If nobody on your team has that sort of experience, it's worth seeking outside support, as even the most seasoned coaches struggle to provide real-time guidance without triggering the sense of personal attack and critique that often precludes people internalizing transformative feedback. As we discussed in Chapters 2 and 3, feedback is love when delivered, and received, in the right ways.

Talking about race isn't the only hard thing you'll do in the course of school transformation, but because that work touches just about every interpersonal nerve possible, it's a helpful focal point for discussions about resistance in general. Schools and faculties must continuously practice having serious, frank, and vulnerable conversations about identity. More often than not, that means talking about the whiteness of the teachers and not the race of the children.

While we've been talking about "Michigan Nice," similar habits of polite evasion manifest everywhere. America was built on a system of racial hierarchy, which Isabel Wilkerson describes in her book *Caste* as "the worn grooves of comforting routines and unthinking expectations, patterns of a social order that have been in place for so long that it looks like the natural order of things." Psychological research indicates that everyone, irrespective of their race, has developed some of those unthinking expectations, creating "unconscious biases." The Harvard Graduate School of Education offers a free online assessment that can help a person unearth their own biases, which is a precursor to combating them.

There are other ways to facilitate discussion on hard issues: racial affinity groups, managerial one-on-one conversations, coaching relationships, and professional therapy, to name a few. Glenn Singleton's *Courageous Conversations About Race* series is a good starting point for educators who are new to this work.

Make no mistake, though: There is no way to improve practice on these issues without confronting the personal and interpersonal dynamics that reinforce systemic racism and oppression. Some of that work will be not just uncomfortable, but downright painful. If our work does not include a deep interrogation of our own personal identities, and the baggage and biases that come with them, we have not yet begun the work of changing ourselves and our dispositions toward the world.

To that point, as you might suspect, a chapter about the complexity inherent in challenging our most deeply held beliefs lacks a tidy ending. Hard stuff is hard, and you will encounter a lot of hard stuff on the path to school improvement. That said, as you can see in the story of Sarah, Palak, Ebony, and the fourth-grade crew, you can survive, thrive, and become stronger through these conversations.

There is, in other words, a next chapter.

It is possible—indeed, necessary—to challenge long-standing norms, cultural taboos, and toxic dynamics, as long as you're surrounded by other folks who are willing to take those steps with you.

Because you cannot do this alone.

When your crew starts to show that there's another way to do things, particularly in a culture that's stuck, amazing things happen. Your culture of inquiry and improvement, when coupled with authentic confrontation of the equity issues that are at the root of our schools' challenges, will become infectious.

How to harness that infectiousness is the work we'll start to unpack together in Chapter 6.

THE CHANGE ISN'T EASY CHECKLIST

- **Acknowledge what is—and is not!—in your sphere of control.** There are entire libraries of books about the complex social challenges that intersect with our desire to provide great love, care, and education to young people. Those challenges are real, ever-present, consequential, and frustrating. And most of them are outside of our immediate control in our role as educators. Crews that want to transform should be mindful of where their energies are likely to drive immediate impact and where they will be tilting at proverbial windmills.

- **Be ready for the unexpected.** Turbulence and discontinuity is the norm in many struggling schools. If you prepare for Plan E, you won't be caught off guard when Plans A through D don't work. Use rapid ROCI cycles to try new things, especially when circumstances prevent you from doing what you had hoped to do.

- **Use teamwork to foster belonging and make it easier for teams to thrive in constant churn.** Grade-level teams are the perfect places to practice cycles of inquiry, but they're also great for cultivating habits that can ease the challenges of rapid turnover. In places where the only constant seems to be change, these structures are indispensable to perpetuating good habits and bringing new change agents into the fold.

- **Continue to build upon what you learned in ed school.** Many of us were prepared to teach in places that do not resemble the schools in which we work. The strategies and practices we learned, while rooted in research, may require adjustments in order to remain relevant. What we learned in ed school should be a starting point for exploration, not a terminus.

- **Use interactive professional learning and skilled facilitators to challenge beliefs and mindsets.** The hardest topics to discuss aren't the ones that push our intellect, but the ones that touch our sense of self and belonging. Challenging your peers to confront those topics requires psychological safety and skilled facilitation. Don't leave anything to chance and use experts to help whenever you can.

(Continued)

(Continued)

- **Practice talking about identity—race in particular.** Our own identities show up all the time in our work. Unfortunately, discussing some of the most critical identity markers—including race, class, ethnicity, and gender—is considered impolite in many communities. There's no way to get better at talking about race without . . . you know . . . talking about race. Transformation crews should use explicit protocols to mitigate the emotional risk of discussing these topics.

- **Unearth biases.** It's easier to address problems once we can name them. While identifying our biases can cause discomfort, the alternative is marinating in our own bad habits. Figure out your own biases, with the help of research-based tools, and work with your peers and experts to address them.

- **Write your own personal racial narrative.** If you don't already know how to talk about your own racial identity, start by writing down your own story. If you don't know where to start, use these questions as prompts: When did you first notice your own race? How has your own race affected you throughout your life? What do you know now that you didn't know before? What do you wish you had known earlier?

CHAPTER 5: DISCUSSION QUESTIONS

1. Can you think of a time when your careful plans were disturbed? How did you deal with the disappointment, and how did you bounce back?

2. Did you, or any of your colleagues, learn as a child that "color blindness" was the preferred method of thinking about race? How did that mindset affect you as a child? As an adult? As a professional?

3. What's something you learned in ed school that has worked for you as a teacher? What about something that hasn't worked?

Culture Eats Strategy for Lunch 6

Tacos El Cuñado sits just a few blocks from Polk Elementary School, and once every other month, Sarah, Birgitte, and Randa trekked there to scarf tacos in a corner booth.

Tacos and ROCI, they had discovered, are complementary, and the excursions provided a useful anchor for a professional ritual. The schedule at Polk was arranged to provide each grade-level team with an open half day each month for planning. The crew, with Palak's support, decided to consolidate their half days into a single full day of team planning every other month.

Those full days were a combination of fun, food, and structured work on cycles of inquiry. They spent the morning in an assistant principal's office, looking at data and talking about which instructional strategies had (and had not) worked the prior month. Then, Tacos El Cuñado for lunch. And after lunch, they identified which strategies to jettison and which would require doubling down, a habit they learned was critical to maintaining momentum for ROCI cycles.

Sarah looked forward to these days with Birgitte and Randa. While the year had gotten off to a crappy start—switching from second to fourth grade before October even arrived—change turned out to be a blessing in disguise. Second-year Sarah, while more worldly than first-year Sarah, was still a novice compared to these veterans, whose collective experience totaled over three decades. Despite their gravitas and

(Continued)

(Continued)

wisdom, they never made Sarah feel stupid for what she didn't know. The team was patient, demanding, warm, and determined.

Most importantly, the team was unafraid to talk about hard stuff, including when the school asked them to do nonsensical things. Their push for schoolwide conversations about race had been a part of that work, but they also were studying instructional challenges across the school.

During one taco trip that next spring, the team was deep in conversation about phonics, a controversial topic. Through examining data, a pattern became apparent to the crew: As the school demographics shifted to include more and more students for whom English was a second language, more students seemed to be reaching upper-elementary grades without foundational reading skills. By the time Sarah started teaching, that population constituted close to 70 percent of Polk. While reading challenges manifested at lower grade levels as well, things got worse by fourth grade, when reading was no longer just a stand-alone subject, but rather the foundational skill necessary to master content across other subject areas, such as social studies and science.

The school's formal curriculum was exacerbating the problem. Their ELA textbooks and associated basal readers had been designed with a homogenous suburban district in mind. There were major gaps in content relevance, to be sure, but the curriculum also failed to acknowledge the realities of teaching students who were coming to school without having learned the basics of decoding written English at home.

To Sarah, Birgitte, and Randa, this discovery was invigorating and frustrating all at once. The crew had decided to spend their afternoon immersed in discussions of what to do with the information. The research on the topic, unfortunately, was rife with inconsistency, contradiction, and even politics. Different schools used divergent philosophies; some experts urged dual-language strategies throughout elementary school, while others called for weaning students from instruction in native languages as soon as possible.

Despite these discrepancies, one thing remained constant in the literature: While excessive focus on decoding can leave multilingual learners behind, most students who come from non-English-speaking families require explicit instruction in phonics and fluency. If those students reach upper grades without mastering those topics, they need to go back to basics, though not at the expense of rigorous instruction in vocabulary-rich content.

This realization put Sarah, who had trained for second-grade teaching, in her comfort zone. Phonemic awareness was central to early-elementary instruction, and she realized she had a lot to add to the conversation. She shared her thoughts and opinions, and her peers listened.

The combination of hard work and camaraderie was infectious.

"This," Sarah thought to herself, "is what I always hoped teaching would be like: tacos with the crew, solving hard problems, adoring my kids, all while making obvious progress."

She would never have expected it just a few months ago, holding back tears in her reading nook, but she was really, really, really happy.

Jumping Into a Warm Pool Requires Little Convincing

There's an old education parable that describes a bunch of people tentatively standing around a cold pool at an outdoor party.

Anyone who went to a pool party as a kid knows the feeling of standing around a cold pool. When the pool is cold, nobody wants to jump in. There's a lot of talking about the pool and discussions about the exact nature of the coldness of the pool. People are peeking at the pool, dipping toes in the pool, dancing around the pool. But very few people end up jumping into that pool.

Why? Because it's a cold pool! Who wants to jump into a cold pool? It's a literal shock to the system, and getting out of the cold pool is even more uncomfortable than getting in. Sure, there's that one person who jumps into the cold pool and then yells, "It's actually not that cold, ya'll, you should try it," but that person is impossible to trust because they're obviously full of it.

Cold pools are a hard sell.

It's a different story, though, when the pool is warm.

Getting people to jump into a warm pool doesn't require much convincing. The water is comfortable, lots of folks are willing to test the waters, and the risks of immersing yourself amidst a bunch of other folks feel manageable.

Healthy group dynamics create an environment that is a lot like the warm pool. Whether a professional organization, a family, a group chat, or a school faculty, when a crew of people jives together, the feeling is infectious. Positive energy feeds on itself, and everyone wants to get in on whatever is going down. Sarah's crew—with their ROCI-infused Taco Tuesdays—had big warm pool energy.

Unfortunately, a lot of the schools we work in are cold pools.

There's no single explanation for the coldness. Some of our schools were warm before and seem to have cooled off, while others have been cold as long as anyone can remember. Lots of places were warm before the pandemic, but now seem far less inviting. Some blame the federal government for enacting blunt public policy regarding teachers, exacting huge emotional and psychological tolls on professionals in the field. Others point to broader trends and widening inequality, which have concentrated more of the responsibility for solving social challenges on schools themselves. Others—wrongly—blame kids and families themselves.

Whatever the reasons for the harsh chill, it's hard to engage people in deep learning and cycles of inquiry if they have to do that work in the shallow end of a cold pool. School transformation work is best conducted in a warm pool with a tight crew.

That's why we're dedicating this chapter to school culture. This is your instruction manual for heating up and maintaining a warm pool. (Be sure to bring inflatable rafts and some of those foam noodle things. *Everyone* loves those.)

Before we can warm up the pool, though, we must acknowledge two facts:

1. A cold pool can, in fact, become warm; and

2. You and your crew have the tools necessary to do so.

These might sound like obvious, even silly, proclamations, but these revelations are critical to your work as a change agent. If you and your crew don't embrace this logic, you will end up spending too much of your time as change agents convincing people to jump into a cold pool. You'll get sidetracked cajoling people to do things that they don't want to do.

That's cold-pool energy.

All the things transformation crews need to do—from improving instructional practice to engaging in collaborative professional learning to celebrating small wins—take time and energy. You don't want to dissipate that energy into the glassy void of the cold pool.

To do as little convincing as possible: show, don't tell.

Crews that engage in transformation should start their work on culture by modeling the kind of vibes to which they aspire. Modeling is easiest when you've already identified the characteristics of positive culture. That's what the fourth-grade crew at Polk did, by embracing both the fun and rigors of teamwork.

Similar situations are a good place to look for inspiration. When we study the culture of schools that achieve significant transformation over time, they share many characteristics. Some are predictable and obvious: Children and adults feel welcome, faculty are supported in achieving their goals, teams learn from each other, and the collective mood is, to overuse a word, warm.

Some elements of strong culture, though, are counterintuitive. Schools that achieve transformation aren't quiet, serene places. Change is often messy, so schools on the path to transformation tend to be vibrant, rambunctious, and sometimes loud. Disciplinarians may worship the quiet hallway, but docile kids aren't thriving kids. In addition, schools that transform embrace constructive conflict among adults. Accepting the discomfort that comes with constructive conflict means recognizing that "niceness" is not tantamount to care. Transformation requires personal growth and school improvement, both of which are impossible without some level of tension.

Some of these characteristics might seem contradictory on paper, but they're not. Educators and academics who study culture sometimes describe the just-right balance as "warm-demanding." The warmth is a necessary precondition, enabling the level of demand required to achieve greatness against difficult odds.

One critical feature of a warm-demanding culture is a deep sense that change is possible, both at a personal and schoolwide level. In her writing about the psychology of school change, Carol Dweck refers to this as a "growth" mindset, which she contrasts with the alternative, a "fixed" mindset. "In the fixed mindset," Dweck argues, "everything is about the outcome . . . the growth mindset allows people to value what they're doing regardless of the outcome. They're tackling problems, charting new courses, working on important issues."

You won't be surprised to discover that a growth mindset is essential to ROCI, where inquiry and learning are rewards unto themselves. Creating a context for behavior change is at the center of transformation; you must believe that change and growth are possible in order to even attempt shifts in practice. If, deep down, you don't believe that both you and your students can do better, you may want to think about a different profession.

The fourth-grade crew was on the verge of shifting practice for themselves. But they didn't want to stop there. They wanted to shift the practices, and the culture, of the whole school.

POLK ELEMENTARY SCHOOL, GRAND RAPIDS, MICHIGAN

The fourth-grade crew went broad and deep into the research on teaching reading to English language learners. Because the research was consistent on the topic of phonics, that's where they decided to focus their energy. Students are supposed to achieve mastery of phonics by second or third grade, but data suggested that lots of students were making it to fourth and fifth grade without mastering these topics.

This disconnect was not unusual for schools that serve large groups of English language learners. Many students at Polk came from Spanish-speaking families. While the English and Spanish alphabets are similar, they are not identical, and subtle differences—like the different pronunciation of the letter "J," for example—made teaching phonemic awareness more challenging than with groups of native-English speakers.

Given what they learned about phonemic awareness, the crew's hypothesis was that lots of students were slipping through the cracks. Kids weren't getting the right dosage of instruction in the early-elementary grades, and because upper-elementary teachers were not used to teaching phonics, students who got to fourth and fifth grade without those skills never built them. Without these foundations, students struggled to develop a real love for reading.

They decided to test this hypothesis using a phonics screening instrument. Their reasoning was twofold. First, they wanted to identify which students were most in need of instructional interventions so that they could deploy those interventions with precision. Just as importantly, though, they wanted to use the results of the tool to generate further buy-in and enthusiasm for the work they were doing. Using the screener was based on a mini theory of action: If they could demonstrate that all students were struggling with basic phonics, then, they reasoned, it would be easier to shift instructional practices among upper-grade-level teams.

The pilot achieved quick results. Their findings were dramatic and confirmed their hypothesis: Large numbers of students in fourth grade required significant support in phonics.

These results raised major technical and cultural questions. On the technical side, they needed to figure out how to build more time for phonics in early-elementary grades to prevent students from reaching fourth grade without those skills in the first place. Beyond that, the information unearthed difficult truths. Why had the culture of the school allowed so many kids to reach upper-elementary grades without foundational skills? Were we coddling our students? Were we kidding ourselves about their progress?

To deal with technical challenges, the crew introduced precise instructional shifts across their team. The centerpiece of those shifts was a dedicated 15-minute phonics section within scheduled literacy blocks. All classrooms had daily literacy blocks, so using the existing time would allow for scaling their strategies later. As with any change in practice, the crew ROCI'd to assess their progress, discuss hiccups, adjust, reflect, and re-up their commitments on a weekly basis.

Things started to improve faster than they expected. Within several weeks, students made measurable progress. Because they were using phonemic awareness to decode with more fluency, overall reading abilities began to flourish.

Sarah and the crew were excited to share their results, so at the next faculty meeting, the crew presented the findings. In particular, they were hoping to win over veteran teachers on the fifth-grade team

(Continued)

(Continued)

because they knew that similar challenges existed across the two grade levels.

The fifth-grade team, though, was a tough nut to crack. These were the teachers in the school with the most experience, gravitas, tenure, and credibility. Their validation of the fourth-grade crew's work could be "make or break" for the broader cultural shifts that they were trying to hasten.

The fifth-grade team's reaction was chilly, to say the least.

"We're fifth-grade teachers," one teacher said somewhat dismissively, after absorbing the presentation. "We focus on reading to learn, not learning to read."

Being an Offline Influencer

Being a change agent is about finding ways to adjust your own behavior, but at its core, transformation also is about the complex work of influencing the behavior of others. As Sarah and the crew discovered when sharing their data from the phonics screener, information alone is insufficient to move hearts and minds. If quantitative results alone were enough to drive lasting change, your Ws would light up an educational scoreboard, and other folks would follow your lead without question.

That's not how change works, though. Change at scale requires collective work, and collective work requires trust. Building trust with and among other humans is hard work. Maintaining that trust is even harder. Leveraging that trust to create collective transformation is just about the hardest thing you can do, but if your crew wants to have an impact beyond the confines of your classrooms, you will have to take intentional steps to encourage, simplify, motivate, and spark similar behaviors among your colleagues.

Put simply, you have to become an influencer.

Influence—unlike control—exists outside of hierarchy. When we influence others, we seek a voluntary response. Influencers do not compel people to comply, but rather inspire people to act in accordance with their aspirations and values. There's a reason the old book is called

How to Win Friends and Influence People and not *Forcing People to Go Along With Your Cray-Cray Ideas.*

Leveraging influence is different from the technical competencies necessary to create structure and process in a school, but it is an important skill that requires cultivation, nonetheless. Margaret Wheatley's "6 Circle Model" describes competencies that are essential to structural change. Three circles are "above the line" and relate to systems: structure, process, and patterns. The other three are "below the line" and deal with beliefs and values: relationships, information, and identity. Influence happens when we harness the "below-the-line" capacities to create the conditions necessary to implement stuff above the line (processes and structures) with fidelity.

While there are few shortcuts in establishing these competencies, in *The Speed of Trust*, Stephen Covey describes a series of behaviors that can help you accelerate the process of building trust, and consequently, influence. Those behaviors involve collaboration, generous contribution to collective work, and listening for understanding. At its core, all of this is good, old-fashioned relationship building: have one-on-one conversations with your colleagues, listen more than you speak, and identify areas where significant common ground exists. The more you can do this from a place of curiosity, and without a hidden agenda, the better.

Becoming influential, though, is just one part of the puzzle. Identifying, channeling, and shaping other channels of informal influence are also critical, especially when it comes to understanding and improving culture. As you might have guessed, influential individuals have a disproportionate effect on the culture of an institution. In the story of Polk, there are a bunch of influencers whose work is at play. Sarah, Palak, Ebony, and their crew are influencers, by virtue of their commitment to, and emphasis on, driving transformational change. They are influencers by choice, not positionality. The fifth-grade teachers, though, are also influencers. Their longevity in the school offers a form of gravitas, which manifests as significant informal authority over how and why things get done.

Truth be told, influence can be wielded both to accelerate transformation or to pump the brakes. If you want to harness influence to drive transformation work, you have to understand the formal and informal channels through which influence travels. One way to do that is to engage in something that community organizers call "decentralized network mapping." While this might sound like a scheme out of a sci-fi novel, network mapping is a straightforward approach to understanding how influence moves. Start this process by putting the names of the folks in your school on a whiteboard. Then, add people outside of the faculty who also affect the way the school works: parents, school board members, and local media figures, for example. Alongside the list of individuals, name all of the organizations and affiliations that are relevant to the school: the district, the PTA, community-based organizations, and the like. Don't forget the informal groups, though! If there's a group of teachers that does karaoke every Wednesday, that counts. So does your taco crew.

After you've identified individuals and affiliations, draw lines between the various organizations and people to illustrate where connections exist. You'll see that some individuals are showing up in lots of groups, while others prefer to play on the periphery. Your network map will serve as a visual illustration of how information and relationships flow. Some of the subtext that you've noticed about how ideas move in and around your school become obvious after you map things out.

Once you have a handle on the sources, patterns, and pockets of influence in your school, you can start thinking about how that information might be harnessed to move transformation objectives. Is there a star influencer in your school who commands the adoration and respect of just about everyone on the faculty? If so, sit down with them and hear what they have to say. Spend more time listening than talking and seek to understand their priorities. Look for places where their ideas and aspirations overlap with yours and use those intersections to drive collaboration.

You also might discover that certain groups—like the fifth-grade team at Polk—wield collective influence. Find ways to build trust with those groups, and whenever possible, do so from a learner's posture. Ask to observe a team meeting or offer to help with an existing project.

As you deepen your understanding of how influence moves, you will start to see the power of including more people in your crew's vision. The process of change management, you will find, isn't about amassing more power and control, but rather creating the deep well of trust and community that allows you to share power with your teammates rather than hoard it.

That's what Sarah, Palak, and the crew aspired to do, which is why they knew they had to crack the code with their trickiest critics: the fifth grade team.

POLK ELEMENTARY SCHOOL, GRAND RAPIDS, MICHIGAN

The fifth-grade teachers at Polk Elementary School taught in a series of detached trailers, the kind that school districts call "portables" to make them seem more palatable. Fifth-grade students and teachers exit the main building, stomp over a blacktop, and climb narrow stairs into one of the two temporary structures that look, from the outside, more like a barracks than a classroom.

The insides of the portables were more inviting, but not by much. A single window in each filtered dim daylight over the weathered tan carpet, while faux wood paneling crept up the walls, serving as a backdrop for graded papers and bulletin boards.

Palak sat in the back of one trailer, as a gesture of both deference and goodwill, observing a reading lesson.

Getting her foot in the door was half the battle. The fourth-grade crew's phonics extravaganza had rubbed some folks the wrong way. Their enthusiasm for change, while captivating to lower-elementary teachers, seemed unrealistic and gauche to the seasoned fifth-grade team.

Palak and the crew realized, though, that the skepticism was understandable. The fifth-grade team was stacked with veteran teachers, a couple of whom had extraordinary teaching talent. They had seen change initiatives come and go, and they weren't enthusiastic about the newest fad emanating from the fourth-grade wing. What looked like resistance and intransigence was more like a rational response to past promises that went unfulfilled.

As an improvement coach, Palak understood this dynamic. She wasn't there to make a hard sell, though. She had been invited on this day not to coach, but to observe and learn. She also had a plan to build bridges. This teacher was known among her colleagues for "word sort" activities, which seemed to be rooted in the same instructional ideas that the fourth-grade crew was trying to advance. Palak wanted to see the activity to determine whether there was something she could learn and also, candidly, to suss out whether her presence might build some

(Continued)

(Continued)

trust. If, in the course of sitting in the back of the classroom, it became clear that Palak did not in fact bite, the crew thought they might make some inroads.

Palak watched the activity without taking notes, narrowing her eyes, or giving off any other body language that might suggest a whiff of judgment. The activity itself was straightforward and fun. The teacher presented students with words with similar-sounding but different long-vowel sounds. Students, then, would work together to sort those words into categories based on which actual vowel sound the words contained. Long Os went in one box and long As in another. Palak saw the value. Students practiced pattern recognition, and there were basic elements of phonemic awareness embedded in the work.

Palak faced a conundrum, though. On the one hand, what she witnessed was engaging instruction. The teacher was in her element throughout the lesson, and the kids were vibing from her energy.

On the other hand, the word sort activity, as structured, didn't achieve the objective that the teacher thought it did. Palak had agreed to visit on the basis that this particular lesson was something that the crew could incorporate into their project of enhancing phonemic awareness. The activity would require significant tweaking to achieve that objective, and Palak wasn't sure whether the teacher would be open to collaborating, especially if that meant making changes to a long-cherished lesson plan.

Later in the afternoon, after dismissal, Palak approached the teacher to reconnect. Rather than confronting her about the content of the lesson, she extended the olive branch that she had prepared. "I saw some really great stuff in your lesson!" Palak said. "I'm working on putting together an instructional leadership team to build bridges across grade levels. Would you be willing to help me do that?"

The request surprised the teacher, who had been expecting another push to adopt the phonics screener.

She smiled. "Let me think about it," she said, in Actual Nice, not just Michigan Nice. "Thank you for asking."

Opening the Classroom Door
Can Do Magical Things

The elementary school classroom is a sacred place, harkening back to when one-room school houses operated out of church basements. This sanctity is both a blessing and a curse. Behind classroom doors, beautiful things happen. Dedicated educators work with impressionable, tiny humans to stimulate, animate, and incubate imaginations. This process has always been a balance of art and science, and you can observe sparks of brilliance in just about every classroom in America.

Unfortunately, though, the closed classroom door also works against our ability and willingness to grow. We now know a great deal more about the science of teaching and learning than we did several decades ago. Whereas we once thought that reading ability was akin to emergent traits that are acquired, like spoken language, we now know that decoding symbolic writing systems requires explicit instruction for most children.

The progress we have made in understanding the cognitive neuroscience of learning often remains unrepresented in classroom instruction. Teachers themselves are not to blame. In one longitudinal study of curriculum standards at schools of education, the National Center on Teacher Quality discovered that, as of 2013, only one-third of colleges provided "adequate instruction" in the scientific underpinnings of reading; by 2020, it was only half. In theory, schools should be able to compensate for these gaps in teacher preparation, but as we discussed in Chapters 4 and 5, professional learning is uneven and not always connected to classroom practice.

As we've said before, you cannot change what you cannot see, and that applies especially to instructional practice. Crews that want to transform must take steps to create a culture of instructional transparency, which is an important precursor to driving systemic change.

That said, for better or worse, veterans like the fifth-grade teachers at Polk have plenty of reasons to be skeptical of observation, especially when conducted by inexperienced outsiders brandishing clipboards and punitive rating systems. To ameliorate this skepticism, transformation crews must reduce the risk of educators exposing themselves to peer observation and feedback. One easy and effective way to do this is to go back to something we learned in Chapter 1 and celebrate small wins. Do your best to find something special and great about the teaching practice of peers and share that practice with the faculty.

"We hear Mrs. C's dividing fractions unit is *the best*, ya'll!"

"Has anyone watched Mr. G's fire mitochondrial energy lesson? Make time for it. Trust me."

Once you've made some progress in building confidence and lowering defenses, ask if you can come observe that lesson. Sometimes, this combination of authentic relationship building and celebration can open the physical and metaphorical doors, even if just a crack.

In addition, while this may sound counterintuitive, another way to encourage greater collaboration and participation is to give leadership roles to the people most resistant to change, like Palak did in the previous vignette. This strategy is effective when working with skilled, veteran educators who have seen dozens of initiatives come and go. We often conflate tentativeness with aversion, but many of the biggest skeptics in your school are also the best teachers. They're not sticks in the mud; they're just exhausted by the constant churn of false promises. If that sounds like someone you know, invite them to lead a training, a data discussion, or even a book club. Even if you don't have a perfect olive branch, camaraderie can be contagious, even for the most grizzled veterans.

Speaking of contagious fun, there's no better way to squash a culture of camaraderie than to force people to do things. "Mandatory" and "fun" rarely find themselves in the same sentence, as most compulsion tends toward compliance and not creativity. Wherever possible, allow teachers and leaders to opt into the culture you are striving to create. Take steps to ensure your team culture is diverse and inclusive and not replicating existing inequitable power structures. This approach will allow you to expand your crew in concentric circles; start with the early adopters, move next to the tentatively curious, and save your outreach to the coolest comrades until you have more people on board.

Finally, and perhaps most importantly, think carefully about the story you want to tell about why you are engaging in change. Too often, our technical strategies for change management are untethered from a broader narrative about why we're engaging in that change in the first place.

Marshall Ganz, a leadership professor at the Harvard Kennedy School, describes public narratives about change as having three distinct parts: a story of self, a story of us, and a story of now. Practice telling and refining your story of self, us, and now so that your colleagues and peers understand the values and motivations that undergird your crew's quest for change. Absent a narrative that you shape, your peers will create their own, which is bound to be more threatening than yours.

Consider the difference between "These upstarts think I'm a crappy teacher and want to tell me how to do a job I've been doing for 20 years" versus "Our school has experienced significant demographic changes in the last two decades that none of us could have predicted, and we *all* have a role in figuring out how to shift our practices and mindsets to respond to those changes."

One is a warm pool, and the other is frighteningly cold.

In practicing your story of self, you are bound to raise challenging questions about your own role in the change process. Am I up for this? Can I sustain this level of energy for the time it will take to really make things different? Why did I choose this work? Am I willing to make the hard changes in my own practice that will lead to transformation?

Because personal growth is precisely where the rubber meets the road, those are exactly the sorts of questions you should be asking yourself at this point.

And we'll wrestle with many of them in Chapter 7.

THE CULTURE CHECKLIST

- **Have fun with your crew. Like, for real.** Change management is fun, but hard. It takes a long time, the path is circuitous, and you will endure setbacks. Persisting through all of that is easier if your crew knows how to kick back together. Grab tacos for lunch, arrange a regular karaoke night, or play video games in someone's basement once in a while.

- **Find the appropriate balance between "warm" and "demanding."** Educators with a disposition toward warmth sometimes worry that adopting a demanding instructional posture can compromise relationships; conversely, demanding educators worry that too much warmth is tantamount to coddling. The truth is in the middle: Great schools that manage to transform find the balance among these characteristics, which are not in tension, but rather are complementary.

- **Cultivate habits that expand your influence.** When you have good ideas, show, don't tell. When collaborating with more experienced colleagues, listen more than you speak. Be generous with praise and recognize when your peers have great ideas. Avoid unnecessary conflict so that you can embrace constructive tension when it's essential to your and others' growth.

(Continued)

(Continued)

- **Create maps of how ideas and relationships move in your school.** Things that seem haphazard and accidental often are rooted in invisible patterns of influence and communication. While you can never—nor should you seek to—control all of those channels, you can use the information you glean from demystifying them in service of transformation.

- **Build opportunities for your peers to "opt in" to new practices.** We can mandate compliance, but we cannot mandate great teaching. Even if you're creating a warm pool, there will always be peers who are skeptical of transformational change. While that skepticism can be rooted in intransigence, it's often a reasonable self-protection mechanism. Creating a culture where teachers and leaders can decide how and when to participate in new ideas is a proven way to generate inclusion, excitement, and enthusiasm, while mitigating pushback and resistance.

- **De-privatize the classroom.** The closed door is one of the classroom teacher's greatest tools, but it can also be a significant cultural barrier to progress and transformation. Work with your crew to create enough psychological and emotional safety for your peers to embrace the sort of constructive love that comes from allowing others to observe and provide feedback on practice.

- **Practice your story of "self," "us," and "now."** Storytelling is a powerful way to influence school culture. Culture, after all, is the accumulation of ideas, habits, practices, rituals, and traditions. In cultivating change and transformation, you are building new ways of doing things, but never forget that you're not starting from scratch. You're always building alongside people and practices that are already there, many of which were there long before you were.

CHAPTER 6: DISCUSSION QUESTIONS

1. Is your school warm, cold, or something in between? How do you know? Do your peers agree with you, or do opinions vary on this topic?

2. When was the last time you collaborated with a peer who wasn't a part of your grade-level team or other formal structure? Do you have personal relationship with folks outside of your team?

3. How do teachers in your school react to observation? Does it feel like a "gotcha" process or an opportunity for professional growth?

School Transformation Requires Personal Transformation

7

David Cohen wasn't sure how many hours of his life as a school principal should involve managing the physical and emotional aftermath of student altercations, but he was pretty sure the answer wasn't "most." It was the spring of 2015, and David was wrapping the second semester of a challenging new principalship. After many years of being in his comfort zone as mediator, motivator, negotiator, and de-escalator, the drama was starting to wear on him.

Early in his career, David had relished—even craved—the daily thrill of knowing that anything could happen during a school day. He had grown up just across the border from Philadelphia, in the Bala Cynwyd section of the "Mainline," where windy suburban roads collide with the final throes of West Philly. He started college, thinking he would become a lawyer, but a year of student teaching was enough to reroute his dreams. He fell in love with being in a school: forging relationships with kids and their families, learning new classroom skills, and becoming a confidant to his fellow teachers. He skipped law school entirely and never looked back.

David came to love the unglamorous "nuts and bolts" parts of running a school, which many of his peers avoided. Processes and procedures made intuitive sense to him, as did building the relationships necessary to implement those systems. His affinity for sweating the small stuff made him an ideal candidate for administration, which is how he ended up at the helm at William E. McBride, a K–8 school in the area.

(Continued)

141

(Continued)

David's penchant for the particularities, though, started to become a burden before his first year at McBride was over. Fights among students were common, which was an unfortunate consequence of broader trends in the neighborhood. McBride's corner of the Philly region often lands on lists that most communities would prefer to avoid, like "American zip codes with highest rates of gun violence."

At an intellectual level, David knew that he couldn't single-handedly stop students from fighting, but that didn't stop him from trying. He personally—and physically—intervened during spats on school grounds. If voices started to escalate in the hallways, David would be there before anyone noticed that he had left the office. If something popped off on the way to school, David wanted to know all the details, conducting detailed post-conflict investigations that gave him a fleeting sense of control.

"Who did what to whom?" he would ask. "Why did this happen? What's going on outside of school that I need to know about? How are we going to make sure this doesn't happen again?"

For all of his professed love for being involved in the nitty-gritty, he started to hit the wall at the end of his first year at McBride. Each day seemed to follow a similar pattern: He showed up at school ready for whatever the morning would bring, but within a few minutes of arrival, a threat to student safety would throw him into crisis mode. He was skipping leadership-team meetings, shortchanging classroom observations, and relegating to the back burner anything that wasn't related to preventing fistfights.

Being so reactive was taking a toll on David's psyche, not to mention his sense of self. He began to realize that the things that had made him great as a novice school leader weren't working anymore. Even more troubling, the same skills that had propelled him to this point in his career now seemed to be the very things holding him back.

One morning, he reached a breaking point. He was standing at the school's front door, greeting students as they arrived on a cool spring day. He was smiling, shaking hands, making eye contact, and enjoying the little interactions he relished having with the hundreds of children who walk to McBride every day.

And then, his neck stiffened as he saw the telltale signs: A group of students running in his direction. Yells from further down the block. Scuffed knees. Papers fluttering out of backpacks. The aftermath of a fight.

He ran toward the action, abandoning his post at the front door.

While he sprinted down the street, preparing to pull kids off each other, he couldn't help hearing a troubled voice inside his head: "This can't be the way this works. Something's gotta give."

Everyone Hits the Wall

The ancient ritual of the marathon is a classic metaphor for describing a person's enduring commitment to long, arduous tasks. But while the analogy has a way of glorifying persistence, it misses the fact that distance running takes an enormous physical toll on human bodies.

When a person trains for a marathon, they are, for all intents and purposes, teaching their body how to sustain long bouts of abuse. The physical integrity of the skeleton is put on trial. The constant pounding of fragile feet on hard pavement wreaks havoc on the tiny bones and ligaments in a person's extremities. The knees absorb the systemic shock of a body's weight collapsing on a single inflection point over and over and over again. Lactic acid accumulates in the muscular system, causing sustained cramps, burning, and other unpleasant sensations.

Preparing for stress in the musculoskeletal system, though, is secondary to the mental trauma. The physical body can accustom itself to relentless force through pain management wizardry, training repetition, and sports snacks. The truly hard part of finishing a marathon, by most accounts, is managing the fragile interaction between one's mental state and long-term energy stores.

Despite advances in shoe technology, sugary beverages, and protein bars, most folks "hit the wall" at some point when they try to run a marathon. Wherever it happens along the 26.2 mile journey, "hitting the wall" is code for that time at which your body can no longer process energy fast enough to keep up with your brain. Some call it "extreme fatigue"; *Runners World* once described it as your brain whispering to your body that it has reached a breaking point.

School transformation work, as we mentioned many chapters before expanding this tortured metaphor, is more of a marathon than a sprint. When you and your crew string together weekly ROCI cycles into monthly reviews, and those monthly reviews become fodder for annual goal setting, and then you come back in the second and third and fourth years of transformation, and there's *still* a lot of work left to do, the relentless reality of the work sets in.

And so, as with marathons, almost everyone who engages in school transformation will "hit the wall." Unlike the neurochemical sensation afflicting distance runners, the educational wall is socioemotional in nature. Symptoms include frequent bouts of crying in the faculty lounge, stress dreams about test prep, snapping at your assistant principal, and asking your spouse to ROCI chore schedules.

Not all the symptoms are so obvious, though. Sometimes, hitting the wall manifests as a mild malaise, which can be just as jarring, as society expects our most passionate change agents to be enthusiastic cheerleaders. Other times, "the wall" looks like cynicism, pessimism, or even regret for having taken up school transformation work in the first place. The feeling may be invisible to others but debilitating to you.

"Why am I bothering to do this?" you might wonder. "Why did I choose to do this? I don't have to be doing this. Nobody is really making me do this. It's so much work. Am I a lunatic?"

First, no, you are not a lunatic.

But you, too, may have hit the wall, as just about every change agent will.

When you do hit the wall, the most important thing to remember is that you are not alone. Every story in this book describes a team effort, and that's intentional; no single person gets to be the savior in the story of school change. We are stronger together, and having a crew ensures that there is no singular person upon whose mental state the entirety of a school's future hinges.

That said, transforming a school requires each of us to reach beyond our current abilities, fears, and limitations. This chapter is about the personal work and growth that must happen in tandem with school transformation.

A big part of personal growth is ensuring that the pursuit of school improvement doesn't overwhelm us beyond our ability to function, so the first step in combating the wall is to take care of yourself. While the concept of "self-care" has become a bit of a buzzword, there are many pragmatic reasons to attend to your own well-being while in pursuit of significant goals. Ancient wisdom teaches that you can't pour from an empty cup, and an anonymous lumberjack (not Abraham Lincoln, to whom the quote is often misattributed) said that, given several hours to chop down a tree, a person should spend the bulk of the time sharpening the saw.

Whichever old saw (pun intended) you prefer, in this chapter we'll talk about filling up your cup, sharpening your tools, and making sure that the work of transformation becomes a self-renewing well of inspiration and not an albatross around your and your crew's collective necks.

WILLIAM E. MCBRIDE SCHOOL, PHILADELPHIA, PENNSYLVANIA

Richard Allen was born into slavery in Delaware in 1760, and when he became a free person for the first time at 20, he did what many newly liberated Black men of the period aspired to do.

He moved to Philly.

Richard made the short trek north because Philadelphia in the late 18th century offered something exceedingly rare: a thriving community of free Black families. Such places were hard to find at the time, even in the North, because while everyone knows how slavery metastasized throughout the South, the noxious institution was still legal throughout the North for most of the 1700s. Pennsylvania finally abolished the practice the year Richard arrived, New York followed suit the following year, and New Jersey moved toward gradual abolition in 1804. Delaware—from whence Richard came—didn't officially abolish chattel slavery until 1901, three decades after the rest of the country ratified the Thirteenth Amendment.

Within a few years of setting up shop in Philly, Richard Allen was a popular local preacher. When local white churches forbade him and other Black pastors from preaching to their flocks, he founded Bethel African Methodist Episcopal Church, the first congregation of what

(Continued)

(Continued)

would become a flourishing global institution and the first free Black denomination of Protestantism in the world.

From his perch at Mother Bethel African Methodist Episcopal Church, Richard rose quickly to become a central organizer and preacher in the burgeoning national abolitionist movement, whose spiritual center was in Philadelphia. When Harriet Tubman escaped from a Maryland plantation in the 1840s, she found refuge among the abolitionist Philadelphians; the city became an indispensable hub for her Underground Railroad activities and a permanent home for her descendants.

Despite this rich, radical history, the City of Brotherly Love hasn't always shared that love back with its Black citizenry. After the Civil War and Reconstruction, when hundreds of thousands of Black Southerners moved north as part of the Great Migration, Philadelphia was one of the most popular destinations due to the perception of widespread equal opportunity.

The perception turned out to be too rosy.

The region's building trades, transportation industry, and military contractors often refused to hire Black laborers, a discriminatory practice cheered on by the city's white-led labor unions. When courts and the federal government intervened in unfair labor practices, the city turned to another tried-and-true form of urban racism: real estate. Redlining, collusion among mortgage lenders, and racial violence divided communities along color lines and created the Philadelphia suburbs, which exploded between 1940 and 1960. In that same period, large sections of Philadelphia went from being mixed race to almost entirely Black. North Philadelphia, with the highest concentration of Black families, went from under 30 percent to almost 70 percent African American during that 20-year period.

The city subsequently made fledgling attempts to drive greater racial understanding and integration, but de facto segregation continued through the 1960s, when the city hired its first Black superintendent of schools. By the time David Cohen—a child of the same suburbs created by racial segregation—became the principal of McBride, the school's neighborhood was almost entirely African American.

David arrived at William E. McBride at an inflection point for both the school and himself. The prior decade of public education around Philadelphia had been turbulent, even by the standards of American schooling. Persistent "fiscal" and "managerial" problems caused the state of Pennsylvania to intervene in some local schools, placing them under the control of a "school reform commission," whose actions only seemed to exacerbate fiscal crises. The problem got so bad that in 2012 the commission issued a "master facilities plan" that included a list of 37 area schools slated to close.

McBride was on the list.

The families of the neighborhood—many of which counted three generations of McBride graduates—had other plans. They organized direct actions, held interventions at community hearings, and collected petitions from residents, making bold arguments for the school to remain open.

Their strategy worked. When the commission announced its final plans later the next school year, the decision to close McBride was reversed.

The community's celebration of grassroots victory was short-lived, however. The revised plan required closing a different school, four blocks from McBride, and sending the dislocated students to a consolidated McBride-based campus. The complications of merging two proximate K–8 schools quickly became apparent. McBride's enrollment doubled overnight, from 300 to 600, and because the region's fiscal problems never abated, consolidation came with a mandate to "do more with less." Instead of getting additional resources, the combined school had fewer counselors, nurses, assistant principals, after-school clubs, secretaries, and school lunch staff than the aggregate schools had before the merger.

David became principal during this fragile transition because of his reputation for attending to detail, caring for communities, and getting in the proverbial weeds. He joined a staff of veterans, and he jumped into the job with vigor. He dove deep into school operations, overseeing the minutiae of lesson planning, classroom bell schedules, and lunch duty assignments.

(Continued)

(Continued)

His dwelling in the details, though, made focusing on long-term challenges harder. When David rushed to stop a fracas, other priorities at the school suffered. Everyone noticed, especially Cynthia Moultrie, the schools' most senior teacher leader. Cynthia had worked at the school for the entirety of her multidecade career, first as a kindergarten teacher and later as an instructional coach. She had grown up in the neighborhood and knew multiple generations of every family in the building.

Cynthia's observation came from a place of love. She could tell that David's heart was in the right place and that he was the right principal for the school, which was saying a lot, given David was a white man coming into a predominantly Black school with a large faculty of experienced educators. Teaching in the community required a long-term commitment, and Cynthia saw that level of dedication in David from day one.

To cultivate that commitment to longevity, Cynthia used her perch as a coach to help the school develop, embrace, and propagate a mantra about student success. "At McBride," Cynthia says, "we are big on the power of YET. If a student can't do something, we don't say that they can't. They just haven't done it YET."

After spending many hours working with David to structure team meetings, build schedules, and talk about data, it was clear that he wanted to work on the big picture. It wasn't that he didn't care about the long-term things that didn't involve the nitty-gritty of day-to-day management.

He just hadn't gotten to them YET.

There Is No Improvement Without Reflection

The power of "YET" is a catchy encapsulation of the growth mindset necessary to engage in school improvement. There are no transformational schools full of stagnant professionals, and a big reason that systemic improvements often stall is that we hit plateaus of personal growth and don't know what to do next. Improvement, though, starts with the self. ROCI was designed to accelerate school transformation, sure, but cycles of inquiry do not happen unless individuals learn and experience concomitant personal transformation.

To this point in the book, we've talked about the ways in which ROCI shapes educational practice. By structuring microtargets for weekly improvement, we set goals, plan, execute strategies, and assess whether or not what we've been doing is working.

But there's a fourth part of ROCI that comes after all the planning, doing, and assessing: It's called "reflect and adjust." The act of reflecting on our practice and then adjusting based on what we've learned is an indispensable part of continuous improvement, but it often takes a back seat to the more technical parts of the process.

This omission is a colossal mistake.

Professionals shortchange reflection for all sorts of reasons. More often than not, "time" is to blame, which we discussed in Chapter 4. When our work feels—and is!—both urgent and important, the act of stepping back can feel like an unearned luxury. We also deprioritize reflection because it can be uncomfortable. When things don't go well, reflection means figuring out where we went wrong, sometimes resulting in finger-pointing and hurt feelings. When we succeed, it may feel superfluous to backtrack and nitpick what could have gone better.

Whatever the reason, no part of the ROCI process experiences as much disinterest and disrespect as the act of reflection, but if you want to live that transformation life, you must reflect.

To ensure that reflection is a part of your daily hygiene, build explicit guardrails for the practice. Find a place amenable to deep mental work, where you won't be interrupted. Make it clear that you intend to use this space for sustained reflection. It might feel strange at first, but block an hour in your calendar every week for "thinking." Keep this time sacred and don't let other people intrude. Your crew should do something similar on a collective basis. You're already meeting in grade-level teams, right? Use some of that time on a monthly basis for reflection.

When you start to reflect habitually, you'll notice changes. First, you will avoid repeating mistakes, thereby preventing bad-habit formation. Fun fact about ROCI: The most common reason that things don't go well the first time a crew commits to a change is that people don't actually do what they said they would do. Why does that happen? There are lots of potential reasons, but you'll never figure it out until you start reflecting and asking why. Some teams even adopt the practice of asking "Five Whys." The logic behind the Five Whys exercise is that you can reach the root cause of just about any problem by asking "Why?" five times. The exercise can feel weird, even a bit childish, but revelatory ideas emerge when we embrace routines that force deeper reflection.

The reflection process also enhances our ability to give and receive feedback. Improvement of the self, and the institutions we inhabit, requires us to be open to hearing uncomfortable things about our practice. One simple protocol that crews can use here is a "Plus/Deltas t-chart." After attempting to try something new, reflect on what went well and what you could do differently next time. On the left side of the chart, list the "Pluses," and on the right side, the "Deltas," or things you might change. Notice that it's not "Pluses" and "Minuses." That's intentional because there's a lot less negativity inherent in discussing what we'd do "differently" versus what we would do "better." Some teams call this "Glows and Grows" or "Pluses and Pushes." No matter what you call it, do the exercise right after the work itself, so the areas for growth are fresh in your mind.

Finally, and for the sake of your prolonged mental state throughout the marathon of school transformation, the act of mandated reflection injects necessary time and space into the cadence of otherwise unyielding transformation work. Derek Mitchell, the CEO of Partners in School Innovation, says, "When you're cooking up important things, sometimes you have to let them sit and simmer." Unfortunately, the world we live in thrives on manufactured urgency and not careful analysis. As a result, our ideas and brains often end up half-cooked.

Doing a half-baked job at school transformation was not in the McBride crew's plans, so Cynthia, David, and their crew went to work reflecting on what they could do better, together.

WILLIAM E. MCBRIDE SCHOOL, PHILADELPHIA, PENNSYLVANIA

The McBride crew came back to school in 2016 knowing that instructional excellence had to be front of mind. David knew that his biggest personal challenge would be pushing beyond his comfort zone to lead that work. His attention to operational detail during the first year had been necessary, but he knew the skills that had made him effective so far might not be the same things that would take the school to the next level.

For support, he turned to Cynthia, other veteran educators, and Mallory Berger, a school improvement coach assigned to the school. David was explicit with the crew about what he needed from himself, and from them, in order to reach the next level. "It's easy to get lost in the sauce of running a school," he said. "We could have all of the processes and procedures in the world, but if learning isn't happening, does the other stuff even matter?"

To create boundaries for himself and others, he jettisoned his physical perch in the building's front office, planting himself on most days in a small, makeshift room that Mallory occupied on the second floor. The room was too small to be a classroom and had no operable windows. There was enough room to push three desks together in the center, and they adorned the walls with calendars describing the school's long-term professional learning plans. It became a vibrant space that cultivated the exact vibe David was craving: heavy on data and instruction, light on drama and distractions.

Meanwhile, Cynthia and Mallory went to work operationalizing the principle of YET. In order for the mantra to become reality, Cynthia knew that the growth mindset needed to encompass not just rhetoric, but every aspect of the school: professional learning, lesson planning, instructional practice, and classroom observation. They built calendars, tools, rubrics, and professional development modules rooted in growth. They formed a data committee composed of the teachers most dedicated to spreading the gospel of continuous improvement.

Cynthia herself became an evangelist for the ROCI cycle. "When we look at data," Cynthia says, "we always have to ask 'what's next?' If we look at data and then never ask any follow-up questions about practice, that data just stops with me, and that's not helping anyone."

David helped ensure that the whole school remained focused on where the data pointed. He chaired instructional meetings and channeled his penchant for process into building instructional improvement protocols. He created a schedule for classroom observations that included everything from the big picture—who would observe which classrooms and when?—to the small factors that often get in the way of translating observations into improvement: Who takes notes during observations? How quickly do those notes get translated into constructive feedback? Who is responsible for making sure that the feedback gets discussed soon enough to make a difference in educator practice?

(Continued)

(Continued)

Beyond doing things outside of his comfort zone, David also made sure he had an accountability process in place to ensure that he changed his behaviors. He was clear and transparent with Cynthia and Mallory about his intentions. "If I'm going to be an instructional leader, I need to spend the time on instruction. Period," he told them. "And if I stray, I need your help to stay the course."

Beyond soliciting input from within the school, David created relationships with peer principals. He assembled a crew of school leaders from other K–8 buildings in the area, and they met to discuss their mutual challenges, often using adult beverages as a conversational lubricant. One principal, Mrs. Z, became a particularly important confidant. Mrs. Z helmed a similar school nearby, which meant that she understood the unique challenges David faced, given that violence from the neighborhood often spilled over into both schools.

With structures in place for both individual and group accountability, it didn't take long for the changes to manifest.

Later that fall, David, Mallory, and a grade-level team were in a ROCI meeting in their dedicated room. Several minutes into the conversation, the dean of students threw open the door of the sacred space. She interrupted the meeting, short of breath, telling them there had been a disturbance on the first floor.

David's adrenaline kicked in, but instead of jumping out of his chair to rush downstairs, he locked eyes with Mallory and waited a beat.

Mallory stared back, saying nothing, waiting to see how he would respond.

David took a breath and glanced at the data on the wall in front of him. Then, he looked back at his dean of students, an experienced administrator, who he knew was capable of de-escalating the situation herself. He reminded himself, in the moment, that his own obsession over details was disempowering the rest of the crew.

"Am I the only person who can solve this problem?" he asked, pulling himself together.

The dean paused and thought about it for a moment. "No," she said, "No, honestly, I guess you're not. I can do it."

"Okay," David said, projecting practiced composure. "I need to finish this meeting. As long as the school isn't burning down, I'm trusting you to put out this fire. You can give me the Cliff's Notes version of what happened later. Cool?"

"Cool," she said, nodding.

The dean of students closed the door, left, and went downstairs to handle the situation. And the instructional team got back to work.

Be the Change, but Never Go It Alone

There's an old saying about humans who have tails and the people who love them: If one person tells you that you have a tail, they're nuts; if two people tell you that you have a tail, they're working together to fool you; but if *three* people tell you that you have a tail, you should probably turn around and look.

The tail tale—in which the unexpected appendage serves as a stand-in for our unexamined imperfections—is powerful because it highlights one of the hardest parts about mitigating said imperfections: admitting that they exist in the first place. All of us have "blind spots" relative to the flaws in our practice, and they are hard to address because they are, by definition, beyond our ability to see.

There are a bunch of ways to identify your blind spots, but perhaps the easiest way is to rely on your crew. That's what David did when he established clear lines of personal accountability. Ask your crew point blank: "What are my blind spots?" or "What am I missing about my own practice that would help me get better?" Unless you're a total jerk—which I'm sure you're not—the responses will be precise, targeted, and gentle. Your crew is not out to get you; they're here to help. If you want to go even deeper, ask your supervisor or coach to create a "360-degree review" process, which incorporates formal feedback from a wide range of stakeholders.

Lacking awareness, however, isn't the only reason we struggle to grow. Racial identity can interfere with addressing blind spots, as folks with racial privilege, especially white men, often get away with downplaying growth areas. Consider, for example, who among your colleagues is allowed to avoid operational tasks by saying, "Sorry, I'm not a detail person," or "I have terrible handwriting, so I shouldn't take notes in this meeting." Ignoring one's weaknesses, even when ostensibly in service of preserving focus on strengths, is a privilege that not everyone is afforded.

Beyond these factors, sometimes we need additional time, knowledge, or experience to improve. You can work through some of these factors with an improvement coach. Many of the educators you've met in this book—Meaghen, Tim, Palak, Ebony, and Mallory, for example—have extensive training as improvement coaches. Coaches are different from bosses and managers, as their relationship to you is based on your improvement and is not supervisory. Most improvement coaches have experience as classroom educators, so their counsel is rooted in practical application of the work you need to do as a teacher or administrator.

If there are experienced coaches in your school, lean on them to help you grow as a professional. Look for someone who has the ability to adjust their posture to your needs. Sometimes, you'll want a tough coach who will "tell it like it is" without a lot of pampering. Other times, you will appreciate a more Socratic process of discovery, where the coach poses questions instead of supplying answers. Often, your coach will need to assign you readings for homework, and once in a while, they'll probably have to listen to you cry. A good coach can adjust to your needs through the art of responsive listening.

Responsiveness and situational awareness matter a great deal because being a change agent is a reciprocal process, where you play different roles at different times. Sometimes, you are the person seeking coaching, while other times *you play the role of coach yourself*. Coaching is not a permanent identity, but rather a disposition that is central to the process of transformational change. You'll get better at accepting and incorporating feedback into your own practice if you work hard at providing that same sort of loving feedback to your crew.

Being a change agent is all about accepting these new, exciting, and sometimes daunting roles. You get to learn new skills, many of which were excluded from your formal training as an educator. This process of discovery can be both exhilarating and scary. At the same time, the work requires you to challenge long-standing practices that have been socialized in your school, often over the course of not just years but generations. Calling attention to this fact can have the side effect of drawing skepticism and irritation from some of your peers and superiors, but that's okay because you're learning how to manage that tension (Chapters 5 and 6).

Being a Change Agent

Five Areas of Focus

MINDSETS

Rooting oneself in an understanding of systemic oppression in our educational system, courageously maintaining a focus on equity and social justice, focusing on results and continuous improvement, and addressing challenges with courage and tenacity.

LEADERSHIP

Inspiring others to work in aligned and deliberate ways to disrupt patterns of inequity; collaborating respectfully with the local community to realize a rigorous and inspiring vision.

ADULT LEARNING

Using coaching and facilitation skills to bring out the best of individuals and groups, guiding others to examine their practice, using data to highlight what is and isn't working, and investing others in making changes that will lead to greater success.

TRANSFORMATION APPROACH

Learning what successful classrooms, schools, and districts do. Holding deep pedagogical knowledge of strategies proven to work for students of color and English learners. Understanding how to design learning systems to support educators.

CHANGE MANAGEMENT

Understanding how the feelings, motivations, points of resistance, and social dynamics of the adults within a system must inform the pace and tactics of change; recognizing that altering the status quo can create discomfort and adjusting to help individuals and institutions embrace more effective practices and structures.

Despite the tallness of this order, it's important to remember that most educators are capable of this work. That's why this book exists in the first place! Each step in this book was calibrated through decades of microexperimentation—not just to hasten school transformation but also to ensure that the process is feasible for regular people, in regular schools, with families, leading regular lives.

This practical research has isolated some major characteristics of individuals who become successful change agents, and those traits can be learned over time. Two interrelated ones are mindset and leadership. To drive change, you have to embrace the notion that something better is possible, even against the headwinds of systemic oppression that we've identified throughout this book. Folks who've adopted that mindset must also be willing to play a role in attracting others to the task of addressing those challenges; that's the leadership part.

Beyond those two areas, you need to learn the tools of change management, understand the basics of adult learning, and develop practical research-based knowledge about what drives student results in schools. At the risk of pulling the curtain back a little bit too far, that's what the first half of this book was about.

Take note, though, of what is *not* on the list of characteristics that make for a great change agent: membership in elite clubs, sophisticated acts of visible heroics, fancy degrees, big egos, or stratospheric standardized test scores. None of those things are a part of a framework for being a change agent because none of those things really matter. The necessity of transforming schools, especially for marginalized children, is too important and widespread for us to rely on the egos of wannabe heroes. If change agency were the provenance only of exceptional superhumans whose otherworldly talents imbue them with untranslatable secrets, there would be no point in trying to spread the word.

This work can only thrive when educators like you decide to turn the tide. So far as we're concerned, the question is not whether or not you are capable of this work; it's whether you're ready YET.

This chapter was all about ensuring that you have the mindset, energy, stamina, wherewithal, and attitude to persist in complex, multiyear change management processes. That persistence requires us to be honest, transparent, and caring with ourselves and others. As bell hooks said in *All About Love*, "Commitment to truth telling lays the groundwork for the openness and honesty that is the heartbeat of love. When we can see ourselves as we truly are . . . we build the necessary foundation for self-love."

That foundation is the basis for the love that we ultimately express out-wardly to our peers, children, and communities. In the next chapter, we'll talk about how to think about that love in the context of school transformation.

THE PERSONAL TRANSFORMATION CHECKLIST

- **Put on your own oxygen mask first.** There's a reason the safety guidelines for air travel ask us to do this: You can't take care of others until you take care of yourself. If you're going to take part in a school transformation process, you need to prepare for the long haul. Prioritize your own well-being and engage in self-care so that you don't burn out when the rubber hits the road.

- **Reflect and adjust to exercise the growth mindset.** Reflection can happen organically, but you will experience the most transcendent personal growth when you create dedicated time for said reflection. Protect the physical and temporal space you use for reflection, and make sure that your grade-level teams build reflection into ROCI cycles.

- **Prioritize after-action feedback.** We know that students can't incorporate feedback on their behaviors unless we provide immediate guidance after a learning opportunity, and adults are no different. Make time to discuss the "pluses and deltas" of your personal projects, even if that means rehashing painful moments.

- **Identify, and work on, your blind spots.** If we've said it once, we've said it a thousand times: You can't fix what you can't identify. Figure out which gaps in your professional practice are opaque to you but apparent to others. Then, take concrete, transparent steps to mitigate those gaps. Reflection without adjustment is an academic exercise.

- **Build interpersonal accountability structures.** Tell your crew what elements of your practice that you're aiming to improve. Then ask them, explicitly, to help you stay the course.

- **Leverage instructional coaches.** Coaching exists to help adults improve practice. Unfortunately, school-based coaches often end up playing lots of roles in schools that are tangential to that project; that diversion of responsibilities has only been exacerbated by pandemic-driven staffing demands. Whenever possible, protect the time necessary for coaches to engage in actual, factual coaching.

- **Be the coach *and* the coachee.** Sometimes, you will be the person in need of a good pep talk. Other times, you will be the motivational speaker delivering that stirring locker room speech that gets the team back on track. Just because you were the coach yesterday doesn't mean that you can't be the person who needs coaching tomorrow. Be prepared to play both roles.

CHAPTER 7: DISCUSSION QUESTIONS

1. What are your habits when things get hard for you at work? Phone a friend? Cry in the break room? Eat a pint of ice cream? Are you able to identify professional stress as it's building because of a propensity to engage in these habits? Reflect on other actions you might take to deal with this stress, as well as how you might keep the stress from building in the first place.

2. Does your day have any built-in time for reflection? Or is it just go-go-go 24/7? What would it take to build in that time?

3. Have you ever made a serious attempt at identifying your professional blind spots? If so, what did you learn? If not, what's holding you back?

Leading With Love 8

WILLIAM E. MCBRIDE SCHOOL, PHILADELPHIA, PENNSYLVANIA

Cynthia Moultrie, like a lot of folks who grew up in the neighborhood, thinks of McBride as the "diamond on the corner of Diamond Street." The two-story brick building wraps around a regular city block, but the colorful murals beckoning you to the sea-green front door are anything but typical: giant butterflies and a human-sized ladybug flank your welcome, while a friendly dragonfly flutters its wings against a setting sun, beckoning you to enter.

The vibrance of the facade is a prelude to the warmth inside. Most city schools experience churn, staff turnover, and the sort of regular cosmetic makeovers that stand in the way of establishing tradition, but despite weathering that sort of turbulence, McBride is a constant for the community in an otherwise unpredictable world. Teachers who come to work there tend to stay. Families with one student in the school send the next one. It is a building of brothers and sisters, caring cousins, families, and multigenerational storylines.

Cultivating that filial love is as much about attitude as attending to details. Cynthia, David, and the rest of the faculty spend time on the finer points of hospitality. McBride has an open-door policy, and everyone at the school—from outside consultants to custodians—know that the standard is not just lip service, but a way of life. When Mom, Dad, Grandma, or Grandpa walks up to the front entrance, someone is waiting to hold the door for them, always with a smile, and often with a hug.

(Continued)

(Continued)

Outside the school's walls, the broader community abounds with history and tradition. Temple University, not far from the school, sends a bevy of student teachers every year. The playgrounds out back constitute the "mecca" of Philly's decades-long tradition of excellence in street basketball. Understanding, partnering with, and wrapping one's arms around the neighborhood experience is a critical part of a successful McBride educator mentality. The school has a way of highlighting the brightest spots in a speckled pattern of uneven earth—not unlike an actual diamond.

No tradition exemplifies this disposition more than the Community Meeting, a habit woven into each day at McBride. Most classrooms hold Community Meeting first thing in the morning, although some teachers wait for the afternoon to debrief daily events. The gathering is a chance to reflect as a class, while synthesizing academic rigor, big concepts, and the typical topics that crop up in the course of a day.

In first-grade classrooms, for example, students might spend Community Meeting parsing sentence structures that describe the day's weather. Rigor escalates with age. Middle school students sometimes use Community Meeting to watch the prior night's evening news before writing journal entries that include their own "first drafts of history." Those accounts can be riven with raw emotion: elation after the Eagles won the 2017 Super Bowl; confusion and fear after the 2016 presidential elections stoked racist fear-mongering.

Younger students also use Community Meeting to practice talking about their emotions, using developmentally appropriate color-coded language as a stand-in for more sophisticated descriptions of mental states. Students who show up to school "ready to go" are "green." Students who show up on "red" are facing challenges and might need a little support. When a kiddo shows up on "yellow" or "red," other students know who might need some extra love on that particular day, even if it's just a friendly face to sit across the table from at lunch.

One day in the fall of 2016, Cynthia sat in the back of a third-grade classroom during Community Meeting, hoping to observe fodder for future feedback. A new student had started at the school the day before, and each child in the class wrote a short letter greeting the newcomer. The letters were packed with both practical advice—"This is

Room 190, and the bathroom is down the hall to the left"—and moral support—"You will like this school; everyone is nice." After the students gave their new classmate a pile of handwritten notes, the newest member of the class couldn't avoid breaking out in a big smile. Neither could Cynthia.

After finishing the letter activity, the teacher transitioned to a temperature check. "How is everyone feeling today?" the teacher asked.

"If you're good, you're green," a helpful, more experienced kiddo whispered to the newbie.

"Then I'm definitely green," the new student beamed, clutching dozens of letters handwritten on wide-ruled notebook paper.

And so a day at McBride started.

What's Love Got to Do With It?

Great schools are full of love and joyful work. This connection between love and work is not incidental, but essential. As the late poet laureate of the United States Dr. Maya Angelou once said, "You can only become truly accomplished at something you love."

Dr. Angelou was neither the first, nor the last, great thinker to consider the intersection of love and transformative work. The philosopher Khalil Gibran said, "Work is love made visible," while early American transcendentalist Ralph Waldo Emerson believed that nothing great is accomplished without love. Oprah Winfrey once said, "Your job is not just to do what your parents say . . . but to figure out what your heart's calling is and to be led by that," while Confucius allegedly advised, "Choose a job you love, and you will never work a day in your life."

While everyone from Confucius to Oprah seems comfortable discussing the universality of love manifesting as work, the intersection of these two ideas is complex. Most people connect to the idea that it is important to do work that feeds us—both literally and spiritually—but different cultures have divergent approaches to the ways that labor and personal well-being interact. Educators know that work in the classroom has an outsized impact on a person's mental state. We spend a huge percentage of our waking lives either at school, thinking about school, or planning for what's going to happen next at school. Our hearts flutter when young people from years past return to tell us that they remember that one essay assignment that made them love writing, and our chests tighten when we know we're struggling to reach a student who needs more than we've yet figured out how to offer.

Despite the obvious emotional weight of our jobs, few of us are comfortable talking in explicit terms about love at work. We wear our professions on our sleeve and make our jobs central to our identities, but we often stop short of acknowledging just how much our deepest socioemotional states depend upon—and ebb and flow in accordance with—our work.

Why is that?

In *The Gifts of Imperfection*, Brené Brown writes, "We cultivate love when we allow our most vulnerable and powerful selves to be deeply seen and known." Being vulnerable is hard, scary even, but the most powerful kinds of relationships become possible only when we open ourselves to the intense vulnerability of loving care. On the one hand, this kind of transcendent connection is a gift to be cherished. On the other hand, it can be downright terrifying to prostrate oneself in a position of such openness, especially in the context of a vibrating school building.

When we talked about school culture in Chapter 6, we discussed the difference between cold pool cultures and warm pool cultures; it should go without saying that it is near impossible to make oneself vulnerable while wading in the discomfort of a cold pool. That said, even when the pool is warm, opening oneself to love requires more than just the promise of psychological safety. Love, especially in a professional context, demands humility, yes, but also an inclination toward growth because love without action is a broken promise.

Because of this, every great school is built on love: love for learning, love for children and families, love for our communities, and not to mention love for the intergenerational work of transferring knowledge across time and space.

Tapping into your whole self—including your capacity to give and receive love—is essential to long-term transformation work. In the last chapter, we talked about the relationship between personal growth and systemic transformation work; the personal growth you experience as a change agent is, in fact, a form of self-love. This chapter is about the different ways love shows up in our schools and how we need to embrace love as a central part of inquiry and improvement.

But beyond just talking about love, we also need to be comfortable expressing love. Tell someone in your school you love them. Today. Make a habit of cultivating an environment where the expression of love is normalized. Does doing that make you feel a little uncomfortable? That's okay. This chapter is going to be about developing comfort with the love we have to give, translating love into transformational growth, and harnessing love in service of our life's work.

WILLIAM E. MCBRIDE SCHOOL, PHILADELPHIA, PENNSYLVANIA

Later that same fall, Cynthia and Mallory sat in the back of a classroom, observing Mrs. P, the school's newest fifth-grade teacher.

There were no two ways around it: Mrs. P was struggling. It was only a few months into the school year, and David, the principal, was starting to lose patience with Mrs. P's approach. Cynthia and Mallory were there to observe, reminding themselves of the power of YET, looking for hints as to how to unleash Mrs. P's talents.

Classroom management was the teacher's biggest challenge. On the one hand, Mrs. P's lack of mastery was not unusual. Younger teachers have little practical experience building, executing, and following through on the rigorous systems that create the context for learning; few teachers "nail it" on their first try—or even their second, to be honest.

On the other hand, observing the work in progress was uncomfortable, even for the veteran coaches. Instructions for activities were vague, and learning objectives for lessons were unclear. There was little evidence of a comprehensive approach for reinforcing student behavior, and while the room wasn't utter chaos, there wasn't much order either.

This was exactly the sort of challenge that made Cynthia love her job. She took mental notes and looked for moments of excellence that could be built upon as she and Mallory observed. While languishing in the early days might be inevitable for novice teachers, Cynthia knew that early intervention with struggling educators was critical for long-term student success.

(Continued)

(Continued)

Coddling, she believed, didn't work for kids, and it certainly didn't work for grown-ups.

This particular tension—between care and coddling—was top of mind for Cynthia and Mallory, as some teachers in the school were confusing comfort for love. It had been two years since McBride and its neighboring school consolidated. David had been hired as principal to support the creation of order, and the building had reached a period of relative stability. That work had been grueling, and some faculty members seemed ready to exhale.

The instructional-leadership team, though, knew that more was possible. Cynthia and the crew insisted that stability was only useful as a prelude to excellence, and not as an excuse for complacency. Yes, there were classrooms where high expectations thrived, but Cynthia liked to remind the faculty that "pockets of excellence don't move the train forward."

To keep the train in motion, the leadership team had made instructional rigor one of the top three priorities in their theory of action. David had come back to school determined that nothing would get in the way of that priority, just as he had put accountability guardrails around his own personal growth the year before.

Mallory, though, was concerned that many teachers didn't have great models for how to balance warmth, rigor, and love in a classroom setting. On one side of the spectrum, there were teachers who seemed to think that "tough love" was the only kind of affection available in schools. Those teachers were strict, unyielding, and tended to rely on harsh forms of discipline that could make an outsider wince. Mallory couldn't help but see these kinds of classrooms as contributing to the overpolicing that drives unhealthy relationships between students and authority figures.

On the other end of the spectrum, though, were teachers who created cocoons. These classrooms, where students were shielded from the troubles of the outside world, felt more comfortable for Mallory to observe, but they were problematic in different ways. In these cases, cuteness and safety crowded out opportunities for academic rigor. Learning, as a process, requires moving beyond one's comfort zone, and the teachers who prioritized sweetness over struggle were depriving students of the mental state necessary for authentic learning.

The crew at McBride faced a classic "Goldilocks and the Three Bears" problem: One kind of classroom was too hard, and the other, too soft.

These priorities, and the challenges of implementing them, were top of mind as Mallory and Cynthia observed Mrs. P's classroom. As the morning's lesson approached its ending, students started to get rambunctious. Kids jumped out of seats, and the children who had been paying attention to Mrs. P became distracted.

The more the kids' energy increased, the more agitated Mrs. P became. She started raising her voice, but her shouted pleas for calm only exacerbated the escalating din.

Mallory and Cynthia watched, wearing poker faces, silently making plans in their heads for what to do next.

Finding the "Just Right" Approach . . . to Both Kids and Adults

The "Goldilocks" conundrum facing Cynthia and Mallory—namely, how to find the appropriate balance of safety and struggle in the classroom—is one that vexes many educators in schools pursuing transformation. While we know that school can and should be a joyful place where children experience physical and emotional safety, we also know that the learning process requires bouts of stretching, striving, and struggle. While none of this needs to come at the expense of children's well-being, there is a perception among some educators that the process of holding young people to high expectations must come at the expense of warmth and love.

Quite the opposite is true. Authentic learning—the kind that emerges from pushing past one's comfort zone—is only possible when we have a deep love for the children in front of us and for the rigors of instructional craft. This love requires not only that we see our children as fully human, but also that we recognize the intersecting cultural contexts in which our classrooms exist.

Unfortunately, our schools often treat love and intellectual demand as mutually exclusive. Part of the challenge is a cultural belief system, rooted in the dominant culture's perpetuation of myths of rugged individualism, which mistakes the contextual circumstances of poverty for human ability. Many of our students come to school from marginalized backgrounds, and too many discussions of American schooling start from the premise that children and their communities require "fixing." The language of failure and brokenness permeates the culture of school improvement policy and literature, and even educators with the most progressive sorts of critical consciousness slip into the language and mindset of "deficit" at times.

While some of this deficit thinking is unique to K–12 institutions, the problem extends beyond the schoolyard. This narrative is rooted in an analytical framework and cultural zeitgeist that places the blame for socioeconomic inequality on the institutions that we ask to solve for those disparities. Blaming schools alone for the social conditions of our communities would be like blaming the fire department for burned-out buildings, and yet serious commentary about schooling often falls for a similarly flawed logic.

We know our schools aren't perfect. This whole book is predicated on the notion that they can be much, much better. At the same time, schools often are fragile crown jewels—diamonds, even—in communities that sustain few other long-standing institutions. To lay the entire tapestry of the social condition at their feet is, to put it plainly, a setup.

On the other end of the spectrum, though, is an equally pernicious problem, which some educators call "loving children to death." This sort of framing—which also is a product of deficit mindsets—posits that children from marginalized communities cannot be expected to achieve at the highest levels because of the very cultural context that our interlocking institutions have created. This framework accepts that schools are the product of explicitly racist policymaking, which is correct, but extrapolates the wrong conclusion from this logic, arguing that classroom-level interventions are hapless against the longitudinal stress effects of poverty. While classrooms alone will never solve America's broader problems of socioeconomic drift, generations of research tell us that school-based interventions have an enormous effect on students' ability to read, write, do math, and become thriving participants in their communities and the world. To negate the impact of classroom teaching, given that reality, is nihilistic.

Race, of course, is at the heart of the deficit framing on both sides of the spectrum, although we are slower to call out the prejudices inherent in coddling. Teachers and administrators who aspire to serve, and become change agents within, communities must grapple with the extent to which they have internalized these narratives. If you're coming to a school to fix something that's broken, save children from the very communities that raised them, or shield them from the realities of the world they must someday navigate without training wheels, you're missing important parts of the story.

As we discussed in earlier chapters, it is important to unearth conscious and unconscious biases in service of loving and seeing the children in our classrooms. We also should anchor our teaching in ideas that reject the narratives of brokenness, while still acknowledging reality. Ferial Pearson, Sandra Rodriguez-Arroyo, and Gabriel Gutiérrez, for example, describe "cariño pedagogy"—loosely translated as "caring pedagogy"—which provides a helpful framework, encouraging teaching that accounts for not just students' humanity and cultural sustenance but also for the trauma inherent in navigating a world in which racism and oppression continue to affect social outcomes.

Beyond unearthing your own biases and anchoring your practice in theory, it's important to interrogate your motivations for engaging in school transformation work. If your work is rooted in love for the people and institutions you aspire to serve, folks will notice. Your actions, as usual, will speak much louder than your words. That doesn't mean, though, that you shouldn't talk openly about your motivations because nature abhors a vacuum. Where gaps exist in your story, others will fill them. Be honest with yourself about when your narrative is, or seems to be, in conflict with your behaviors. Learn from that conflict and embrace processes that hold you accountable for growth. All of this is much easier if you've spent time with your crew talking about racial identity and blind spots, which we discussed in Chapters 4, 5, 6, and 7.

If you don't know whether you're finding the "just right" balance in the classroom, talk to families and veteran educators in your school. If you don't have a strong enough relationship with anyone to get a frank response, that's a good sign that something is off. Your biggest allies in cultivating and expressing love will be those folks who have called the community home for a long, long time. Even amidst the forces of gentrification and displacement, our schools continue to serve intergenerational communities of extended families. Building real relationships with those families, whose love for a place is not learned but inherited, is essential to your work.

Solving the Goldilocks problem in our relationship with children, though, is just one part of the puzzle. The same logic applies to our relationships with adults, particularly when we play the role of coach. Finding the "just right" balance with adults isn't just about having the technical wherewithal to help improve instructional rigor. It's about having enough love for our peers to believe in their capacity to grow, while committing the professional and emotional bandwidth to the project of that learning.

WILLIAM E. MCBRIDE SCHOOL, PHILADELPHIA, PENNSYLVANIA

After observing Mrs. P's classroom, Cynthia and Mallory worked together to craft a plan for coaching the new teacher toward a more effective approach.

Knowing they couldn't address everything at once, they zeroed in on the specific topic of classroom management. They anchored their plan in an overall vision for what they wanted to see in classrooms at McBride, based on an ongoing conversation among teachers and leaders about what constituted the "just right" classroom vibe. Some components of the vision related to mindset: the power of YET, believing that students are capable of extraordinary things, and ensuring that instructional priorities are sufficiently high to drive the right amount of constructive discomfort for kids. Beyond mindset, they considered practices: routines that cultivate engagement, constructive dialogue among students, and differentiated lesson planning, for example.

They approached Mrs. P's growth from a position of love, which allowed them to see where she evinced bright spots. Students in her classroom, for example, were encouraged to work together in small groups. While her approach to establishing group routines was a bit disorganized, the emphasis on collaboration held promise. Beyond that, Mrs. P demonstrated commitment. She was not afraid of hard conversations and had already started making connections with families and the community. She never talked down to kids and parents or acted as if she had all the answers.

Cynthia knew that she could work with someone who had this combination of humility and willingness to learn.

When Cynthia sat down with Mrs. P to have a follow-up conversation, she approached it Socratically, as was her preference for coaching. Cynthia first asked questions about the lesson she observed, without being evaluative. "What did you hope would happen when you gave those particular instructions for group work?" she asked. "And was the outcome in the classroom what you had hoped for?"

In asking probing questions, Cynthia opened the door to self-reflection. Sometimes, coaching means having an extra set of eyes present to illuminate what's invisible to the teacher at the front of the classroom, but there was nothing subtle about the disarray she had witnessed in Mrs. P's class. Cynthia suspected that Mrs. P, more than anyone, recognized that something had gone awry.

Mrs. P wasn't surprised by the question and had clearly been thinking about what went wrong. "I know, I know," she said. "It was a mess, and I wish I could tell you it was a one-time thing. I feel like every time I have a handle on this classroom, it just slips away. I'm trying lots of things, I promise."

Cynthia continued probing, asking Mrs. P to go deeper. She inquired about the various ways that she had attempted to create a healthy classroom environment. She asked whether she had evidence that any of those steps had been successful. Then, they talked about what the ideal classroom environment would look and feel like so that they had a shared picture of what might manifest once some new routines had been established.

As they approached the end of the coaching session, Mrs. P pushed Cynthia to provide some concrete direction. "You've been doing this much longer than I have," she said. "There have to be a few pointers you can give me so that this doesn't keep happening."

Cynthia demurred. "I can tell you what I think you should do next," Cynthia said, "but who is that helping? Me? You? Neither of us really." Cynthia believed that imparting expertise in a coaching session was something to be done rarely—and typically only when all else had failed. She continued to brainstorm with Mrs. P, in a collaborative manner, to identify some things to try next. She casually inserted a few tips throughout the debrief, in ways that were complementary to Mrs. P's disposition and approach.

As they wrapped up the session, Mrs. P thanked Cynthia for making the time to debrief. "This is hard," Mrs. P said, fatigued from the intensity of the conversation.

"Of course it is," Cynthia said. "Because this is our craft. I can give you articles and send you to PD sessions or give you a lecture about the finer points of equity in the classroom. But nobody gets better at their craft without working on that craft. That's what I'm here to support you in doing."

They agreed to check in again several weeks later, and both educators left the conversation hopeful that progress was imminent.

Adjusting Your Posture to Help Others Thrive

Helping other adults to find the outer limits of their comfort zones is an act of love because until a person finds those limits, growth is not possible.

The social scientist Judith Bardwick describes the "comfort zone" as a mental state of "neutral anxiety," wherein a person's socioemotional stores are more or less untaxed. There is little risk in the comfort zone, and as such, most folks experience steady, unremarkable performance when situated in this kind of psychological space.

Learning and growth, however, require us to stretch beyond the comfort zone, which introduces an element of risk-taking. Just as the act of love requires vulnerability, so does the process of learning. In opening yourself up to personal and professional growth, you exit the comfort zone, putting elements of your psychological and emotional safety on the line.

The growth process, however, is not about exposing oneself to thoughtless, uncalculated risks. Growth doesn't flourish in the comfort zone, but it also doesn't manifest in the "danger zone," where our well-being and safety are threatened. Authentic learning requires finding a sweet spot—you guessed it, the "just right" balance—which exists beyond the limits of comfort, but short of legitimate peril.

In Chapter 7, we introduced the notion that every change agent needs to toggle between coach and coachee during a transformation process. When you are acting as a coach to someone else in your crew, that role will require you to express love in the form of cultivating the conditions for personal growth. That's what Cynthia did with Mrs. P, as she led a Socratic process of pedagogical dialogue, aimed at unearthing a combination of beliefs, mindsets, and mental blocks. Doing that kind of work requires instructional skills, a working knowledge of how adults learn, and leadership capabilities, to be sure. It also requires, though, a series of relational abilities that allow you to adjust your approach based on the contours of the context in which you find yourself counseling.

Put simply, you need enough situational awareness to figure out different coaching "postures."

Knowing which kind of posture to adopt when coaching is as much art as science, and you will likely adopt multiple postures during a single coaching session. Before you adopt any posture, though, be sure to create a transparent objective for the coaching conversation. In the previous vignette, for example, Cynthia and Mrs. P agreed that they were going to work on classroom management structure, which created the appropriate entry point for asking challenging questions about how Mrs. P might shift her practice in service of that goal.

Once an objective is established, there are a handful of different postures you can adopt to elicit transformative coaching conversations. One is to *expand* the situation beyond the current context. Expanding means looking at the situation through a different lens, eliminating existing constraints in our conception of the challenge, and imagining new possibilities. Using an expansive posture is helpful when a colleague is stuck in a rut or is too deep in the weeds to perceive the bigger picture.

Another related posture is to *inquire*. When you coach from a position of inquiry, you seek to elicit beliefs and emotions that can lead to self-awareness. Use an inquiry posture when someone hasn't yet gotten to the root of their challenges or maybe even has a blind spot about how their personal belief system is getting in the way of technical progress. Inquiry was a significant part of Cynthia's coaching process with Mrs. P.

The *affirm* posture is deployed to validate a person's strengths, while helping them to build toward new successes. Affirmation is useful when someone is on the right track but needs to be reminded that there is still work left to be done. You affirm to reinforce good habits and patterns. The corollary posture to affirm is *confront*. We use confrontation when someone needs to let go of an ineffective behavior or break a bad habit. While affirming conversations seek to identify the factors contributing to good outcomes, confronting conversations seek to understand why someone persists in doing something that is not working.

Coaches adopt a *synthesize* posture to organize ideas and build consensus for next steps. Taking a synthesis approach often means restating core ideas from a conversation or creating visual artifacts that capture the major contours of a coaching session.

A final posture coaches can use is to *consult*. Consultation is useful to help people develop new ways of thinking or problem-solving. Coaches using this posture might share resources, provide supporting research for a new instructional approach, or introduce another expert into the conversation.

Coaching Postures

POSTURE	INTENTION	TAKING THIS POSTURE SOUNDS LIKE . . .
Expand	Broaden or push thinking beyond the current state	— How could we look at this differently? — If you could let go of your current constraints, what would your practice look like?
Inquire	Develop insights that will support problem-solving, self-discovery, and self-directed learning	— What problem are we trying to solve? — I heard you say ____. What do you mean by that?
Affirm	Validate or build on what's working	— What has contributed to that success? — How can we build on this strength?
Confront	Help someone let go of an ineffective way of working	— We've spent time talking about this concern before. What might be keeping you from acting on that? — Here's a disconnect I see . . .
Synthesize	Make thinking explicit, help organize and clarify ideas, and build consensus in a group	— What I hear you saying is . . . — Let me make sure I've captured our conversation. I'm hearing ____. Is that correct?
Consult	Support a new way of thinking, enable someone to learn an unfamiliar process, or help build a vision of what is possible	— One possible approach is . . . — Research indicates . . . — Our experience with successful schools . . .

To that last point, it's important to note that only the "consult" posture involves the dispensing of knowledge or expertise. Once in a while, coaching will require the impartation of new information, but most of the time, coaching is about aligning beliefs and motivations to meet personal goals. That's what Cynthia hoped to do when working with Mrs. P to improve her classroom management practice. Mrs. P already possessed a deep intellectual understanding of the challenges in front of her; she just hadn't figured out how to align her behaviors to that knowledge.

Yet.

While the postures described here do not constitute an exhaustive list of how educators in a coaching role can cultivate their peers' learning, honing each of these positions will make you better at both giving and receiving love and feedback. Keep in mind, though, that the postures alone don't make for good coaching. Your spirit, generosity, personality, and disposition are critical to the process as well. Or as Megan Kizer of Partners in School Innovation puts it, good coaches "add value, make jokes, and bring cake."

There is inherent value in the reciprocal coaching process, sure. But the real magic happens when the love we give and receive is reciprocated as growth . . . in our pedagogical practice and in our students' learning.

WILLIAM E. MCBRIDE SCHOOL, PHILADELPHIA, PENNSYLVANIA

Later that school year, Cynthia and Mallory had a unique chance to assess whether their work with Mrs. P was bearing fruit. A network of schools throughout the area was engaged in a professional learning community to share learnings from their respective transformation efforts. Principals from that network rotated their meeting locations to observe progress at the network's schools.

One day in the early spring, the gathering happened at McBride.

On the afternoon of the meeting, leaders from a dozen schools across the Philly region, including an assistant superintendent supporting their efforts, trickled into Mallory and David's tiny second-floor room, making the already cramped space feel like a sardine can. School

(Continued)

(Continued)

leaders tossed their bulky coats and laptop bags onto chairs, radiators, and whatever other surfaces they could find. A few principals walked in while still having animated cell phone discussions with administrative staff; one figured out her walkie-talkie could still reach her home school and continued managing lunch dismissals from the McBride hallways.

Once everyone arrived, Cynthia, Mallory, and David welcomed the crew that had assembled. After almost a year of work together, the network of principals was beginning to hit a rhythm. The mood was collegial, curious, and energetic. To kick off the gathering, David and Mallory offered a short presentation on the school's theory of action and their approach to ROCI before Cynthia took the group on an observational walk to see classroom instruction.

Cynthia was craving serious feedback, so she structured a tour that would include teachers at various levels of comfort in the classroom: Several would demonstrate master teaching, a couple were in need of improvement, and one or two were hard to pinpoint, including Mrs. P. The novice teacher had made significant progress in the intervening months, but Cynthia wanted to use this opportunity to garner some outside perspectives.

When the group got to Mrs. P's classroom, Cynthia held her breath a bit. The group entered the room, and they saw what to a lay observer might still seem like modest madness. A few students sprawled on beanbag chairs, reading chapter books. Four kids sat together at a small table, all with laptops open, discussing a group project in borderline outdoor voices. Mrs. P herself was perched on a fuzzy armchair, conducting a targeted reading intervention with a group that had struggled the prior week. The room was intense, but not disorderly, pulsing with the kinetic energy of small bodies in motion.

When the group concluded the walk-through, they returned to the small office to debrief. Cynthia set out a few bowls of hard candies, which disappeared quickly, and asked, "So what did we think?" while drawing a "Glows/Grows" t-chart on a nearby whiteboard.

Principals shared their unvarnished thoughts, in a way that might have felt threatening without the level of trust the group had built together. They pointed out where they saw teachers at their best. They also noted where there was obvious room for improvement: worksheets taking the place of legitimate instruction, and middle school teachers delivering content with insufficient rigor, for example.

After a few minutes of conversation, the assistant superintendent, John Tupponce, piped up. John was responsible for coordinating the work of this collaborative network. His perspective carried weight—not just because of his positional authority, but because he had a long track record in school improvement and a perch that allowed him to see transformation work across dozens of different schools. "Can we talk about Mrs. P's classroom?" he asked. "Because that was different."

Mallory and Cynthia shared a quick look, equal parts curiosity and surprise. "Sure," Cynthia said. "Could you say more?"

"Sometimes in large districts," John began, "you have so many factors coming together—compliance, red tape, everything else—that when it all trickles down to the classroom things become rote and overly structured. And then you walk into this room and see something different. It's a little chaotic, and you hear this hum of energy. It had the feeling of a neighborhood coffee shop, where a bunch of creative people are working together. Sometimes, you see that kind of stuff happen in college spaces. But in a K–8 school? Almost never. What I saw in there is sticking with me, in a good way."

This crew of principals, who often used constructive disagreement and argumentation as a growth strategy, were in a rare state of consensus on this topic. "I'm with you," another K–8 principal said. "It's not perfect, and it wouldn't necessarily show up on an evaluation rubric, but that teacher is doing something special with her kids." They continued to unpack the experience, offering tips for Cynthia and Mallory as they further coached Mrs. P toward mastery.

Then, the group moved on to other topics, and as the debrief wound down, Cynthia and Mallory helped people locate their errant belongings and reminded folks how to find the front door. Once everyone had left the room, David asked Cynthia and Mallory to stay behind and huddle.

"Okay, so you two were right about Mrs. P," David said. "She's getting there. And you know I was a little bit skeptical." They continued to talk, and David went on to reflect on how his bias toward structure and order

(Continued)

(Continued)

might affect his ability to see emerging instructional practice that is somewhat outside the norm.

Cynthia smiled and thanked David for his reflection. "Look," she said, "her heart was in the right place. And the results speak for themselves. She had the capacity to organize a vibrant learning environment. She just hadn't gotten there—yet."

Real Love Is Lasting

The technical aspects of the ROCI approach to school transformation are built on an internal logic about how humans experience change, which is hard work. The difficulty is compounded because many schools gauge progress on lagging indicators that can take months—if not years—to process. As such, many efforts at transformation fizzle before we even know if they're working. Without microindications that things are moving in the right direction, we might jettison promising initiatives before they have time to flourish.

The technical stuff, however, only gets us so far, as most stakeholders who aren't already policy nerds will struggle to remain excited for the long haul of transformation solely on the basis of your crew's newfound obsession with improvement science. The long-term project of sustaining excellence across years and decades, which is far more complex than weekly ROCI cycles, is a tall mountain that is impossible to climb if our emotional disposition toward the work is lukewarm.

ROCI can get you through the next week. An instructional-leadership team's goal-setting process can illuminate the month to come, and a school's theory of action can describe our aspirations for what might happen in a year or two.

But staying the course for years and years and years? Only love can do that.

The further we look into the future, the less precise our technical planning becomes. If we've learned anything from managing the COVID-19 pandemic, it's that figuring out what's going to happen next Tuesday is hard enough, let alone determining what our school will look like 200 Tuesdays from now.

Where our technical tools fall short, love bears some of the burden. Love is the power of YET in action, acting as faith that the energy we pour into our colleagues right now will bear fruit in the future. Love is a force that occupies the gap between where we are today and where we know we can arrive later. Love for our children sustains us on days when nothing else seems to be going right. Love for our peers allows us to see their strengths, even when their growth areas are fighting for center stage. Love for our families allows us to see the totality of what our children bring to school, while love for our communities provides psychological safety and emotional interconnectedness, which can sustain us through the inevitable highs, lows, successes, and disappointments of a school transformation process.

Love is fuel, love is relief, and love is roots.

When our school transformation is rooted in love, change agency becomes infectious. That's important because change implies some level of disruption, which is palatable when coming from a place of love but can be threatening when motivations are less clear. While you might see the need for change as self-evident in a school community, other stakeholders might not view your quest as so urgent. To folks whose investment in a place is rooted in long-standing love, change might seem suspect. What you and your crew view as the urgent need for improvement could be seen as an existential threat to an institution that other folks already view as inherently worthy. In that light, your crusade might seem unnecessary—or worse, threatening.

Love is hard to fake, and the families and community members you serve will know when your expressions of love are coming from a place of legitimate care. Find ways to embed acts of love into even your most technical strategies. School transformation reviews are a good case in point. In Chapter 3, we discussed leveraging that process to identify momentum that can be built upon. You should also use that process to identify what people love about the school and the individuals whose love has allowed those things to flourish. Every school has a cadre of educators, boosters, and elders whose love for the place transcends the measurable. As a change agent, one of your goals should be to learn from that experience. Find ways to see the school through their eyes. Learn the history of the school and community from their words. Perhaps most importantly, make yourself vulnerable in the presence of that love, and do your best to reciprocate.

When our technical work is rooted in love, those roots spread, creating a community context for growth and transformation that lives beyond our individual schools. When change begins from the ground up, there is a stable base on which to build for the future. Other schools can leverage that foundation to start their own transformation processes. Broader communities start to see your school, and your leadership, as inspiration for a broader project of supporting thriving neighborhoods.

And sometimes, once in a while, whole school systems even begin to change.

When that happens, the potential for transformation seems limitless. In the next chapter, we'll talk about what happens when whole districts embrace that possibility and how districts that are on the cusp of radical transformation can help create the conditions for ground–up change.

THE LEADING WITH LOVE CHECKLIST

- **Express love openly while doing your work.** As strange as it may feel to dwell on deep emotions in a work setting, your work will be more fulfilling, and your quest for transformation more infectious, if the love starts with you.

- **Fight deficit-based language and mindsets.** We talked about adopting an asset-based mindset in Chapter 3. Unfortunately, prejudiced narratives about low-income communities, communities of color, and the children we serve manifest not just as backward mindsets but also as policy and practice in our schools. We have all internalized elements of the deficit narrative, just by virtue of living in this culture; the classroom is not immune to these ideas, and keeping them at bay requires active work.

- **Reject dichotomies that treat love and rigor as mutually exclusive.** It's not hard to identify and reject classroom approaches where children are treated like problems, but we must also be vigilant about not perpetuating "happy schools" where everybody seems content, but nobody is learning a thing. Neither is good for creating long-term opportunities for children, even though one might seem more comfortable to observe.

- **Repeat after me: "I am not a savior or a missionary."** You are, though, an educator, and if you approach that role through a lens of service and humility, magical things can happen.

- **Show more than you tell but don't be afraid to express your motivations.** If you don't tell your own story, someone else will, so practice becoming comfortable with owning your personal narrative, parts of which we talked about in Chapter 5. If you come to a school from outside of a community, it's especially important to be clear about what forces drew you there; but even if you come from the community itself, that doesn't mean your motivations are automatically pure.

- **Identify the traditions, people, and ideas that make love real in your school.** Seek to build on those foundations, not to replace them. Embrace the spirit behind those traditions and do your best to embody the ethos they imply. Learn from educational elders, be humble with veteran teachers, and be proactive in forging relationships with community members outside of the school.

CHAPTER 8: DISCUSSION QUESTIONS

1. What is one thing that just about everybody loves about your school? What's something you love about your school that you suspect is unique to you?

2. What does "just right" instruction look like, in your own words? What about "just right" professional coaching?

3. How comfortable are you expressing your love and motivations at work to colleagues, students, parents, community members, and so on? What would it take to increase your comfort with doing so?

Hi, I'm From the Central Office. And I'm Here to Help.

9

It was a few weeks before Thanksgiving in 2013, and dense aromas were wafting from the rear of the administration building. Frankie Blackmon walked with caution toward the large conference room at the back end of the school district central office, not quite knowing what to expect when she opened the door.

The sense of uncertainty was unusual for Frankie. Navigating educational mazes was something like her superpower, and public schooling had always been a place of joy and comfort for her. As a child in Ethel, Mississippi, she had excelled in the classroom and on the basketball court, the latter of which she knowingly attributes—at least in part—to being 6'3". She continued her command on and off the court in college, then followed her passions for athletics and academics into public education leadership. She had already spent most of her multidecade career in the Mississippi Delta, teaching, coaching, designing curricula, and facing down thorny challenges.

The epicurean arts, on the other hand, were way outside of her comfort zone. But on this fall day, in the Delta district of Indianola, Mississippi, Frankie was willing to swallow her pride to be a good teammate.

Because the district's leadership team had decided to hold a chili cook-off.

(Continued)

(Continued)

The concept behind the cook-off was simple: Each member of the system's leadership, which included both central office staff and school administrators, was assigned at random to a team. Each team would be responsible for preparing a spread that included three separate dishes: chili, cornbread, and banana pudding.

Frankie's team—"The Red Hot Chili Peppers"—drew its name not from the eponymous rock band, but from a mash-up of Frankie's favorite color and the main ingredient in their signature dish. Due to her culinary limitations, Frankie abstained from cooking and assumed the role of decorator-in-chief. She had binged the television show *Chopped* for inspiration and knew that a dish's presentation was a critical component of a cooking competition, so she went to the Dollar Store and picked out some red streamers that would complement the team's color palette.

While Frankie meandered toward the cook-off, William Hill and Emily Schriber were in a small office further down the hall. The two educators were acting as district improvement coaches, whom system leaders had tapped to help navigate some major challenges they were confronting. Emily and William came to Indianola every few weeks and were knee-deep in supporting the rollout of school and district transformation reviews. The two coaches sat, huddled over a pile of charts and graphs, preparing for an upcoming strategy session with the district's leadership team.

Frankie passed the small office on the way to the event and stopped to call out to them. "Hey, you two, welcome back!" she said. "Are you coming to the cook-off?"

Emily looked up from her stack of papers, a little confused. "I would love to," she said, "but we didn't make anything."

"Oh, that's no problem," Frankie replied. "You can be judges!"

"Wait, what, are you serious?" Emily asked, as Frankie ushered the conscripted chili officiants into the conference room, where a dozen manic, makeshift teams of amateur cooks materialized before them. The room, which echoed like a cavern on a normal day, felt miniscule when packed with giddy teams of aspiring sous chefs. Emily and William surveyed the conference room, their eyes panning across the offerings that they would be tasting, then savoring, then judging in the course of an afternoon.

Emily felt excitement laced with anxiety. On the one hand, in front of her was a once-in-a-lifetime opportunity to really, really experience home-cooked southern food. On the other hand, each cook-off dish held a sacred place in Black southern food culture, which Emily felt ill-equipped to adjudicate. "I'm a white woman from New Mexico," she mused aloud. "Why are you putting me in the position of judging this food?"

Frankie reassured her. "Seriously, don't worry. It's a team-building event. There's no pressure. I got these streamers at the Dollar Store—see?" she said, waving her arms in front of her team's table. "This is low pressure."

Emily nodded, while she and William steeled themselves. The two of them had worked with school districts all throughout the country. They coached superintendents, cultivated transformation efforts, and facilitated extraordinarily difficult conversations among fragile school leadership teams about the most fraught interpersonal topics. As professionals, they were seasoned.

As cook-off judges, though, they were novices.

Frankie, William, and Emily surveyed the room together, reflecting on the work they were undertaking as a crew. Among them flickered an unspoken responsibility: to support transformational change for a whole region of children, not just in one or two schools.

At the same time, they saw the joy in their colleagues' faces as educators laughed, compared recipes, traded playful barbs, and stuffed their faces with pudding and cornbread.

"Well," William said, taking a deep breath and turning to Emily.

Emily glanced up at William, narrowed her eyes, and nodded.

"Okay, then. Let's do this thing," he said, and they made their way to the first table.

Districts Can Set the Metaphorical Table for School Transformation

Being a school-based crew in the throes of transformation is an exhilarating exercise: The camaraderie fuels little bursts of adrenaline, weekly ROCI cycles ensure that the work never becomes stagnant, and the fruits of your labor manifest in surprising ways—not just in your class-room, but often across your entire school.

At the same time, the work can be lonely and isolating. While the urgency and necessity of your mission might seem self-evident from the trenches, other educators and administrators might not understand the significance of your undertaking. A lack of recognition can be frustrating, surely, but a dearth of systemic support is by no means fatal to your efforts. We built this book, and the practices herein, based on the understanding that you can achieve extraordinary results without reaching too far beyond your own school.

That said, the most extraordinary transformations happen when schools and districts work together, in concert, to cultivate heretofore unthinkable outcomes.

Now, I know what you may be thinking. Central offices and their schools are notorious for having a relationship status that hovers closer to "It's Complicated" than "Heart Emoji." There are myriad reasons for the complexity, but dwelling on downsides is counterproductive. Meanwhile, partnerships built on truth, collaboration, clarity of vision, and mutual respect are essential to delivering great outcomes for children.

It's also critical to acknowledge that district officials manage just as many competing demands as their schools do. When states and the feds mandate intensive interventions, districts bear the brunt of responding. Ambitious national policies around teacher evaluation, curriculum adoption, and school improvement were hatched to drive practical changes in schools; but in the months and years between legislation and execution, district officials were responsible for translating complex—sometimes misguided and conflicting—mandates into manageable tasks for schools and educators.

Meanwhile, school districts are large, complex, multilayered organizations that must respond not just to said government mandates but also to communities' preferences, parents' demands, students' needs, and educators' voices. Standout districts conduct this work while delivering great results for children, but even the most competent central offices struggle to juggle competing pressures. The COVID-19 pandemic only added additional wrinkles, as districts are now charged with interpreting conflicting state, federal, and global guidance on the science of immunology and disease prevention. Not to mention that managing virtual schooling, which used to be a peripheral activity for traditional school systems, became an industry standard overnight. While some school systems are used to managing chronic uncertainty, many are not.

Even the most historically high-functioning systems have experienced unprecedented teacher burnout and dissatisfaction in the last couple of years, making explicit attentiveness to culture and morale that much more important.

Enter activities like the first annual Indianola District Chili Cook-Off.

While team building alone cannot solve international public health crises, chili, cornbread, and banana pudding are pretty delicious. And from an organizational development standpoint, food and culture are intensely intertwined. (It's not a coincidence that so many of the crews in this book have done their best work surrounded by tacos.) Holding communal events built around food cultivates team building, stretches people beyond their comfort zones, amplifies excitement, and reduces stress. In providing the opportunity for people to know each other as people, and not just functions, we create deeper understanding, fostering persistence when discussions get hard. One of the most powerful, subtle roles that a school district can play in advancing transformation is modeling vibrant cultures where performance is valued, risk-taking is encouraged, creativity is celebrated, and missteps are accepted as a core principle of improvement.

You could attempt to encourage those qualities with spreadsheets and presentations, but why make a PowerPoint when pudding will prove the point?

Although most of the stories in this book deal with the power of ground-up transformation, culture change gets a booster shot when people in systemic leadership facilitate and nurture the process. This chapter is all about the magic that happens when districts embrace that role as core to their identities. Establishing a culture that embraces learning, novelty, and collaboration is just one of many things a district can do in setting the metaphorical table for transformation; in this chapter, we will focus on the many roles that district officials can play in that work.

Trust and collaboration are essential, as it's critical for districts and their schools to work as partners in this endeavor. While conventional wisdom among educators often suggests that schools are islands unto themselves, the deepest transformation emerges from intensive cooperation and alignment among schools and their central offices. There are unheralded change agents in each district office in this country, and while most of this book focuses on classroom educators, there have been district folks working in the background in every instance, offering a quasi-invisible hand to guide the work of transformation. In

Chapter 1, for example, José Manzo, the Alum Rock superintendent, lights a fire under René to jump-start a change process. Guadalupe's motivating guidance in Chapter 3 accelerates Tamitrice's plans, while John's network strategy creates the context for interschool collaboration in Chapter 8. These visible actions are accompanied by hundreds more that happen behind the scenes; the district role we unveil in this book is but the tip of the proverbial iceberg.

To make some of this critical background work more visible, this chapter and the next, unlike the others, emphasize the work of districts and central office employees. That said, it also offers hints for how classroom educators and school leaders can collaborate in service of school-based transformation goals. We will talk about things districts should do to support improvement at the school level, and at times, we will be explicit about what districts should definitely *not* do.

As you consider this guidance, it's important to keep in mind that this chapter is not a comprehensive handbook for how to run a school district. There are myriad district responsibilities that are supportive of school transformation—like budgeting, human resources, facilities management, enrollment, and procurement—that we will not discuss here. These omissions are not a verdict on their importance, but an acquiescence to the limitations of a single book.

We should also remind ourselves that, while no two districts are alike, there are patterns that we can observe across state and county lines. Recognizing symmetries, however, is no replacement for understanding the deep history of the particular places in which we are working. The story behind the story always reveals important truths, while providing clues for where to go next.

 ## INDIANOLA, MISSISSIPPI

The Mississippi Delta is a fertile crescent of rich alluvial soil, situated between the Mississippi and Yazoo Rivers, a place dense with roots of all kinds.

The region's unforgiving heat and humidity, coupled with its fecund earth, create ideal conditions for agricultural undertakings. Native people planted corn, beans, and squash. Beginning in the early 18th century, European colonizers forced enslaved people to plant sugar and rice. By the 19th century, cotton had become the monocrop staple of the region, unleashing the violent proliferation of chattel slavery. The brutal plantation system erected cruelty on top of fertility, and by the dawn of the Civil War, there were almost a half a million enslaved people living in Mississippi, more than in any other state. The abolition of slavery after the Civil War offered fleeting, yet unfulfilled, feints at freedom; sharecropping, economic serfdom, and the Jim Crow caste system ended up replacing the institution.

These cycles of joy and pain are hard to capture in words alone, which is part of the reason the Delta Blues became so popular. "People all over the world have problems," said B. B. King, perhaps the most famous of all blues musicians, "and as long as people have problems, the blues can never die."

Situated in the geographic center of the Mississippi Delta, Indianola is the town B. B. King once called home. One of the biggest problems people continue to have here is disentangling the lasting impact of systemic racism from all other facets of human life.

Unlike the de facto, covert flavor of racial segregation that characterizes schooling in the American North, racial separation has been flagrant and overt in Mississippi throughout most of history. A decade after the Supreme Court ruling in *Brown v. Board of Education* made school segregation illegal, the U.S. government sued the city of Indianola for the inadequacy of its desegregation plans. The district's approach, while not dissimilar from what other systems throughout the country did, was equal parts typical and farcical: The school board had drawn a single line—along a set of literal railroad tracks—establishing two attendance zones: one north of and one south of "the tracks." All but eight of the town's African American children lived on one side.

Segregation was not simply the systemic expression of personal prejudices, but rather the institutionalization of pilfered communal wealth. Multiple generations of push and pull among the district, state, and courts over the role of the schools in either perpetuating or ameliorating historic funding inadequacies was destabilizing to the operations and finances of the schools. By 2013, the district was several years into "conservatorship," a system created to give the state

(Continued)

(Continued)

financial authority over districts with persistent financial challenges. The state had appointed a seasoned Mississippi educator as "conservator" superintendent of the Indianola schools, and as part of conservatorship, the school board had agreed to merge with a larger, neighboring district, Sunflower County Public Schools.

When the district leadership instated the chili cook-off in 2013, it was against this backdrop and history. The conservator had recruited an extraordinary team of educators from the local community to lead the transformation efforts, including Frankie, special education expert Cindy Taylor, and deputies Sammie Crigler and Shamica Pitts. Their talents were supplemented with select experts from other parts of the state. The crew viewed their shared history as but a prelude. While the mostly African American leadership team was well aware that the current predicament was the product of an unjust history, they also knew that the Indianola and Sunflower County communities had vested their educational leaders with the power to lead for the future, while striving to break the cycles of the past.

Schools, more than any other local institution, exemplified to the community the ways in which freedom, civil rights, and policy can intersect to accelerate justice. That responsibility weighed heavily on the people charged with leadership in the Delta.

As such, the Indianola crew intended to examine every little detail of how the district operated—to better serve the children and to live up to the aspirations of the broader community. They intended to use the power they had at this particular moment in history to make as much of a dent in educational inequity as possible.

The question for the crew, then, wasn't whether transformation was necessary. The question was how to get started.

Allow Me to Reintroduce Myself: My Name Is ROCI (District Remix)

Many of the challenges we face in public schooling seem beyond our capacity to comprehend. The more of the picture we see, the less straightforward the solutions appear. When we widen our aperture beyond schools—to include districts, cities, counties, states, race, class, and history—the depth and breadth of oppression threaten to over-whelm us. We can become paralyzed by our relative smallness in the face of historic injustice.

While this reaction is understandable, we have a responsibility to start somewhere and to do something.

The technical and relational tools we've deployed throughout this book cannot solve all the world's problems. They do, however, offer manage-able ways to tackle seemingly unmanageable challenges. As such, when districts launch into the work of transformation, much of what we've counseled heretofore remains true. Districts need to start somewhere, pick measurable targets for improvement, use data to set time-bound goals, assess progress, act in accordance with learnings, and make time for deep reflection and adjustment on an ongoing basis. Do ROCI, while always rooting that work in considerations of equity.

Same name. Same game. Different playing field.

That said, as we consider the role of the district in inquiry and improve-ment, there are a few important adjustments to keep in mind. First, while ROCI remains the central technology of the process, districts cannot ROCI on behalf of schools. School-level educators must do that work for themselves, as the magic of the process is in the shared learning that occurs among the adults who participate.

Districts should, though, *create the conditions and the time* for schools to embrace ROCI as a process. From a cultural standpoint, that means establishing the importance of continuous improvement cycles, creating incentives for grade-level teams to embrace the approach, and provid-ing training opportunities for educators to practice firsthand. Because remember, as we discussed in Chapter 6, voluntary adoption will always lead to greater fidelity than mandated participation.

Beyond being a general booster for the concept of inquiry, there are technical changes that districts can make to foster collaboration. Those changes include amending school schedule requirements to create reg-ular collaborative meeting times, allowing teachers to participate in noninstructional responsibilities by videoconference, aligning district-mandated professional development with monthly ROCI cycles, and freeing up resources to facilitate flexibility at the school level.

In addition to cultivating school-level ROCI, districts should ROCI their own work. Does the district want to reimagine school assign-ment to better reflect racial equity? How will we know it's having the intended effect, and on what timeline? Improvement cycles are likely to be longer at the district level because changes take more time to permeate an entire system. That's not a reason, though, to eschew time-bound vigilance; it's actually a good reason to be even more attentive. Reforms that take months or years to manifest require ongoing scrutiny; otherwise, they risk becoming just another binder on a shelf somewhere in the central office.

Speaking of old binders, another way that districts can support school improvement is through clearing out the underbrush of prior programs that overwhelms time-strapped educators. Time has become an even more precious resource since the onset of the COVID-19 pandemic, and educators have little of it available for extraneous work, let alone academic initiatives with no clear connections to their current priorities. In Chapter 4, we talked about the failure of the "Christmas tree" approach to school improvement; this diagnosis applies to districts too. If we want school crews to engage in ROCI cycles, their plates must be cleared of superfluous stuff to provide maximum time for a small number of actual priorities.

To figure out what schools can stop doing, conduct an audit to determine how many hours per week the average principal spends responding to central office requests. Research has indicated that this number can creep up to half of a principal's entire workweek. You should also keep track of how many emails and forms you send to educators and administrators on a weekly basis. Ask yourself how many of those requests are necessary and eliminate anything that isn't either a legal requirement or contributes to the immediate improvement of instruction.

To that last point, when dealing with a district's role in administering federal and state requirements, it's important to verify that central office interpretations of law and regulation are factual and not the result of a long game of "Telephone." Sometimes, districts claim to do things a particular way because of "the state" or "the feds," when in reality the practice is just something habitual that nobody ever bothered to check. One common example is the appropriate use of federal Title I funds. Many districts use unspent Title I funds for end-of-year field trips, believing that federal "supplement, not supplant" financial rules forbid spending those funds on curricular resources. That's untrue, but word-of-mouth approaches to understanding compliance can prevent creative programming.

Finally, districts need to trust schools to do their work, while figuring out the appropriate "loose/tight" balance of program choice and service delivery. In some areas, districts will have strong perspectives about the specifics of school-level work and be "tight" on those topics; in other areas, a "loose" posture will allow schools to have more autonomy. There is no one right answer to addressing the loose/tight challenge, but districts and schools must create transparency about who decides what, and when.

A comprehensive review of district practices, through the lens of identifying which habits are supportive of and aligned to improvement at the school level, is an essential part of finding that balance. A strong district transformation review will pose questions about a range of topics: a district's ability to support ROCI, professional learning connected to that approach, and core curricula with a strong research basis. Conducting a district review should happen alongside school-level reviews for the fullest perspective on a system's readiness for growth.

Which brings us back to Indianola, where Frankie, Cindy, Shamica, and their district crew were in the midst of conducting exactly that kind of review. While they weren't exactly sure how to transform the whole system, like good change agents they were willing to let inspiration, data, context, research, and collaboration be their guides.

INDIANOLA, MISSISSIPPI

Some members of the Indianola leadership team wanted to take a nap after overdosing on pudding and cornbread at the cook-off, but the team-building event was merely a prelude to some intensive group work. Throughout the rest of the week, the district crew and their school-based counterparts would be reviewing and generating next steps from data collected during school and district transformation reviews.

The leadership team had started to set the table for this endeavor earlier in the fall. Frankie, William, and Emily led teams in conducting reviews at the district's schools. Cooperation with the buildings wasn't always easy. Frankie knew that the culture of the district in the past had been one where central office employees visited schools for unannounced performance appraisals. These visits could feel like "gotcha" sessions, and some teachers had even started calling district visitors "snitches."

(Continued)

(Continued)

To calm nerves, Frankie worked with principals and their instructional-leadership teams to build protocols that would minimize distrust while building a collaborative spirit. Review teams overcommunicated the purposes of the process, gave immediate "Glows and Grows" to each classroom, and made the observation rubrics transparent. They also took pains to note that the reviews would have no role in teacher-performance evaluation, which took the edge off with most educators.

In addition to coordinating school-based efforts, Emily and William spent several days with the central office staff to structure a thorough district transformation review. They interviewed district staff while cross-referencing central office perspectives with school leadership teams to corroborate findings.

On the day that the district had set aside to debrief the findings from the various reviews, leadership teams from schools filed into the conference room, which still smelled strongly of chili. School teams sat at individual tables, littered with snacks, data printouts, helpful craft supplies, and notated review rubrics. Frankie, the conservator, and the leadership team—a handful of directors and assistant superintendents—sat at a separate table, reviewing their district diagnostic.

William and Emily had prepared a daylong agenda, designed to unearth the core instructional challenges facing the district. Literacy was at the top of the list. The conservator had noticed enormous differences between what constituted basic reading ability in Indianola versus what existed in other parts of Mississippi, where he had participated in successful transformation efforts. The results of the transformation reviews had confirmed that anecdotal assessment: Schools lacked a clear theory of action with respect to teaching reading, and the central office wasn't helping much.

To tease out greater collective understanding of these issues, William took the lead as facilitator for the day. His presence served as a powerful symbol for what it would look like to change the dynamics in the community, as most "national experts" didn't look like the Indianola leadership team. William, on the other hand, was an African American man with extensive credibility. Having a national expert in town who shared this core identity with the leadership team was an important factor that people noticed.

As the teams started to dig into the results of the various reviews, William stood at the front of the room, guiding that exploration with a protocol he and Emily had developed in partnership with Frankie and other members of the central office team. He asked intermittent questions to the whole group, hoping to elicit provocative responses and reactions.

"If you're a high school, how will you work with feeder middle schools to align your approach to reading?"

"How will you discuss these results with your grade-level teams, knowing that some folks might get defensive about the results?"

"How do adult expectations, rooted in race and class dynamics, show up in this data?"

Almost every time William asked a question, though, the conservator was the first to share his thoughts. Even when he didn't say a word, the conservator possessed a well-earned reputation for having a lot of answers. He had led successful transformation efforts in other districts, including in the state's largest city, and the state had appointed him to leadership in Indianola because of that track record. The goal of the activity, though, wasn't just to unearth solutions to the district's challenges; it was also designed to cultivate buy-in, understanding, and consensus around next steps.

William noticed that the dynamic was having a silencing effect on the rest of the team. He tried to direct his questions at others, but the conservator persisted in answering. Finally, William decided to switch postures.

He made direct eye contact with the conservator and nodded at him.

The conservator nodded back slowly, as if to say, "Do what you have to do."

"I'm going to ask another question," William said, "but I don't want the conservator to answer this one. Got it? This has to be a team effort. Can we try that?"

The conservator stared at William, and the rest of the room went silent.

Then, the conservator stood up. He walked over to a table full of supplies, grabbed a large piece of masking tape, and put it directly over his own mouth.

The rest of the room broke out in waves of relief and laughter, while Cindy, the special education director, snapped a photo for posterity.

Teamwork Makes the Dream Work

Transformation tales often overindulge in the oversimplified story of the solitary hero. This overrepresentation happens not just when talking about schools, but across leadership domains and literary genres, particularly in Eurocentric traditions. Stories ranging from the *Iliad* to the biography of Steve Jobs to Batman comics conspire to perpetuate the illusion that individual effort is the antidote to complex social problems.

The simplicity of these stories is part of their appeal, as most share the same tidy structure:

> *Act 1*: An extraordinary problem exists. Whatever will we do? Oh, look, a hero!
>
> *Act 2*: Hi! I am the hero. Through trials, tribulations, and so on, I have developed supernatural talents and am finally here to help! You're welcome.
>
> *Act 3*: Magic is deployed! Problem is solved! Peasants rejoice! Ready the parade!

As we all know, real life, real work, and real problems do not fit into such a structure, yet we continue the search for singular figures in our quest to solve multidimensional problems.

We do this, in part, because at some level we crave the simplicity that the hero narrative offers. Because real life is messy as all get-out. We fumble in teams with other humans, manage interpersonal conflict, take losses, move multiple steps backward, pause to lick wounds, get distracted, and discover additional problems that we didn't even know existed along the way.

And when we do get wins, they're rarely as clear and unmitigated as we want them to be, and no single person even gets to claim the "W." All significant transformation work requires a crew of folks pulling together, and that's just as true at the district level as it is at the school level.

When we discussed building a crew for school-level ROCI cycles, starting in Chapter 2, the assemblage of aggregate core competencies emerged as central to that project. Great school crews need educators with deep content knowledge, instructional coaches with adult-learning chops, and data geeks with analytical experience, to name a few important dimensions. Building a crew at the district level requires related, but different, skill sets. You need people who can manage relationships with state education agencies, build robust community ties, understand special education, design student assignment schematics, deploy legislative and legal expertise, and produce complex budgets. While some individuals will know a little bit about many of these topics, no one person knows everything about all of them.

With the importance of teamwork in mind, accountable leadership remains a critical part of almost all institutional arrangements, and some individuals will end up in the "hot seat," like the conservator was in Indianola. As a state-appointed district conservator, he had direct accountability to the most senior officials in Mississippi—not just for managing activities, but for delivering student results in the midst of significant systemic disruption. His energy in the previous vignette reveals a level of urgency about tackling the challenges in front of him.

And like all successful transformation leaders, when put to the test, he understood the wisdom inherent in the ancient adage that going fast happens alone, while going the distance happens together.

In putting literal tape over his mouth, the conservator simultaneously modeled multiple lessons that reinforce the importance of teamwork in solving complex problems. First, he accepted difficult feedback, in real time, in front of his team. In doing so, he opened the door for robust truth-telling among the rest of the crew. Second, he did that modeling quickly, and with levity, which is essential when staring down immense challenges. Some interpersonal dynamics are so problematic that they require that our collective work grind to a halt while we hash them out; most feedback, though, can be accepted in the moment and without drama so that the rest of the group can plow forward. Third, he practiced an important skill we discussed in Chapter 2: "stepping back." Building strong teams is more about listening than dispensing expertise, and by modeling silence, he made room for others to participate in constructive dialogue.

Last, and perhaps most importantly, the actions in the last vignette demonstrate how everyone in a transformation effort must experience growth: from the student in the classroom to the person whose name is on the ballot, and everyone in between. There are significant power dynamics that exist among district leaders and classroom educators, which can complicate our ability to engage in honest, authentic expression.

When we take steps to flatten those relationships through humility and relationship building, we unlock the potential for uncharted growth.

After the large-group session, Frankie, Emily, and William took time to reflect on what topics popped out in teams' debriefs of their transformation reviews.

Student literacy kept rising to the top of everyone's list.

On that issue, they faced a tall hill to climb. Dramatic literacy gains are difficult in any educational context, but Indianola was teetering on unusually fragile conditions. Basic literacy was a significant challenge for all of the district's schools. The Indianola central office alone had deployed multiple reading interventions of varying success in the prior five years, and joining with Sunflower County meant creating exponential complexity in managing systemwide service delivery and fidelity of implementation.

The first thing Frankie wanted to determine was why their existing interventions didn't seem to be working. During the school transformation reviews, the crew had identified a large cohort of 10th, 11th, and 12th graders at the local high school who were reading at very low levels. The size of the group was surprising, as the district had spent hundreds of thousands of dollars on specialty reading intervention programs the year before. The central office had hoped those programs would deliver results more quickly, but almost nothing had changed in the interim months.

Shamica, William, and Emily created a quick plan for assessing the root of the challenges. They went to the local high school and talked to some of the kids who were struggling with reading. They also conducted a quick exercise—anonymously—to determine exactly how significant the reading challenges were. They showed the high school students flashcards with letters and asked them to identify the accompanying sounds. A striking number of high schoolers were unable to complete the task, something they should have learned in early-elementary school.

The literacy challenge, then, clearly included the need to address the very fundamentals of decoding and fluency. Unfortunately, when the crew looked at the district's intervention programs, there was a mismatch. Emily and William sat in a small district office conference room with Frankie, Shamica Pitts, Cindy Taylor, and other members of the district crew, sorting through mountains of curriculum materials.

"This is a program designed to address comprehension issues," William said, his head buried in scientific studies outlining the research base for the program the district had spent hundreds of thousands of dollars procuring.

"The young people we talked to at the high school aren't even decoding," Frankie said, looking equal parts relieved and frustrated. "A comprehension intervention alone is never going to be enough for them."

The crew realized at that moment that high school teachers could remediate higher-level comprehension skills until the cows came home, but without basic fluency and decoding, students would never be able to read with confidence. This realization created additional complications for how they would roll out any eventual solutions, as high school teachers are not trained to teach the foundational skills of reading. Not to mention the fact that many teenagers who make it to high school without reading skills develop compensatory—often counterproductive—behaviors that get in the way of instruction, often as an emotional response to their educational needs being minimized in earlier years.

In short, their realization meant not just making some hard decisions in the moment, but planning for increasingly difficult execution and collaboration with schools further down the road.

Frankie, Shamica, and Cindy brought their findings to the conservator to make sure he was okay with abandoning the expensive interventions that weren't working.

He immediately understood and supported their tough decisions. "It looks like we need to make every teacher in this district a reading teacher," the conservator said. "Figuring out how to do that is the real challenge. Materials are secondary. There's more to selecting them than simply the question of whether the curriculum is research-based."

And with that, the district made the hard decision to stop doing something that was never going to work in the first place.

Accountability Means
Much More Than Testing

Accountability comes in many different shapes and sizes.

While many seasoned education professionals are still nursing a collective hangover from a generation of overemphasizing high-stakes testing, it's important to remember that "high-stakes testing" and the concept of "accountability" are completely different things.

Accountability is a good thing. The idea of being in a state of profound accountability to the people who depend on you is central to interpersonal and institutional relationships of all kinds, as we discussed in Chapters 7 and 8. Being accountable, and having a community supportive of accountability behaviors, is central to group health, organizational behavior, friendships, marriages, restorative approaches to justice, and all sorts of human dynamics.

Not to mention, measuring progress on a regular basis—although not necessarily through test scores—is central to the work of inquiry and improvement.

The question, then, isn't whether or not to hold ourselves accountable for measurable outcomes. The better question, rather, is for what, and to whom, do we hold ourselves accountable, and why?

Enter the district change agent.

One of the critical roles of a district supporting school transformation is to drive accountability for the right things, while aligning district resources toward those goals.

The Indianola crew demonstrated their commitment to collective accountability through measuring the right things and then making hard decisions based on those measurements. These behaviors speak louder than any words ever can. Sometimes, alignment means adding new programs to address unmet needs. Once in a while, it means canceling programs that we started because they no longer fit within stated priorities, which is what happened in the previous vignette.

That last part is a particular challenge, as school district programming often resembles an archeological site, where the deeper you dig, the more evidence you find of the influence of administrations past. Dig one layer down, and there's a phonics initiative; go a little deeper, and there's a direct-instruction program; below that, you'll find evidence of a balanced literacy approach.

Your goal as a district leader, though, isn't to leave your personal mark on a system: it's to unleash greatness among classroom educators.

After all, alignment is about creating the context for teachers to focus on their priorities. This is an enormous social responsibility because your priorities aren't just a template for an inquiry process; school district objectives set the tone for the values of entire communities. If your approach to schooling is lax and undemanding, that culture will permeate beyond the school. Similarly, if your district routinely invests in privileged students and parents without attending to the needs and aspirations of historically marginalized kids, how your community grows and develops (or doesn't) will reflect those disparities.

Communities and schools flourish together, making it critical to understand how our schools are enmeshed in the broader sweep of history and policy. Our schools aren't just a reflection of historical trends; they are a central part of shaping them.

That's why we're going to spend the final chapters of this book discussing the lasting effects of racist policymaking on our schools, how schools interact with the often unjust systems around them, and the role that educators can play in changing those relationships, systems, and communities while pursuing school transformation goals.

THE DISTRICT TRANSFORMATION CHECKLIST

- **Cultivate a culture of infectious curiosity.** District change agents should create regular opportunities for schools and their leadership teams to experience the impact of a positive culture, while cultivating a sense of belonging. Little gestures go a long way, and consistency is critical. Don't skimp on the details, and don't be afraid to get a little bit corny.

- **ROCI your district initiatives. System-level changes should receive the same level of results-oriented scrutiny as school-level work.** The higher the stakes of an initiative, the more important it is to develop a regular cadence of assessing efficacy. Keep doing things that seem to be driving student outcomes. Stop doing things that are just adding work and red tape.

- **Conduct school and district transformation reviews.** It's hard to figure out where to start without a vivid picture of the current state of your system. Use a comprehensive instrument to determine what's going well, what needs work, and what hasn't gotten off the ground yet. Be sure to cross-reference your findings with school personnel in order to corroborate findings and to cultivate a service-oriented mindset.

- **Make space for school-level ROCI.** Do whatever you can to make ROCI easy for your schools. Allow principals to use professional development funds for projects aligned to their theories of action. Free up schedules to facilitate grade-level collaboration. Eliminate unnecessary forms, requirements, and compliance hurdles that don't add substantive value to schools' work.

- **When it comes to the law, trust but verify.** Make sure you really know the laws, rules, regulations, and policies that govern your work. Doing things differently and creatively will require the interrogation—and often the abandonment—of long-standing norms. Sometimes, those norms are rooted in actual law, but lots of times they're not, even though someone claims they are.

- **Align district systems to school needs.** Driving student results is hard enough without competing priorities. District leaders should pick a small number of high-leverage activities to support and then clear the way for schools to execute. The best way to do this is through making sure that your district central office understands your schools' theories of action and can get behind those plans with real resources.

- **Use precise accountability to drive desired behaviors.** When done with care and respect, accountability—like feedback—is a form of love. Remember to disentangle the idea of accountability from its least nuanced manifestation: high-stakes testing. Once you untangle those ideas, figure out how you want to build systems and structures that hold you, your schools, and your fellow educators accountable not just for student outcomes but also for your own personal growth.

CHAPTER 9: DISCUSSION QUESTIONS

1. When was a time when you experienced authentic collaboration between a school and district? What did that look and feel like? What were the contextual factors that made such collaboration possible?

2. Have you ever stopped using an academic program because it was no longer meeting your needs? Was that hard? Did you face resistance?

3. How do you like to be held accountable? What does it look like when that sort of accountability works?

The Practice of Freedom 10

Once Frankie, William, Emily, and the Indianola crew better understood the roots of their district's literacy challenges, they were ready to support their schools in teaching students how to read with mastery.

And then, the state of Mississippi threw a legal wrench into their plans.

While the crew conducted transformation reviews, the state legislature passed a law, mandating new approaches to reading instruction that affected every district in Mississippi. The intent of the law made some intuitive sense. Adults in the state have literacy rates among the lowest in the country, and historical racial divisions meant that the state often ignored underinvestment in teaching reading to Black children. The new law mandated early intervention for students deemed off track, the adoption of research-validated training for teachers, and strict accountability measures for failure to meet the new standards.

The last part, though, had the crew scrambling and a bit confused. The law required districts to retain students in third grade if they failed to meet basic proficiency standards. Some research indicated that failing to achieve basic reading skills by third grade was devastating to adult literacy, but other studies argued that the third-grade threshold was arbitrary, driven less by the neuroscience of learning and more by the intervals of standardized testing regimes. Research was more consistent, however, on the notion that retaining kids, even for a single grade, was detrimental to all kinds of life outcomes. In that light, implementing retention in Indianola could be devastating: Frankie had examined

(Continued)

(Continued)

interim assessment data and found that almost 90 percent of third graders in Indianola were testing below what the state considered to be basic proficiency.

The lopsided reading data made it hard to ignore the other challenge staring Frankie in the face, which was the lasting impact of racial divisions in the community. In addition to unearthing challenges related to reading instruction, the transformation review process also shone light on issues related to race and equity. While about 95 percent of the district's children were African American, about half of the teaching force was white. Explicit conversations about the lasting impact of race on literacy, investment, and opportunity in the community were rare in professional settings, particularly among mixed-race groups of adults.

Frankie, for her part, had been shocked by the level of racial division still evident in the Delta. As a child in Mississippi, she had attended mixed-race public schools, but when she moved to Indianola to work for the school system, friends quizzed her about where she planned to send her son. The not-so-subtle implication was that the district was good enough to be her employer but not good enough to educate her African American child. Frankie enrolled him in the Indianola public schools and never looked back, although she was quick to note that none of her white colleagues seemed to have done the same.

All of these topics and more would need to be on the table as the district contemplated the ramifications of merging with the Sunflower County school system, which was dealing with a related but unique set of legacy challenges.

In preparation for that merger, Frankie and the Indianola crew were coordinating with the leadership team at the Sunflower County schools, including Dr. Charles Barron, who had been appointed conservator superintendent in Sunflower. The two districts were building a collective plan, coordinating with the state government, and engaging the broader community in discussions about what consolidation should look like.

With these complexities front of mind, Frankie, the districts' conservators, William, Emily, and a broader crew met together at a local middle school in preparation for a large community meeting that was scheduled for later in the spring. The community meeting would be a chance to incorporate the broader aspirations and visions of community members in the long-term planning for the new consolidated school district.

The district teams came together in unity to develop a work plan and agenda for community collaboration that would highlight collective bright spots, while addressing potential pain points that could present themselves in the coming years. They sat in a classroom, repurposed as a "situation room," surrounded by budget printouts, student achievement data, and district maps.

Because of their experience working with districts at critical inflection points, William and Emily agreed to support preparation for the community engagement. The goal was to be transparent and honest about historical challenges while building support for doing things differently in the future. Emily looked across the two districts to determine the relative compatibility of their reading programs, while William studied the staffing ramifications of consolidation.

The discussions that day were intense, but constructive. Both districts wanted to ensure extraordinary outcomes for the children of the broader community against the background of many years of inequitable resourcing. The community had demanded, and deserved, more. The district teams were eager to deliver.

At the end of that day's work session, the team agreed to adjourn for dinner. Emily was compiling the last of the notes from the meeting, lost in her own thoughts, when Charles, the Sunflower County conservator, tapped her on the shoulder.

"Do you need a ride?" he asked. "Dinner's in the next town, and it's a bit of a drive."

"Yes," she said, snapping back to reality. "Yes, that would be great, thank you."

They left the classroom, and Emily hopped in the passenger seat of the car. After a few minutes of driving, they were outside of Indianola and meandering amidst miles of farmland, undulating in irregular parcels that had been cotton plantations through the 20th century.

As they got closer to downtown, Charles pointed out the driver's-side window. "See that building?" he said.

(Continued)

(Continued)

Emily nodded. "Yup."

"That's the old county jail," he said. "I spent the night there in the 1960s."

"Really?" Emily asked. "Why? What happened?"

"Oh, you know, I got into the usual kind of trouble," he said, gazing into the distance. "We were registering Black people to vote."

The Unbroken Connection Between Education and Freedom

No matter how much progress we make erasing the stain of racism on this country's fabric, we are offered regular reminders that our history is anything but past.

That the education leaders of today were instrumental figures in the freedom fights of the past should not surprise us. The collective memory of the generation of Americans that fought for liberation during the civil rights era continues to be a blessing. From that generation, we learn not just how history moves but also how to preserve pragmatic optimism in the face of incalculable cycles of cruelty and violence.

From those leaders, we also learn the physics of American racial progress, where every tilt toward justice elicits an equal and opposite reaction from forces that seek to preserve oppression. Lynching and Jim Crow followed abolition and reconstruction, just as redlining and mass incarceration were reactions to desegregation and voting rights. As American journalist Adam Serwer notes, "Great strides toward equality are possible . . . at least until the inevitable backlash consumes it."

America in 2022 is reckoning with a moment of such backlash.

The stories and vignettes that animate this book take place in the decade between 2010 and 2020. During that period, through the proliferation of digital video and social media, millions of white folks, including some who were profiled in this book, woke up to facets of reality that were already transparent to people without racial privilege: the fact that the American criminal legal system routinely commits extrajudicial executions of Black people, that organized white supremacists continue to apply pressure on domestic electoral politics, and that the racial disparities created by chattel slavery continue to manifest in the distribution of public and private resources.

During that same period, as if to put an exclamation point on the very notion of backlash, America went from having its first African American president to having a chief executive who expressed anti-Black racism as a governing strategy.

Meanwhile, in response to the aforementioned raising of cultural consciousness among white folks on topics of race, political actors with roots in the American conservative movement began a campaign to eradicate the discussion of said issues through the demonization of a legal framework which heretofore had been the provenance of law school scholarship and not K–12 school board meetings. "'Critical race theory' is the perfect villain," claimed Christopher Rufo of the Manhattan Institute, whose advocacy played a central role in instigating a moral panic that materialized almost overnight in 2021. Villainizing this legal-policy framework made the hunt for evidence of race-conscious discussions in schools a cause celebre; while Benjamin Wallace-Wells, writing in *The New Yorker,* called it an "invented conflict," the consequences were real. States passed half-baked laws banning the teaching of triggering terminology, while lawmakers asked parents to act as censorship vigilantes, leading to books being banned and educators losing their jobs.

All of this happened against the backdrop of a global pandemic, which only exacerbated the exact disparities that honest discussions of racial inequity sought to illuminate.

All conflicts, at some level, are invented, but that doesn't make them any less profound. As long as public schools have existed, they have been a primary arena for cultural battles about racism. *Weaponizing discussions about race* is just a new addition to a centuries-old toolkit that people in power have used to exclude Black people *on the basis of race*. Before the Civil War, most Southern states passed laws that prevented African Americans from learning how to read; people were routinely killed for teaching reading to enslaved people. Ongoing racial segregation in schools perpetuates racial disparities in wealth accumulation, and the privileged continue to protect that system, which weds private real estate to structural power.

In that light, we can see that the contemporary fear-mongering about critical race theory is just the newest move in what Kimberlé Crenshaw and others call a very old, very dangerous, and very racist playbook. In the coming years, if history is our guide, the struggle will surely morph into something else, and educators need to recognize patterns and be prepared for the inevitable shifting sands of oppression's various manifestations.

James Baldwin once said, "To accept one's past—one's history—is not the same thing as drowning in it." This book has aspired to heed Baldwin's words by offering specific guidance toward delivering more equitable educational outcomes while not ignoring the most egregious facets of our past and present that complicate said project. Our work as educators requires us to stare unflinchingly at the truth, in all of its ugliness, while imbuing our work with the unbridled joy and optimism that our children deserve.

Describing that tension in the work is a balancing act. Living that tension is even harder.

In this chapter, we will deepen our exploration of conducting school transformation against the backdrop of centuries of racist policymaking, with a unique focus on the American Deep South, a region that often is excluded from national discussions of education policy and practice. We will examine the linkages between past and present struggles, the ways in which freedom and literacy intersect, and the importance of individual acts of courage in the face of systemic injustices.

Understanding the specific history of your local context is essential. Throughout this book, we have drawn narrative threads that connect the past and present. We did this not just to honor the experiences of our ancestors; we also did it to illuminate how public policy and individual practice interact, over the course of generations, to deliver disparate outcomes.

Sometimes, that history is buried, and you will have to dig deep to find it.

Other times, it's hiding in plain sight.

INDIANOLA, MISSISSIPPI

Charles Barron, the Sunflower County superintendent, was one of many freedom fighters of the 1960s who put their lives at risk in pursuit of the right to vote, and the city of Indianola played an outsized, almost mythical role in some of the most turbulent episodes of the civil rights era.

By the early 1960s, the national civil rights movement had secured some major wins, but progress on the ground in the Deep South, and in Mississippi in particular, felt fragile. Lynching remained rampant, school districts dragged their feet implementing *Brown v. Board*, private employers continued blatant discrimination against African Americans, and the right to vote remained elusive. The Civil War had ended a hundred years prior, but a Black person had not served in the Mississippi legislature since the end of Reconstruction in 1896.

Slavery might have been abolished in theory, but all signs pointed to the fact that it had mutated into something like apartheid.

The lack of political inclusion was especially striking around Indianola and Sunflower County, where African Americans outnumbered white folks by large margins. Amzie Moore, a Delta elder and NAACP leader, liked to note that the census had never even bothered to count all the Black folks who lived in the region. In light of such lopsided misrepresentation, Amzie, Dorie Ladner, and other local leaders of the early 1960s wanted to make voting rights in Mississippi a central component of national movement strategy. They invited the Student Nonviolent Coordinating Committee and other national organizations to support voter registration efforts in the Delta.

The rest of the country answered the call. During an organizing meeting in 1962, at the Jackson headquarters of national civil rights organizations, Medgar Evers and Dr. Martin Luther King Jr. explained the situation in the Delta to a group of aspiring student activists, including college freshman Charles "Mac" McLaurin. Mac immediately joined a vanguard group that drove from Jackson to Indianola later that week. They recruited Fannie Lou Hamer and other brave locals, who marched into the notoriously hostile Indianola courthouse with voter registration papers in hand. Their courage crescendoed into the now-legendary "Freedom Summer" of 1964.

That work, led by regular folks, was bold, difficult, and world-changing. Their efforts were instrumental in mounting the political pressure that led to the passage of the Civil Rights Act of 1964 and the Voting Rights Act of 1965, perhaps the greatest civil rights victories in the history of the United States.

(Continued)

(Continued)

Fannie Lou, Mac, and their crew experienced intimidation, violence, and bureaucratic nightmares in their efforts to register Black Mississippians in Sunflower County. Organizers were murdered for leading registration drives, while armed white men in pickup trucks forced buses full of would-be Black voters into roadside ditches. Even when aspiring registrants made it to the Indianola courthouse to file their papers, local officials administered arcane and arbitrary "literacy tests" designed to exclude even the most highly educated individuals. The state's refusal to provide adequate schooling to Black children meant that the control and definition of what constituted literacy was just another tool through which the state preserved white supremacy.

Beyond using the definition of literacy as a tool of oppression, the white community used other forms of violence and intimidation to protect artificial electoral dominance. After the passage of the Voting Rights Act, the Sunflower County Sheriff took headshots of every Black person who registered to vote, then fed their names and home addresses to local papers. Being identified as a voter could be a literal death sentence—at the very least, an economic one.

Indianola also was home to the first chapter of the now-notorious "Citizens' Councils," otherwise known as the "Uptown Klan." Members of the Citizens' Councils worked in public, in contrast to their hooded counterparts in the actual Klan; they were business owners, political leaders, movers, and shakers who placed ads in Mississippi papers, asking white readers to donate to the cause of "personally maintaining segregation."

Those donations were used to create "Segregation Academies," which proliferated throughout the South in the mid-20th century. When the courts ordered the integration of Indianola schools in 1969, the Citizens' Council opened the private "Indianola Academy" almost overnight, as they had been raising money for the project since the Supreme Court decided *Brown* in the mid-1950s. According to locals who attended the Indianola high school, the 1969 court order came on a Friday, and almost all white students had fled the public schools by the following Monday.

Despite white families abandoning the public school system en masse, the governance of public schools in Sunflower County was controlled by white power brokers through the 1980s; by then, over 90 percent of the students in the school system were Black, and the majority of the school board was white. The situation came to a head in 1986, when the board passed over a qualified Black leader to be superintendent, appointing instead a white administrator from another county. Local organizers, working in the civil rights tradition, called a boycott of local businesses in protest. Their direct action coincided with a national conversation about political representation, attracting global attention, including from *The New York Times*, which characterized the situation as yet another instance of southern African American students being, in the paper's words, "ruled by whites."

Black and white communities started working together more closely in subsequent years, making efforts to better integrate public and private life. The schools, though, continued to experience "financial issues" through the early 2000s, when the conservator superintendents were appointed to manage consolidation. In *Let the People Decide*, a history of Sunflower County by J. Todd Moye, the author notes that "financial issues" often are code for the inevitable consequences of generations of racial exclusion. The Indianola tax base never included payments from plantations just outside of city limits, the owners of which continue to bear responsibility for—and reap the financial benefits of—generations of racial oppression.

Moye goes on to note, dryly, that Sunflower County, its schools, and its public officials have not yet single-handedly "solved the problems created by a society based on the institution of slavery." Most white families—three generations after the decision in *Brown v. Board*— continue to send their children to the private Indianola Academy. The Academy's sports teams still have exclusive rights to using the city's "public" recreational spaces, a potent symbol of the enduring, pedestrian flagrancy of racial segregation.

Ordinary People, Extraordinary Things

When racial justice prevails in America, in hindsight those victories can be made to look like the inevitable outcome of applied strategic brilliance, executed in sequential fashion by heroic individuals following a preordained playbook.

In real time, though, organizing for freedom is messy and anything but linear. People take two steps forward, and prejudice pushes back. Tactics are tried and discarded. Leaders rise and fall, just as groups accumulate power and then dissipate. Alliances are formed, relationships are nurtured, trust is cultivated. And all of that can break overnight.

Systems do improve, though, when enough regular people keep, for lack of a better phrase, "doing stuff."

That's how some of the greatest human rights victories in the history of the world were secured by the brave freedom fighters of the Mississippi Delta.

In the early 1960s, Amzie Moore, Dorie Ladner, Medgar Evers, and other Black Mississippians faced incalculable odds as they fought for the right to vote by any means necessary. Some of us remember Medgar's name, but how many people outside of Mississippi know the stories of Amzie and Dorie? Their brand of unheralded work is what this whole book is about. For every Rosa Parks, there are dozens of church ladies whose names we don't know who drove their neighbors to courthouses; for every Medgar Evers, there's a Mac. Even the people whose names we still sing—like Fannie Lou Hamer's—were regular folks taking one step at a time, embracing the risk of failure or even death, all in the face of odds that seemed outlandishly out of favor.

Transforming our schools into centers of justice and not allowing them to be complicit in regenerating the inequitable status quo is now, and has always been, a central part of that struggle. Finding your place in that work does not mean having a title, donning a cape, or understanding the precise means of our collective liberation.

You do, though, have to do things. Ideally, every day. And those things should explicitly challenge the racist norms of oppressive systems.

You can't challenge those norms, however, without understanding them, which is why studying our collective history and making active decisions to challenge dominant cultural narratives is so critical. Nikole Hannah-Jones, working with dozens of scholars of American history, created *The 1619 Project* to shed light on the versions of history whose prior relegation to the academic margins obscures our understanding. Other contemporary scholars connect the sins of the past to the inequities of the present, like Isabel Wilkerson, who in her book *Caste* notes that "Slavery was not merely an unfortunate thing that happened to [B]lack people. It was an American innovation, an American institution created by and for the benefit of the elites." Wilkerson, Michelle

Alexander, Ibram X. Kendi, and other social scientists describe how slavery morphed and metastasized into the contemporary American institutions that perpetuate racial division: the criminal legal system, segregated housing, and yes, schools.

If the onus is on regular folks to carry the mantle of fighting racism, the uncomfortable flip side of that notion is that the people who bar the doors and stand in the way of justice—while sometimes memorialized as cartoonish supervillains in stock photos—also are regular people making conscious decisions in the face of the exact same system. The protectors of the institutions that regenerate white supremacy, generation after generation, are not anonymous foot soldiers in a fantasy battle; they are our neighbors, family members, business owners, community leaders, and, yes, teachers.

That's why Dr. Beverly Tatum, whose work we discussed in Chapter 5, describes racism as a "moving walkway," where standing still moves us, passively, in the direction of injustice. The walkway is a visual illustration of Desmond Tutu's admonition that adopting neutrality in situations of injustice causes you to side with the oppressor. While some folks in the present are active perpetrators of conscious racist deeds, many others are passive inheritors of generational advantage who are not *yet* privy to how their participation validates injustice.

Breaking racist patterns, in the context of our schools, means being able to identify when we are enabling racism's moving walkway. These stories, and the oppressions they underscore, will be old news to many of you. Some of you who picked up this book, though, when you started reading might not yet have had the emotional, intellectual, or historical tools to describe, dissect, and discuss the lasting impact of racism in our schools. In hearing these stories, discussing them with your colleagues, and doing the personal work we described in Chapters 5, 6, 7, and 8, hopefully you feel somewhat more equipped now.

But what will we do with that newfound knowledge and understanding?

When we see racism—either as subtle microaggressions or as glaring student disparities—will we speak up, or will we let things slide?

When our colleagues look the other way from these issues, will we view them as lost causes, or do we try to shift their perspectives?

Will we have the courage to admit when we perpetuated these very disparities in the past, or will we judge our peers for holding beliefs that we only managed to shed several months ago?

Being a change agent means taking a leadership role in confronting these issues. When you see racial disparities, be the first to speak up. When race is the subtext in a conversation, take a step back and make it the text. If you struggle to talk about race, that's okay—lots of people do; but that's not an excuse to delegate the work of social change to others. Learn the history, understand your role in it, and practice speaking so that, when the time comes, you're not concerned about whether or not you're using the right words, but with whether or not you are identifying and interrupting cycles of injustice and violence.

As we've said many times throughout this book, you yourself cannot single-handedly right history's wrongs from inside of your classroom or school.

That said, nothing has ever changed—not in this country or the world—without the concerted work of regular folks pushing back, day in and day out, trying and failing, striving and flailing, against forces that once seemed unconquerable.

INDIANOLA, MISSISSIPPI

Frankie, Shamica, Emily, and the rest of their crew knew that part of their job as change agents was to face the truth, and the reality in Indianola was that too many children in the community still could not read.

The crew knew that this reality manifested due to generations of underinvestment in schools serving Black children and that the levers of state power, not to mention school finance authority, were well beyond their reach.

That said, building district systems that enable children's reading skills to flourish was well within their purview, and they intended to do something about that.

The first part of their challenge required confronting difficult truths, including the actual data, which Frankie had uncovered in the course of planning for the transformation reviews. Local reading evaluations, which the crew trusted, indicated that the vast majority of elementary school students in the system were not reading at grade level. By the time students got to high school, the challenges became even more difficult, though not impossible, to remedy.

Another uncomfortable reality that required facing was that the district's current approach to remediation and intervention was not addressing the root of literacy challenges. Their brutal analysis of their remediation strategies already had led to scratching some programs at a central level, but there remained school-based challenges as well. Frankie in particular was dismayed to realize that the district was using summer school as a remediation strategy for high schoolers; but students who attended summer programming were mostly placed in the same classrooms—with the same teachers—as they had been assigned to during the regular school year.

To that point, the attitudes of teachers in the classroom were perhaps the biggest challenge the crew needed to confront, particularly given the demographic differences that existed between the teacher workforce and the student population. Emily noticed that some novice teachers, who had little experience working in African American communities, struggled to communicate with their kids in an authentic way. On the extreme side of this, one teacher more or less parked herself behind her desk every morning and never moved. Getting teachers to come out from behind their literal desks, and out of their virtual shells, was a major part of the work. At a more foundational level, helping educators learn to talk openly about race and how their own personal identities interacted with their teaching and relational capabilities was an uphill climb that was well worth the effort.

After confronting the facts on the ground, the crew went to work identifying potential solutions and next steps. Shamica worked with Emily to build a plan that would introduce teachers and staff from across the district to the most relevant contemporary cognitive science informing reading instruction. Once the crew had built some systemic understanding of the relevant science, they built rubrics for identifying new curricula and interventions. With concrete rubrics created, they were able to illustrate, definitively, that the current programs were ill-suited to their challenges. In the process of building and vetting curricula as a crew, they were able to build buy-in and consensus, not just from central office staff but also from school-based educators.

(Continued)

(Continued)

To deepen the schools' engagement in the process, the central office crew carved out significant chunks of districtwide professional development time for individual school teams to build theories of action related to literacy. Each of the schools in the district built a one-page document that outlined specific "if/then" statements related to the improvement of literacy instruction. The high school described how they would use professional learning networks within their school to build teachers' competencies in, and comfort with, reading instruction. An elementary school described how they would use explicit vocabulary building strategies to build bridges between reading instruction and other core content areas.

Frankie and the rest of the crew saw real promise in the school's literacy theories of action. The strategic vision and attention to detail in the plans was emblematic of the sort of intentionality that they hoped to cultivate in a consolidated Indianola–Sunflower district. The central office curriculum staff subsequently built beautiful visualizations of how the school's plans connected to the broader district strategy; the central office also organized the rest of the year's inservice programs around skill-building to support the plans.

Schools and teachers noticed and appreciated both the clarity and the attentiveness to their needs.

The level of sophistication—not to mention school and district alignment—in the literacy plans was so evident that Emily and William suggested sharing them as a model during the big spring community event. The community meeting was being structured to provide the broader civic leadership of Sunflower County with an opportunity to share perspectives about the culture and future of the consolidated school district. In responding directly to the state's new mandates, while building local knowledge about the science of reading, the literacy plans seemed like a perfect bright spot to highlight.

Frankie and the crew agreed, and the team got to work preparing an agenda that would engage, motivate, and inspire the community's broader leadership to continue their support of systemic growth.

Facing History and Facing the Truth

It is impossible to improve what we're too timid to face, and there are a lot of things in our work as change agents that are frightening to confront.

One of those things, which we've discussed at length in this chapter, is our shared, fraught history as American people. If we do not face our history and how that history prefaces our contemporary struggles to deliver racial justice, we have no shared starting place or moral standing for propagating the project of public education. A failure to reckon with systemic injustice creates not just moral problems, but tactical ones, as our ignorance causes us to miss enormous, consequential parts of our students' and communities' stories. Those failures in turn place severe limits on the efficacy of our interventions: We end up answering the wrong questions, designing solutions to the wrong problems, and erecting structural supports on top of fragile foundations.

At the same time, the work of being an educator requires facing the immense genius and potential of our country's children. We must not be afraid to acknowledge and recognize when we are falling short of respecting that genius. Educators must adopt mental models that position children as equal parts curious and capable. While historical injustices create barriers to understanding our children in that light, so do our own prejudices and predispositions. Many of our children receive an inadequate, unscientific, second-rate education because of the color of their skin, the wealth of their parents, or the zip code in which they were born.

And if we do not rise, as individuals, to meet our children's inherent brilliance, we remain complicit in that arrangement.

Our efforts matter a great deal to the children in front of us, despite the fact that there will always be deep tension between the consequences of structural oppression and the limitations of individual effort. There are no bootstraps thick enough to overcome four centuries of overt racism. It is because of that truth—not in spite of it—that public schooling must manifest in ways that are culturally sustaining, research-validated, teacher-friendly, and results-oriented.

We do not need to make either/or decisions about whether we focus on student results or the legacy of systemic racism.

The reality, as with so many things in life and in this book, is that we need to do both/and.

In *We Want to Do More Than Survive: Abolitionist Teaching and the Pursuit of Educational Freedom*, Bettina L. Love outlines the tension inherent in that notion. She describes the cognitive dissonance of teachers striving to

> *achieve incremental changes in their classrooms and schools for students in the present day, while simultaneously freedom dreaming and vigorously creating a vision for what schools will be when the educational survival complex is destroyed.*

Such is the burden for change agents who dream of a different world, who must hold onto multiple (often conflicting) truths simultaneously, while taking steps each day to confront and shape reality in the direction of justice.

The work you do—either in the classroom or in the central office or somewhere in between—to inspire material changes in the educational conditions for children today is not counter to the long-term project of revolutionary change.

It is, rather, the essential precursor: the small wheel that turns the bigger, more daunting wheel.

INDIANOLA, MISSISSIPPI

While the Delta districts were engaged in complex internal planning processes, the long-term success of those systems depended, more than anything, on the ongoing support, love, strength, and resolve of the local community.

The community, its leaders, its stories, and its traditions had sustained the schools through the ups, downs, joys, and pains of the past. And only the community could lead the combined school systems into the future.

In recognition of that ongoing role in shaping the future, the transformation crew from the two districts had spent the winter preparing to host a large community gathering that would provide opportunities for civic leadership and the broader population alike to share their input on the evolving plans to create a consolidated local school system.

In preparation for the meeting, Frankie, Emily, and William had prepared detailed presentations on finances, enrollment patterns, personnel, and performance trends. They planned to share the Indianola schools' literacy plans as examples of how to align community needs to government resources, while also preparing engaging activities that would allow participants to generate a collective vision for what the future might hold.

To help with that part of the presentation, William had invited Derek Mitchell, the CEO of Partners in School Innovation, to share some reflections on how other systems across the country had managed similarly complex undertakings. Derek had spent considerable time consulting with local officials on the consolidation plans, and his national expertise in school and district transformation would be an asset in navigating the community conversation.

The meeting was held at a local community college on an evening in the spring of 2014, and the conversation was both positive and spirited. Educators who attended seemed focused on the brass-tacks technical complexities of managing the merger of adjacent, yet dissimilar, school systems. Which curriculum will we use, and who will make those decisions? Will there be one school board or multiple overlapping boards? How will student assignment to schools work? If there are overlapping and duplicate functions in central offices, what will happen to the people who hold those roles?

Local civil rights organizers, meanwhile, situated the contours of the current discussion in a multigenerational story of racial progress in the Delta. They pointed to the successes of the past generation, including the presence of more African American school board members and elected officials in the community, the existence of a thriving Black middle class, and the dissipation of the most overt forms of interpersonal racism.

The leaders of those organizations, however, counseled the districts against seeing those changes as a sign that racism was a thing of the past. The head of the local NAACP noted that a small number of white families continued to own a disproportionate number of local businesses and that their approach as employers often carried overtones of the unjust labor arrangements of the past. In that spirit, another attendee felt it was important to note that the meeting itself was taking place in a building—the Charles Capp Center—named for a recently deceased

(Continued)

(Continued)

Mississippi legislator, who himself had been president of a Citizens' Council.

Despite the weight of the conversation, difficult issues had been approached in a spirit of moving toward a more just future. The rest of the meeting was equally fruitful. Small groups broke out to discuss what characteristics the consolidated district would seek in a new superintendent; community members cocreated asset maps of local resources that the systems might draw upon; and school board members held question-and-answer sessions about their current theories of action.

When the meeting closed, the crew exhaled. Frankie thanked William and Emily for helping her to prepare, and the group decided to take the night off.

William and Derek drove to a small restaurant in downtown Indianola to debrief the conversation. While dining, they reflected on the extraordinary feeling of being Black men with advanced degrees— both of whom had spent a lifetime working toward, and studying the history of, the trials and tribulations of American schools; both having the opportunity to shift the long arc of justice, year in and year out, in community after community, throughout the United States. They talked about how much had changed and how much had not.

After the meal, they got in their rental car to drive back to the hotel where they were staying, a few miles outside of town.

As Derek drove, cautiously, down the same dark, country roads where Mac, Fannie Lou, and the freedom fighters of the past had staged their stands for human rights, all of a sudden William saw bright red and blue lights in his rearview mirror.

"Cops," William said.

Derek looked at William. "Did I do anything? Am I speeding?"

"No, man," William said, "You're barely driving the speed limit."

The police car sped up to catch the rental car, directing Derek and William to pull off the road. Two police officers, both white, got out of the cruiser. With hands perched on their gun holsters, they approached the rental car from opposite sides.

Derek sat in his dark suit, tie still knotted, one hand fixed on the steering wheel, shaking. This was not their first rodeo; both men had been stopped by police in many states, both in the North and South. But something about this time—the dead of the night in the middle of the Mississippi Delta, with the history described by local leaders fresh in their minds—made this feel more harrowing than the others.

Derek rolled down the window.

"Where are you two going?" the first officer asked.

"We're just headed to our hotel," Derek said, reaching for his license.

The officer tightened his grip on his gun. "What are you reaching for?"

"Just my license," Derek said, as every encounter he had ever seen or heard or felt about Black men and police on dark roads flashed through his and William's collective consciousness.

"Don't make any movements," the officer ordered. "What are you doing here?"

"We're here on a business trip," Derek said. "That's why we have out-of-state plates."

"Show me your license," the officer said, "and the rental car agreement."

As Derek reached for the documents, William shook his head. The officer looked over the paperwork and looked back at the two men.

"Is something wrong?" Derek asked.

"We were just wondering who you were and where you were going," the officer said. "That's all. Stay here."

"That's all," William repeated back to himself. As if the casual dismissal could erase the fact that they, two Black men with the highest of educational credentials, fresh from a meeting with the community's elected political leaders, were dealing with the danger and indignity of explaining to the police, cruising down the road in the middle of catfish farms, where, exactly, they were headed that night.

(Continued)

(Continued)

The two officers conferred behind them as Derek and William sat in silence in the car. After a few minutes, the first officer walked back to the driver's window.

"Okay," the officer said, handing the papers back to Derek and looking the two men over once more. "You're free."

"Are we?" pondered Derek, as he put his license back in his pocket, started the car, and pulled back onto the country road.

THE EDUCATING FOR FREEDOM CHECKLIST

- **Learn the truth of history.** When we fail to understand the past, we are, in fact, condemned to repeat its worst injustices. That said, possessing historical knowledge alone is insufficient to hasten material change. Once you understand history's violent, oppressive cycles, you must take steps to break them.

- **Recognize patterns.** Political fights today are being waged to prevent classroom discussions about the history of race, but next year, there will be a different set of arguments mounted to protect white supremacy. By recognizing that there are structural forces at play—not to mention individuals—that benefit from perpetuating inequity, you as a change agent will equip yourself to recognize when the next battle emerges.

- **Listen to elders.** Some of the most victorious and egregious moments in American history have happened during the lifetimes of people that are still living today. Learn history from them and be sure to thank them for the gift of their presence.

- **Play your role.** Everyone has a part to play in unwinding systems of oppression and injustice. Yours, as an educator, must involve *both* recognizing the harm of structural *racism and* teaching children in ways that deliver results. There is no either/or here.

- **Embrace the power and love of community.** Oppressive systems derive their strength from creating arrangements that offer some people power at the expense of others. The only way to combat that kind of injustice—both technically and spiritually—is to work together in community, in ways that are deep, profound, respectful, and mutually affirming.

CHAPTER 10: DISCUSSION QUESTIONS

1. Do people in your community speak openly and frequently about the history of race and racism? Are there racial differences in who is willing to address these topics?

2. Are there elements of your local history that you wish you knew more about? What steps can you take today to enrich your understanding about local history?

3. When was the last time you talked to an elder in your community about their experiences with the schools? What did you learn?

Thriving Schools, Thriving Communities

11

The fourth-grade crew at César Chávez Elementary School began a trend.

Within a few years of their initiating grade-level teaming, five additional schools across San Jose were engaged in intensive transformation work. The principals of those schools started a tradition of eating carnitas and burritos at a local restaurant, La Perla, whenever they needed to debrief challenges. By then, those schools had something in common: ROCI. The improvement cycles that had begun in Paradise Breeze—the supply closet masquerading as office space at Chávez—had become infectious.

The successes of scale, however, brought once-buried challenges to the surface. Some folks in the district central office had expressed curiosity about the level of autonomy exerted by Chávez and the other transformation schools. The idea of teachers collaborating to set their own interim goals, with the support of school-based instructional-leadership teams, was a new concept that wasn't entirely comfortable for folks more accustomed to top–down leadership. While a few teachers experimenting in a janitor's closet could fly below the radar, *six whole schools*—not to mention, the very schools in the district under the most state and federal scrutiny—couldn't avoid attracting attention.

(Continued)

223

(Continued)

René Sanchez, the Chávez principal, and his peers were wrestling with this conundrum one evening at La Perla, while preparing for a day of district-sponsored professional learning. The group was struggling with how to address these challenges with their partners at the central office. Most of the six schools were using grade-level collaborative planning rooted in dissecting standards, while minimizing the use of district pacing guides. The process was working, but they were concerned that their results might be overshadowed by deviating from systemic norms.

After some candid chat over carnitas, no clear conclusion was reached. The principals decided to see if the district would offer an opening for a critical conversation. The professional development session happened the following week at the district's training center on Rough and Ready Road, behind a local middle school. The teams from the transformation schools piled into the auditorium and sat at their respective tables, wondering what to expect.

The first surprise came during the opening plenary session when the superintendent introduced a new deputy, a man by the name of Tom Green, who had recently joined the district from the faculty of a local university to oversee school transformation and innovation. The introduction created a buzz, as a few of the principals knew Tom already. He had built an academic reputation studying school-based empowerment as an approach to serving marginalized young people. This focus made him a local folk hero to change agents.

Tom's hiring was the exact signal the principals had been awaiting, so when the floor opened for discussion, René jumped. He asked Tom a pointed question. "We're doing things differently at some schools, particularly related to standards-based instruction," René said. "We've been hesitant to say much about it because we don't want to start an unnecessary beef with the district. If you're going to be overseeing our schools, what's your response to that?"

Tom, finding himself immediately in the hot seat, didn't hesitate. "There's a long history of tension between districts and schools that want to be innovative and try different things," Tom said. "I'm your champion. I'm here to protect what you want to do. If you get results, I'll do whatever is in my power to make sure nobody can get in the way of that."

The crowd murmured a positive response, and a few people even clapped. More importantly, Tom's bold edict turned out to be true in practice. The transformation schools had the district's explicit blessing to continue down the road they had started, so they doubled their efforts. ROCI moved from the background to the foreground. Tom even became an ambassador to the local grantmaking community, making a point of finding philanthropic partners who had an appetite for systemic change.

The combination of district support and school-level energy was transformative for Chávez. After three years of building ROCI into grade-level teamwork, the school experienced multiple consecutive years of double-digit growth in reading and math proficiency.

And for the first time since the state of California started designating schools as needing improvement, in 2014 Chavez moved off the state's watch list.

On the day they got the news, the staff was ecstatic. René—never eager to rest on laurels—reluctantly agreed to let Meaghen and Tiara stage a celebration. They bought a giant cake at the local Costco and procured a case of sparkling apple cider. They decorated the teachers' lounge with streamers and balloons, setting out dozens of tiny plastic glasses that mimicked champagne flutes.

The lounge, whose dour energy had once been potent enough to scare away even the most grizzled faculty member, effloresced with energy. Ecstatic educators clinked cups of cider, hugged, laughed, cheered, and celebrated, without reservations.

Little Wins Can Add Up to Big Wins

Not every team that engages in school transformation work will have a moment of celebration so clear and profound as the mock-champagne popping at Chávez. And yet, as we come full circle and revisit the same community where we started this book, it is important to recall the foundational premise that animates the hard work we've been discussing: A different world is, in fact, possible, and your efforts are central to shepherding that world into existence.

Consider the arc of the Alum Rock experience. When we met the educators at Chávez, the faculty was in a collective rut, and the school had been identified as one of the lowest-performing schools in all of California. Trust among peers was low, collegiality was a joke, and the children who came to school each day absorbed that lackluster energy.

Within several years, the school was in an utterly different place. Between 2010 and 2015, the school went from a score of 645 to 812 on California's performance index, meaning it was one of the most improved schools in the entire state. The school's demographics remained unchanged in that time, with close to 90 percent of families coming from socioeconomically marginalized backgrounds. While bureaucratic accountability regimes and the assessments that undergird them are far from the only measures that matter in schools, crawling out of the hole of state and federal sanctions is an enormous task that warrants celebration.

During those years of sustained, measurable progress, the school used ROCI as the centerpiece of a school transformation framework. Teachers started working on grade-level collaboration first, then added schoolwide professional learning modules the following year. By the 2012–2013 school year, ROCI was so embedded in their approach to professional growth that the district had created new teacher inservice schedules to foster the weekly and monthly improvement cycles.

While Chávez is only one school in the story, everyone who was involved in the Alum Rock transformation agrees that the level of collaboration between the district and its schools was essential to achieving break-through results. In the early days of the work, educators at Chávez felt they had to tiptoe around their colleagues in the central office for fear that departing from norms might trigger backlash.

Their concerns, though rooted in complicated historical dynamics, turned out to be unnecessary. José Manzo, the superintendent, and Nora Guerra, another top deputy, ensured that the district acted as an enabler from the beginning. The hiring of Tom Green, who had innovation in his DNA, was another game changer. Beyond support-ing departures from district-mandated pacing, district leaders helped to acquire substitutes for professional learning days, reorient the district calendar toward ROCI cycles, and attract resources from other parts of the community. In a conference presentation on their "lessons learned" from many years of transformation work, René, José, Tom, and Nora outlined the core lessons that continue to animate their work: "invest in people not programs; prioritize core instruction; limit distractions; and use data to reflect and adjust."

In other words, ROCI, rinse, repeat. Because when something is work-ing, you shouldn't just ignore it. You should try to do more of it.

That's the lesson folks learned in San Francisco too.

School Transformation Framework

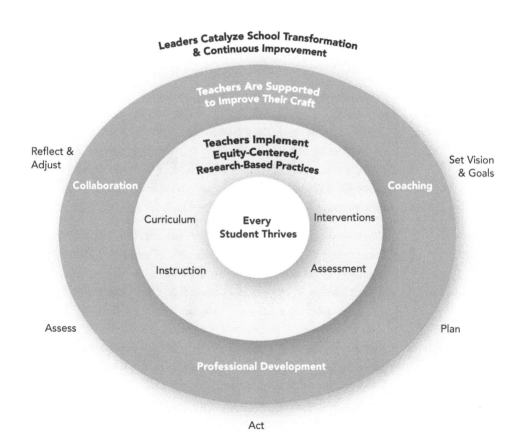

Guadalupe Guerrero, the Bay Area leader responsible for transformation work, could see that something special was happening at Steward, Freeman, and the other schools that had adopted ROCI as a way of life.

That secret sauce wasn't just evident in test scores, even though the numbers were strikingly good: double-digit math gains at Steward in just a couple of years, not to mention double-digit math and reading gains across another seven schools in a community of professional practice that had adopted the ROCI approach.

What seemed even more important to Guadalupe, though, was the culture of trust, care, and excellence that was evident across the schools. The just right "warm-demanding" balance was palpable to him upon entering buildings, and when he dug a little deeper, it was clear that the culture of continuous improvement had permeated beyond grade-level teams to encompass just about every aspect of the schools' operations.

When working toward his doctorate in education leadership, Guadalupe had studied the role of district leadership in supporting school improvement at scale. He had experienced a hands-off approach from district leaders when he was a principal and was determined to find a more collaborative balance. He appreciated that ROCI provided a unique way to distill improvement science into discrete chunks of work that were accessible to frontline educators and saw how the process could be leveraged to create constructive relationships at a systemic level. The clarity of purpose and alignment he witnessed at schools like Steward and Freeman made him excited—even a little bit jealous. "My life would have been so much easier as a newly appointed turnaround principal working in isolation so many years ago," he reflected, "if I would have had the benefit of this brand of school improvement coaching, this more collective approach, and the benefit of the ROCI framework to guide our school community's work."

Seeing the work in action made it clear to Guadalupe that the ROCI framework, coupled with ongoing coaching support for educators, were essential enabling conditions that could not be separated. He wanted to systematize this work and took two critical steps to broaden the influence of the improvement framework. First, he and his colleagues at the central office built continuous improvement into the district's overall strategic plan. He had been asked to facilitate districtwide improvement efforts due to the successes in the Mission and Bayview neighborhoods, and he didn't see any reason that the principles playing out at the school level couldn't be leveraged for citywide gains.

Second, he helped create something called the "Superintendent's Zone," which would be the basis for the district's most intensive work in chronically underresourced schools. Guadalupe described the Zone framework in the district's application for school improvement grants, a federal school-funding program that expanded during the Obama administration. Securing those grants required promising significant reforms in exchange for federal dollars. In those plans, his district crew grouped the district's struggling schools into the virtual "Zone," building on national research detailing the operational conditions necessary for transformation to thrive.

The Superintendent's Zone inverted the way folks normally think about schools in marginalized communities.

"Schools in the Zone went from being low status to suddenly being The Place Where Things Were Happening," Guadalupe said. "If you wanted to challenge yourself as an educator and were prepared to make the level of commitment demanded in this particular set of schools, then you understood that you would have the benefit of significant resources dedicated to this collective effort—that you would have access to the best professional development, coaching, and wraparound supports available anywhere. Working in a Zone school brought status; you were in the arena, embarking on a deliberate mission of transformation, to raise outcomes and create a positive counternarrative for the students of these school communities."

Transformation: The "Club You Want to Join"

In describing the "Superintendent's Zone" strategy, Guadalupe captures something critical that we haven't already mentioned about the work of being a change agent: If you do it right, it can be kind of cool.

It's hard to overstate just how revolutionary an idea this is. Most schools in marginalized communities struggle for resources, turn off the strongest educators, and form reputations as places to be avoided. By adopting the ROCI approach and making that framework central to broader systemic improvement strategies, the San Francisco crew turned conventional wisdom on its head.

The Zone strategy itself is another important part of the story. Zones as a concept have roots in not just school improvement but also in community empowerment and global economic development. Sometimes called Empowerment Zones or Opportunity Zones, these policy structures offer opportunities for innovative leaders to try new things outside of normal rules and regulations. When school districts create a Zone, they provide some level of autonomy to schools, with the understanding that those schools should achieve stronger results as a result. In essence, the Zone is a way of formalizing the benign rule-stretching in which René and his peers engaged.

Beyond creating new rules for transformation schools, a Zone is a statement about systemic priorities. By giving struggling schools special status, system leaders send a signal about what is important to them while also adjusting rules and regulations to accelerate progress. Guadalupe's Superintendent's Zone included a series of incentives and trade-offs: Schools received more resources and more attention, with the expectation that they collaborate, try new things, and make measurable progress.

Many districts tried similar strategies in the last decade, and the overall success of the federal school improvement grant program remains a controversial topic. The results in the Superintendent's Zone, however, were incontrovertibly strong and consistent. Independent teams of academic experts at Stanford, the University of California at Irvine, Brown University, and the University of Washington studied the San Francisco approach and found that systematic alignment between the district and schools led to consistent improvements over time. Families that once fled transformation schools now clamored to attend them. Test scores went up, teacher retention improved, student absences decreased, and professional learning resources became more aligned to overall school goals.

Perhaps most importantly, the researchers discovered that the longer schools engaged in continuous improvement work, the stronger they became. The most critical factor in that improvement seems to be the overall increase in staff capacity through intensive processes of personal growth and reflection. These are critical findings for a couple of reasons. First, too often school improvement efforts are quick, flashy endeavors that fizzle after breakthrough results aren't achieved within a single school year. To expect immediate results in a school that has experienced generations of socioeconomic trauma is unrealistic; policy initiatives that seek quantitative outcomes on such a short cycle are, to revisit an expression from Chapter 1, "pre-failed strategies."

Second, it's important to note that these results came because of increasing educator capacity and not through draconian staff replacement measures. If we harken back to Chapters 1 and 2, we remember that Chávez Elementary School was facing "staff reconstitution" if transformation efforts stalled. Many of the schools in this book were operating under similar trade-offs, hemmed in by state and federal school improvement requirements. Replacing tons of educators is destabilizing for teachers, students, families, and the broader community culture, not to mention impractical for policymakers. Even if you believe that replacing teachers is a viable school improvement strategy, hard-fought labor rules, coupled with district teacher assignment policies, mean that replacing staff en masse in one school is bound to create disruption in others.

It is hard to overstate the importance of these findings, as the results suggest that our best shot for improving schools at scale is to invest—consistently, dramatically, and intentionally—in the professional growth of teachers. There are millions of classroom educators in America. If the next generation of education policy embraces the enormous transformative potential in harnessing their collective greatness, the possibilities seem limitless.

One final important finding from the longitudinal research on San Francisco relates to the sustainability of the habits we describe throughout this book. The schools here continued their improvements for three to four years after federal funding dissipated. This result is striking, as the conventional wisdom in school improvement work is that "fiscal cliffs"—sharp, sudden declines in funding—can cause academic regression. That seems not to have happened here, and the researchers suspect that the habits of continuous improvement play a large part in the durability of gains. By building consistent routines of data examination, collaboration, execution, and reflection across an entire faculty, schools can create insulation against future events that might otherwise threaten hard-won changes.

While these results are worth celebrating, we must keep in mind that the retrospective examination of complicated journeys can create the illusion of inevitability. Real school improvement work, as we've learned throughout this book, requires patience and resilience. Once in a while, we reach what we think is the mountaintop, but the vista from the new peak only reveals new challenges that require renewed sources of energy. Sometimes, our biggest wins are followed by unmitigated losses. We navigate hilltops and valleys, riverbends and secret passages. We achieve, we fail, we bounce back, we recover, we learn, we mend, and we heal.

In light of that, keep in mind that your own personal growth is the one thing in your control.

It's not unusual, quite common actually, to experience extraordinary personal breakthroughs, even against the backdrop of institutional inertia. At times, our individual growth outpaces the transformational capacity of our schools and districts.

That's okay too.

GRAND RAPIDS, MICHIGAN

Sarah Hundt bloomed where she was planted because the soil was so rich. Every year that she was at Polk Elementary School, Sarah grew into a stronger teacher. Surrounded by caring veterans—and supported by Palak and other coaches who were attentive to her professional growth—Sarah had just about everything a novice teacher could want to thrive.

As Sarah became a more experienced educator, the lines between her classroom and the wonders of the world became blurrier and blurrier. Her crew started planning field trips to supplement classroom work. One year after a science lesson on climate change, they took students to the local recycling plant to observe the single-stream sorting process. While not everyone sees the inherent magic in garbage disposal, Sarah's fourth graders were enrapt, watching hunks of household metal getting pressed into dense little cubes.

The success of the sojourn to the recycling center was inspiration for bolder ventures. Sarah's crew organized field trips whenever they could, building tight bonds with parents and grandparents who were eager to serve as chaperones. At the end of one year, the fourth-grade crew went to the nearby town of Holland to visit Lake Michigan. Sarah had been surprised to learn that most students had never seen the Great Lake, despite living just a few miles away. When they arrived, she was sure to register the look on their faces, as shocked kiddos absorbed the immensity of a body of water that was larger than many countries they had studied.

In Sarah's third year at Polk, the fourth-grade crew planned a field trip to see a movie that was based on the book *Wonder*, which she read aloud with her students each year. One of their teammates, Randa, had just moved to a different school, and a new teacher had replaced her, so Sarah thought it might be a constructive bonding experience to do the book–movie combo as a team. She raised the topic in a grade-level meeting. While Palak and most of her peers were enthusiastic, the new teacher was chilly to the idea. She didn't want to add a new book to her repertoire and couldn't see the value in going to the movie.

In a meeting later that week with her fellow instructional coaches, Palak worked with her peers to troubleshoot. "Is anyone else experiencing similar resistance among more veteran teachers?" she asked.

A chorus of "yes" followed.

The assembled coaches discussed mitigation strategies while comparing notes across buildings. While some teachers and leadership teams embraced ROCI, others preferred more traditional, solitary approaches to solving the complex challenges of educational justice.

While some of those older habits were rooted in objective research about how to improve schools, most were not. Palak suspected that perpetuating unproven habits would exacerbate existing systematic disparities, but she also knew that districtwide change couldn't happen overnight and that the pathway to long-term progress was likely to look more serpentine than linear.

It was hard to stomach the setbacks, though. One day, a local central office leader called a meeting of struggling schools to discuss progress monitoring and data. There was nothing notable about this sort of meeting, except that the person who called the meeting was unusually skeptical of ideas that were not his own.

(Continued)

(Continued)

To prepare for what was likely to be a tense discussion, Palak and the district's other coaches prepared a dazzling array of useful information to share at the session. They built school-by-school graphs of longitudinal student data, colorful charts illustrating how the district's performance stood up to comparable systems, and case studies rooted in grade-level practice at schools that were making outsized progress.

When Palak and her peers got to the meeting, though, many of them didn't even have a chance to participate. While many instructional coaches were employees of the school district, some were technically employed by nonprofit organizations that had built partnerships with the school system. The district had adopted a stringent rule around data access, and the person holding the meeting had decided to invoke that authority to exclude employees of partner organizations from the discussion, even though neither law nor policy required such exclusion.

"You have to leave," he said, as he ushered a handful of educators to the door.

"But we're in these schools every day and have a lot to add," one coach said. "What's the point of keeping us at arm's length?"

"We'll be fine," he said, motioning to the door. "You can come back in when we're done discussing the data."

The excluded coaches huddled out the door, and he closed it behind them.

ROCI Is a Cycle: What Feels Like an Ending Might Be a Beginning

The measurement of progress and success is highly dependent on one's point of view. Achievements can be recast as setbacks, and stumbles can be opportunities.

Consider student academic data, for example. If we know that only one in four children in an elementary school—25 percent—can read at grade level, that might sound like a devastatingly bad statistic. If we find out, however, that in the prior year only 10 percent of students could meet that goal, the statistics take on a different character altogether.

The same principle applies to qualitative indicators of improvement. Perspective matters. The goal of school transformation is not to achieve some ephemeral measure of executional perfection, but to always be in the process of learning, improving, and reflecting. That last vignette—in which a bunch of educators were kicked out of a meeting for no real reason—sounds demoralizing. It confirms our worst assumptions about how our hard work will be received by remote sources of authority, while reinforcing top–down models of hierarchy.

We don't know, however, what happened next.

That's because the next chapter in the school transformation story is waiting to be written, perhaps by you and your crew.

In Chapter 7, we compared the work of school improvement to a marathon. At Mile 13 of a marathon—the exact middle—one can look either forward or backward and see equally long, problematic roads. In the case of Sarah, Palak, and the Polk crew, we already know that the path leading up to the final vignette was anything but direct: There was the saga of Sarah's pillows, endless educator reassignment, cringeworthy Fishbowl sessions, and consistent resistance to collaboration. The next phase of their transformation journey—heck, any school improvement endeavor—is bound to be beset by just as many obstacles. To end each story in this book with a tidy coda is not just unrealistic; it's dishonest.

Despite all of this, Polk Elementary School, and the other schools in the greater Grand Rapids region that adopted ROCI, experienced breakthrough results. In the time that Sarah was a teacher, Polk more than doubled the percentage of students scoring above the district norm in math. When teachers were surveyed, they expressed "surprise" at how much their practices changed when they were exposed to real data, disaggregated by student demographics. Researchers from the University of California at Los Angeles studied their work and came to a striking conclusion:

> *Time to meet and talk with your peers ("thought partnering") appears to be the single most important driver of success. . . . This seemingly basic concept has driven tremendous change . . . . Time during the day is filled with responding to demands, crises, and administrative minutia. Carving out a space for professional conversation with skilled, informed partners is a luxury in far too many schools. Simply having a [coach] present, pushing for undivided attention and reflection has fundamentally altered the culture in each of the schools and led to changed practice*

among staff. **The challenge for the districts going forward is to maintain and sustain the culture of collaboration, preserving the time needed for professional conversations.**

I added the bold emphasis on that final part because the researchers at UCLA really captured the gist of this entire book in a single sentence. At some level, the entire ROCI process is about formalizing and institutionalizing these simple ideas, which should be taken for granted in schools but unfortunately are rare.

These characteristics are so hard to find in American public schools because we've spent more than 30 years focused on just about everything except for improving the objective quality of teaching on a daily basis.

During the course of a multigenerational search for silver-bullet solutions, the field of public education lost sight of the basic elements that make for great teaching at scale. Instead of cultivating schools and districts where inexperienced teachers could become good, and good teachers great, innovators sought to make schools "teacher proof." Publishers created rote curricula that relied on memorization instead of instruction; software engineers invented algorithms that aspired to replace the classroom teacher; and entrepreneurs cooked up cookie-cutter school designs optimized for mass replication. Much of this was done without ill intent, but the cumulative effect was to marginalize the idea of consistent, incremental professional improvement for frontline educators.

Fortunately, through the work of schools and educators like the ones we followed in this book, the work of improvement science is experiencing a renaissance throughout the field. The approach is attractive not just because it works but also because it provides a plausible alternative to more faddish approaches. Or as Tony Bryk says in *Improvement in Action,* which highlights practical research on continuous improvement in schools,

> [C]ontinuous improvement is not the next "new program" to be embraced by school systems alongside other initiatives such as introducing a new curriculum, a technology, or some additional new services. All of these may be thought of as the *what of schooling. . . . In contrast, continuous improvement focuses on* how *schools can both make current programs work better and take best advantage of whatever new initiatives they might introduce to secure quality outcomes.*

When we learn *how* to improve, we're bound to get better at *whatever* the world throws our way.

John Tupponce left the principals' walk-through at William E. McBride K–8 school knowing that he had seen something special. As a local assistant superintendent responsible for transformation, he spent most days traveling between schools at different points of the improvement process. While he saw something eyebrow-raising just about every day, it was rare to see something that reoriented his way of thinking about schools.

The visit at McBride had done that.

John had been an educator for more than 20 years and spent most of his life in schools and communities that looked a lot like McBride. In his view, the emphasis on compliance in schools was creating cookie-cutter conditions across the country; the level of sameness in classrooms and schools serving marginalized children had started to get under his skin.

The slightly off-kilter creativity at McBride had inspired him though. The classroom he observed offered a different mental model for what it might look like for children to express their genius outside of a system of command and control. Finding new approaches was of some practical urgency for him; John and his crew had responsibility for more than 30 schools, many of which had challenges similar to McBride's.

John knew, however, that improvement at scale was more complicated than waving a magic wand to replicate what was happening at McBride, where educators achieved significant increases on Common Core-aligned literacy assessments within just two years of initiating transformation work. As a district leader, he wanted to create the conditions for educators to thrive, not dictate their jobs to them. As such, figuring out the critical underlying factors germane to the McBride story seemed critical.

One important ingredient was the school's multifaceted leadership crew. In David, the principal, the school had a seasoned operational leader with relational skills; John had been instrumental in coaching David toward the growth he experienced. Cynthia, the senior teacher leader, was a master coach, had decades of experience in the community, and possessed an unwavering belief in the human capacity to grow

(Continued)

(Continued)

and learn at all stages of life. Mallory, the improvement coach, was a systems thinker who could translate long-term goals into daily priorities. Together, they possessed the tools and the talents necessary for transformation, while none of them could have done the work alone.

In addition, McBride demonstrated the extraordinary value of being open to the broader community. Steppingstone, a program at Temple University that supports college and career pathways, was embedded in the school's academic programming. AmeriCorps volunteers, trained by the nonprofit organization City Year, supported tutoring at McBride. Even Mallory herself, who worked in the school every single day, was a coach trained and employed by Partners in School Innovation. John recognized the value that these partnerships brought to the table and saw how those relationships flourished with the right leadership at the school level.

As a system leader, John saw an opportunity to leverage these lessons in service of broader goals. When a local district decided to roll out a systemwide initiative to improve middle school math teaching, he encouraged the adoption of a continuous improvement approach. Instead of mandating new curricula from the top down, his district crew adopted a ground-up approach. They cultivated a professional learning community made up of the leadership teams from schools that opted to participate. They leveraged nonprofit experts—like Partners in School Innovation—to build content and materials for the network.

And they used ROCI to drive progress.

Alongside these technical choices, the schools made racial equity and cultural responsiveness central to the work of improving math instruction. Ryan Stewart, who helped design the math networks before becoming secretary of education in New Mexico, likes to dispel the myth that math and science are somehow outside of the realm of equity work. "It's not just about the content, even though the content has to be relevant," Ryan says. "It's about bias and stereotype threat. Why are African American boys and girls not represented in the sciences? Why are there systemic gaps for our English language learners in math? Are we really setting our kids up to be successful in these fields? It needs to be more than putting up a poster of a person of color in the classroom."

Through using ROCI and equity to drive innovation in math instruction, the same principles that drive school improvement are creating a new paradigm for math teaching across Philadelphia. School leadership teams come together, share their struggles, play math games, and reflect as a community. What started in just a few classrooms now has tentacles across an entire region.

All of this makes Cynthia Moultrie very happy. "When our teachers or administrators are excelling at something, they cannot become the gatekeepers of great ideas," she says. "If my classroom is on fire with great instruction but the teacher across the city is struggling, that's not something to celebrate. I'll say this over and over again to remind you: Pockets of excellence don't move the train forward."

Putting It All Together

We are the ones we've been waiting for.

—*June Jordan*

Educators in this book, working in all corners of the country, decided to take matters into their own hands, with striking success. To revisit a critical adage from Chapter 1, the data cannot tell the whole story, but numbers don't lie: Chávez Elementary School made some of the most significant gains in the state California; the San Francisco transformation schools serve as a national model for the immense possibilities of improvement; Polk Elementary School dramatically outperformed peers; and the work at William E. McBride was so striking that ROCI rolled out across the region.

Meanwhile, the Sunflower County Public Schools of Mississippi continue to shatter educational norms: After consolidation, and through the strength of their improvement strategies, the district achieved double-digit growth on state tests in both reading and math. The Delta district still has a long road ahead, but for the first time in history, Sunflower County schools are outperforming the schools in Jackson, the state capital.

None of these stories is over, but the big wheel turns in every community in this book.

So what do you think? Now that we've painted a realistic, pull-no-punches, warts-and-all picture of school transformation, are you ready for the work? Can you be one of the catalysts who takes the plunge into the warm pool, sets an example for your peers, and kicks off the series of chain reactions that leads to student success?

In short, are you a change agent?

You don't have to answer that question right away. That said, I hope you've at least been entertaining the possibility already.

If your answer is an unequivocal yes, then I have a few next steps for you. First, go back to the beginning of the book and get started. Pick a topic that gets your juices flowing and enlist a few peers to join your first ROCI session (Chapters 1–2). Once you achieve and celebrate some early wins, recruit a slightly larger group within your school to help write a strategic theory of action (Chapters 3–4). Figure out how to manage pushback (Chapter 5), cultivate a schoolwide culture that can embrace the work you're doing (Chapter 6), and don't forget to attend to your own personal growth in the process (Chapter 7).

While you're doing the work, keep in mind the contextual factors that have an outsized impact on progress. Keep love at the center of what you do (Chapter 8). Look for allies outside of your school building (Chapter 9). Always be explicit about, and mindful of, the complex history of race and exclusion that forms the backdrop for our work (Chapter 10); and paint a long-term vision for school transformation rooted in a coherent framework (Chapter 11).

At the risk of being repetitive, this work is not linear, so it's unlikely you'll do these things in the exact order in which they're presented. It's a good idea to read the whole book once and then revisit chapters on an as-needed basis. Pull out Chapter 1 every time you introduce new people to ROCI, for example, and reread Chapter 7 when your nerves are frayed.

If you're a "maybe" or a "hard no" on the change agent thing, I understand. This work isn't for everyone. If you've made it this far and still can't decide, I'm not sure what else we can say to convince you.

Either way, I believe in you and know you can do this work.

But more important than my faith in you is this: It is essential that you—and other people like you—take on this challenge. Margaret Mead once said, "Never doubt that a small group of thoughtful, committed citizens can change the world; indeed, it's the only thing that ever has."

The work of school transformation is nothing less than world-changing.

On a planet as unpredictable as the one we inhabit, the inevitability of change is perhaps the only thing we can predict with confidence. How that change manifests is up to us.

You can wait for the change and follow when it arrives.

But wouldn't you rather *be* the change?

INDIANOLA, MISSISSIPPI

The day after the large Sunflower County community meeting, William and Emily were slated to lead a full day of professional learning. A big chunk of their agenda was designed around incorporating insights from the community into the strategic plan for the district consolidation. Part of the community gathering had been an exercise in asset mapping, which was fodder for that discussion.

Emily had gone home afterward to synthesize the information they had gleaned. She organized the various community-based organizations and leaders into categories, while taking a first pass at aligning some of those entities with needs that had been identified in the school and district transformation reviews. She put her initial thoughts on large pieces of chart paper, drawing lines and placing colorful dots for emphasis.

She was already hanging charts in the district's big conference room the next morning when William arrived, obviously shaken.

"Are you okay?" she asked.

"Not really," he said and then explained the previous night's encounter with the police.

Emily's face fell as she listened with a combination of anger, fear, and understanding. "I'm so sorry that happened to you and Derek," she said. "Is there anything I can do?"

"Thanks for asking," he said, thinking for a minute. "Maybe just follow my lead this morning. I might do things a little differently than we had planned."

(Continued)

(Continued)

She agreed, and as the rest of the district leadership team arrived, William stood at the front of the room and decided to abandon the icebreaker he and Emily had planned for the day. "Do you all mind if I go off script a bit?" he asked, as the group nodded and murmured agreement back at him.

"I'm going to tell you the story of what happened to me last night after the community meeting," he said, "and I wonder if what I share sounds familiar to anyone here."

William described his experience of being pulled over on a dark country road by white police officers, for no reason. He described the pain, the fear, the anger, and the shame he felt. He expressed that he was coming to this meeting still sitting in all of that, and he wondered if anyone else could relate to the experience of showing up at school, or at work, marinating in such a complex stew of raw emotions, rooted in experiencing the contemporary realities of systemic oppression.

As it turned out, the group could, in fact, relate.

The first hour of that daylong meeting became a session of collective truth telling, about people's lives, their families, the community in which they lived and worked. Every Black man in the room had at least one police-related story to share. Most of the Black women did as well. A few decided to use the forum to tell their stories for the first time. Several other folks declined to share their tales, deciding not to retraumatize themselves through the process of storytelling . . . while still expressing gratitude that the doors had been opened to the discussion.

After a time, William suggested they move to other topics. "Thank you for allowing us to have that space together," William said, as he shifted the group's focus back to the planned agenda.

The collective sharing ended up being a gift to the broader work of transformation. The level of personal vulnerability required to engage in the topic strengthened connections within the leadership crew. The rest of the day was livelier and more honest as a result. People laughed and cried with ease. Hours that might have otherwise dragged passed like minutes.

The team experienced joy in the process of unearthing their shared humanity.

William doesn't think the shift was coincidental. His and his colleagues' framework for school transformation rests on the belief that the technical work of improving schools can only flourish when situated within the truth, however difficult that truth may be.

"You have to do the work, *and* you have to deal with the trauma," William says. "If we can't do it for ourselves, we cannot expect our kids to do it. Many of them walk into a world that's hostile to them just because of the color of their skin. It's our job as educators to make sure that we ourselves are aware of that reality. That way, we can shape the kids' awareness of that reality in a way that still allows them to have agency in, and navigate, that world."

"And if we can do that really well," he says smiling, "they'll end up living each day in that world with some joy."

Bibliography

Chapter 1

Brunson, Q., & Einhorn, R. (2021). *Abbott elementary*. Delicious Non-Sequitur Productions, ABC.

Bryk, A. S., Gomez, L. M., Grunow, A., & LeMahieu, P. G. (2015). *Learning to improve: How America's schools can get better at getting better.* Harvard Education Press.

Cuban, L. (1997). Change without reform: The case of Stanford University School of Medicine, 1908–1990. *American Educational Research Journal, 34*(1), 83–112. https://doi.org/10.3102/00028312034001083

Hite, J. E., & McGahey, J. T. (2015). Implementation and effectiveness of the response to intervention program. *Georgia School Counselor Association, 22,* 28–40. https://files.eric.ed.gov/fulltext/EJ1099646.pdf

Ibarra, N. (2020). High poverty schools can be high performing. *Brown Political Review.* https://brownpoliticalreview.org/2020/12/high-poverty-schools-can-be-high-performing/

Kannapel, P. J., & Clements, S. K. (2005). *Inside the black box of high-performing high-poverty schools.* The Prichard Committee for Academic Excellence.

Kantamneni, N. (2020). The impact of the COVID-19 pandemic on marginalized populations in the United States: A research agenda. *Journal of Vocational Behavior, 119,* 103439. https://doi.org/10.1016/j.jvb.2020.103439

Kowal, J., & Ableidinger, J. (2011). *Leading indicators of school turnarounds.* Public Impact & University of Virginia.

Kutash, J., Nico, E., Gorin, E., Rahmatullah, S., & Tallant K. (2010). *The school turnaround field guide.* FSG Social Impact Advisors.

Langley, G. L., Moen, R., Nolan, K. M., Nolan, T. W., Norman, C. L., & Provost, L. P. (2009). *The improvement guide: A practical approach to enhancing organizational performance* (2nd ed.). Jossey-Bass.

Leachman, M., Masterson, K., & Figueroa, E. (2017). *A punishing decade for school funding.* Center for budget and policy priorities. https://www.cbpp.org/research/state-budget-and-tax/a-punishing-decade-for-school-funding

Loewus, L. (2012). Survey: Teacher job satisfaction hits a low point. *Education Week.* https://www.edweek.org/teaching-learning/survey-teacher-job-satisfaction-hits-a-low-point/2012/03

Mora-Ruano, J. G., Heine, J. H., & Gebhardt, M. (2012). Does teacher collaboration improve student achievement? Analysis of the German PISA 2012 sample. *Frontiers in Education.* https://doi.org/10.3389/feduc.2019.00085

Sampath, B., Baldoza, K., Lenoci-Edwards, J., & Barker, P. (2021). An integrated approach to quality. *Healthcare Executive, 36*(6), 52–53.

Smarick, A. (2010). The turnaround fallacy. *Education Next, 10*(1), 20–26.

Sun, M., Kennedy, A. I., & Loeb, S. (2021). The longitudinal effects of school improvement grants. *Educational Evaluation and Policy Analysis, 43*(4), 647–667. https://doi.org/10.3102/01623737211012440

Sunderman, G. L. (2007) *Supplemental educational services under NCLB: Charting implementation.* The Civil Rights Project, UCLA.

Torres, B. (2005). Tutoring becomes a hot commodity. *The Baltimore Sun*, July 24. https://www.baltimoresun.com/news/bs-xpm-2005-07-24-0507230207-story.html

Vangrieken, K., Dochy, F., Raes, E., & Kyndt, E. (2015). Teacher collaboration: A systematic review. *Educational Research Review, 15*, 17–40. https://doi.org/10.1016/j.edurev.2015.04.002

Chapter 2

Alinsky, S. D. (1971). *Rules for radicals.* Random House.

Brown, A. M. (2017). *Emergent strategy.* AK Press.

Collins, J. (2001). *Good to great.* Harper Collins.

Covey, S. (2006). *The speed of trust.* Free Press.

Dubbs, N., & McGeary, K. A. (2014). Four ways to spread ideas. *Stanford Social Innovation Review.* https://ssir.org/articles/entry/four_ways_to_spread_ideas#

Engler, M., & Engler, P. (2016). *This is an uprising: How nonviolent revolt is shaping the twenty-first century.* Nation Books.

Jeynes, W. (2012). A meta-analysis of the efficacy of different types of parental involvement programs for urban students. *Urban Education, 47*(4), 706–742.

King, M. L. (1963). *Letter from a Birmingham jail.* https://www.africa.upenn.edu/Articles_Gen/Letter_Birmingham.html

Krakovsky, M. (2013). Why do some ideas spread? *Insights: Stanford Graduate School of Business.* https://www.gsb.stanford.edu/insights/why-do-some-ideas-spread

Matthiessen, P. (2014). *Sal si puedes.* University of California Press.

Nicolaides, A., & Poell, R. F. (2020). "The only option is failure": Growing safe to fail workplaces for critical reflection. *Advances in Developing Human Resources, 22*(3), 264–277. https://doi.org/10.1177/1523422320927296

Patterson, K., Granny, J., McMillan, R., & Switzler, A. (2002). *Crucial conversations: Tools for talking when stakes are high.* Hill Education.

Pentland, A. (2014). *Social physics: How social networks can make us smarter.* Penguin Books.

Reinhardt, R., & Gurtner, S. (2015). Differences between early adopters of disruptive and sustaining innovations. *Journal of Business Research, 68*(1), 137–145. https://doi.org/10.1016/j.jbusres.2014.04.007

Seeley, T. D., Passino, K., & Visscher, K. (2006). Group decision making in honey bee swarms.

American Scientist, 94(3), 220. https://doi.org/10.1511/2006.59.220

Warren, M. R., & Mapp, K. L. (2011). *A match on dry grass: Community organizing as a catalyst for school reform.* Oxford University Press.

Weiss, H. B., Lopez, M. E., & Rosenberg, H. (2010). *Beyond random acts: Family, school, and community engagement as an integral part of education reform.* Harvard Family Research Project.

Chapter 3

Allensworth, E. M., & Hart, H. (2018). *How do principals influence student achievement?* University of Chicago Consortium on School Research.

Baldwin, J. (1962). *The fire next time.* Random House.

Brinklow, A. (2020). San Francisco has one everything to the Bayview except fix its problems. *Curbed San Francisco.* https://sf.curbed.com/2020/2/18/21142590/bayview-black-population-sfmta-transit-report

Deming, W. E. (2012). *The essential Deming.* McGraw Hill.

Garcia Contreras, A. F., Ceberio, M., & Kreinovich, V. (2017). *Plans are worthless but planning is everything: A theoretical explanation of Eisenhower's observation.* Departmental Technical Reports (CS). https://scholarworks.utep.edu/cs_techrep/1102

Hirsch, S., & Hord, S. (2010). Building hope, giving affirmation: Learning communities that address social justice issues bring equity to the classroom. *Journal of Staff Development, 31*(4), 10–17.

Iruka, I. U. (2013). The Black family: Re-imagining family support and engagement. In L. Hogan (Ed.), *Being Black is not a risk factor: A strengths-based look at the state of the Black child* (pp. 18–23). National Black Child Development Institute.

Ladson-Billings, G. (2021). *Culturally relevant pedagogy: Asking a different question.* Teachers College Press.

Livingston, M. M. (2011). *The rise and fall of the dream schools: Equity and local politics in the San Francisco unified school district* [UC Berkeley Electronic Theses and Dissertations]. https://escholarship.org/uc/item/3614s924

Moore, R. O. (1964). *Take this hammer.* KQED.

Nafici, S. (2006). *The people or the place?: Revitalization/gentrification in San Francisco's Bayview Hunters Point* [Thesis (M.C.P.]. Massachusetts

Institute of Technology, Department of Urban Studies and Planning. https://dspace.mit.edu/handle/1721.1/37868

Newman, F. M., Smith, B., Allensworth, E., & Bryk, T. (2001). Instructional program coherence: What it is and why it should guide school improvement policy. *Educational Evaluation and Policy Analysis, 23*(4), 297–321.

Oatman-Stanford, H. (2018). Demolishing the California dream: How San Francisco planned its own housing crisis. *Collectors Weekly.* https://www.collectorsweekly.com/articles/demolishing-the-california-dream/

Rothstein, R. (2017). *The color of law.* W. W. Norton.

Wilkerson, I. (2010). *The warmth of other suns.* Random House.

Yoon, K. S., Duncan, T., Lee, S. W. Y., Scarloss, B., & Shapley, K. (2007). *Reviewing the evidence on how teacher professional development affects student achievement (Issues & Answers Report, REL 2007–No. 033).* U.S. Department of Education, Institute of Education Sciences, National Center for Education Evaluation and Regional Assistance, Regional Educational Laboratory Southwest. http://ies.ed.gov/ncee/edlabs

Chapter 4

Ball, D. L., & Cohen, D. K. (1999). Developing practice, developing practitioners: Toward a practice-based theory of professional education. In L. Darling Hammond and G. Sykes (Eds.), *Teaching as the learning profession.* Jossey-Bass.

Bossidy, L., & Charan, R. (2002). *Execution: The discipline of getting things done.* Crown Business.

Darling-Hammond, L., & Bransford, J. (2017). *Preparing teachers for a changing world: What teachers should learn and be able to do.* Jossey-Bass.

Gordon, N. (2018). *Disproportionality in student discipline: Connecting policy to research.* Brookings. https://www.brookings.edu/research/disproportionality-in-student-discipline-connecting-policy-to-research/

Jayaram, K., Moffit, A., & Scott, D. (2012). *Breaking the habit of ineffective professional development for teachers.* McKinsey & Company.

Lenger Kang, R. (2020). *Don't take it personally: De-escalating conflicts in the classroom.* Columbia Teachers College. https://cpet.tc.columbia.edu/news-press/dont-take-it-personally-de-escalating-conflicts-in-the-classroom

LiCalsi, C., Osher, D., & Bailey, P. (2021). *An empirical examination of the effects of suspension and suspension severity on behavioral and academic outcomes.* American Institutes for Research.

Schwartz, K. (2017). *A whole school approach to behavior issues.* KQED.

Tucker, J. (2016). In bid to reduce suspensions, schools try de-escalation. *San Francisco Chronicle,* August 19.

Chapter 5

Devine, P., Forscher, P., Austin, A., & Cox, W. (2012). Long-term reduction in implicit race bias: A prejudice habit breaking intervention. *Journal of Experiential Social Psychology, 48*(6), 1267–1278.

DiAngelo, R. (2018). *White fragility.* Beacon Press.

Figlio, D. (2017). *The importance of a diverse teaching force.* Brookings. https://www.brookings.edu/research/the-importance-of-a-diverse-teaching-force/

Gershenson, S., Hart, C. M. D., Lindsay, C., & Papageorge, N. W. (2017). The long-run impacts of same-race teachers. *The IZA Institute of Labor Economics.*

Hammond, Z. (2014). *Culturally responsive teaching & the brain.* Corwin.

Perry, A. (2020). The educational value of a Black teacher. *The Hechinger Report.* https://hechingerreport.org/the-educational-value-of-a-black-teacher/

Robinson, T. E. (2012). *A city within a city: The Black freedom struggle in Grand Rapids, Michigan.* Temple University Press.

Singleton, G. E. (2005). *Courageous conversations about race.* Corwin.

Tatum, B. (1997). *Why are all the Black kids sitting together in the cafeteria?* Basic Books.

Ward, F. (1966, November 24). Mustache ban on Negro students stirs protest. *Jet Magazine,* 18–25.

Wilkerson, I. (2020). *Caste: The origins of our discontents.* Random House.

Chapter 6

Calderón, M., Slavin, R., & Sánchez, M. (2011). Effective instruction for English learners. *The Future of Children, 21*(1), 103–127.

Carnegie, D. (1936). *How to win friends and influence people.* Simon & Schuster.

Castro, J. C. (2015). Visualizing the collective learner through decentralized networks. *International Journal of Education & the Arts, 16*(4), 1–31. http://www.ijea.org/v16n4/

Deheane, S. (2009). *Reading in the brain: The new science of how we read.* Penguin Books.

Drake, G., Ellis, C., Moorer, A., & Walsh, K. (2021). *Teacher prep review: Program diversity and admissions.* National Council on Teacher Quality. www.nctq.org/publications/Teacher-Prep-Review:-Program-Diversity-and-Admissions-2021

Dweck, C. (2006). *Mindset: The new psychology of success.* Random House.

Ganz, M. (2008). *What is public narrative?* https://changemakerspodcast.org/wp-content/uploads/2017/09/Ganz-WhatIsPublic Narrative08.pdf

Safir, S. (2019). *Becoming a warm demander.* ASCD. https://www.ascd.org/el/articles/becoming-a-warm-demander

Wheatley, M., & Dalmau, T. (1983). *Leading for equity: The six circle model.* Dalmau Consulting.

Wheatley, M. (2006). *Leadership and the new science: Discovering order in a chaotic world* (3rd ed.). Berret-Koehler.

Chapter 7

Christman, J. B., Gold, E., & Herold, B. (2005). *Privatization "Philly style."* Research for Action.

Clay, R. A. (2020). Self-care has never been more important. *Monitor on Psychology, 51*(5), 60.

Graham, K. (2013). 10 schools spared in revised closing list. *The Philadelphia Inquirer*, February 19.

hooks, b. (2000). *All about love.* Harper Collins.

Kimeldorf, H., & Penney, R. (1997). "Excluded" by choice: Dynamics of interracial unionism on the Philadelphia waterfront 1910–1930. *International Labor and Working-Class History, 51,* 50–71. http://www.jstor.org/stable/27672354

Newman, R. A. (2008). *Freedom's prophet: Bishop Richard Allen, the AME church, and the Black founding fathers.* New York University Press.

Philadelphia Department of Public Health. (2021). Chronic male unemployment and gun violence in Philadelphia *CHART, 6*(7), 1–7.

Polinco, S., & Back, A. J. (2004). The heart of the matter: Coaching as a vehicle for professional development. *Phi Delta Kappan, 85*(5), 398–400.

Runner's World. (2019). *What is hitting the wall during a marathon and how can you avoid it?* https://www.runnersworld.com/uk/training/marathon/a774858/how-to-avoid-the-wall-and-cope-if-you-hit-it/

Travers, E. (2003). Philadelphia school reform: Historical roots and reflections on the 2002–2003 school year under state takeover. *Penn GSE Perspectives on Urban Education, 2*(2). https://urbanedjournal.gse.upenn.edu/archive/volume-2-issue-2-fall-2003/philadelphia-school-reform-historical-roots-and-reflections-2002-

Zenger, J., & Folkman, J. (2020). What makes a 360-degree review successful? *Harvard Business Review.* https://hbr.org/2020/12/what-makes-a-360-degree-review-successful

Chapter 8

Aguilar, E. (2016). *The art of coaching teams: Building resilient communities that transform schools.* Jossey-Bass.

Bardwick, J. M. (1995). *Danger in the comfort zone.* Amacom.

Brown, B. (2010). *The gifts of imperfection.* Hazelden.

Freire, P. (1972). *Pedagogy of the oppressed.* Herder and Herder.

Knight, J (2008). *Coaching approaches and perspectives.* Corwin Press.

Pearson, F., Rodriguez-Arroyo, S., & Gutiérrez, G. (2021). Cariño pedagogy: A framework of Corazón. *Journal of Curriculum, Teaching, Learning and Leadership in Education, 6*(1), 82–91. https://digitalcommons.unomaha.edu/ctlle/vol6/iss1/7

Valenzuela, A. (2017). *Grow your own educator programs: A review of the literature with an emphasis on equity-based approaches* (pp. 1–17). Instructural Development Research Association, EAC-South.

Chapter 9

Farrington, C. A., Roderick, M., Allensworth, E., Nagaoka, J., & Seneca Keyes, T. (2012). *Teaching adolescents to become learners. The role of noncognitive factors in shaping school performance: A critical review of the research.* The University of Chicago Consortium on Chicago School Research.

Finn, C. E., & Petrilli, M. J. (2007) *The autonomy gap.* Thomas B. Fordham Institute.

Smith, J. (1988). *Off the record: An oral history of popular music.* Grand Central.

Roza, M. (2019). *New education department guidance on supplement-not-supplant: Sorry not sorry.* Brookings. https://www.brookings.edu/blog/brown-center-chalkboard/2019/02/20/new-education-department-guidance-on-supplement-not-supplant-sorry-not-sorry/

Wise, D. (2015). Emerging challenges facing school principals. *National Council of Professors of Educational Administration Leadership Review, 16*(2), 103–115.

Chapter 10

Alexander, M. (2010). *The new Jim Crow: Mass incarceration in the age of color blindness.* The New Press.

Clendinen, D. (1986). White grip on southern schools: Keeping control. *The New York Times,* June 23.

Crenshaw, K. (1991). Mapping the margins: Intersectionality, identity politics, and violence against women of color. *Stanford Law Review, 43*(6), 1241–1299.

Dennis, D. J. Sr. (2014). Unsung heroes of 1964 Mississippi freedom summer. *The Southern Quarterly, 52*(1), 44–50. https://www.muse.jhu.edu/article/567248

Fiester, L. (2010). *Early warning! Why reading by the end of third grade matters.* The Annie E. Casey Foundation.

Hannah-Jones, N. (2021). *The 1619 project.* Random House.

Harris, B. (2019). Reckoning with Mississippi's "segregation academies." *The Hechinger Report.* https://hechingerreport.org/reckoning-with-mississippis-segregation-academies/

hooks, b. (1994). *Teaching to transgress.* Routledge.

Hughes, J. N., West, S. G., Kim, H., & Bauer, S. S. (2018). Effect of early grade retention on school completion: A prospective study. *Journal of Educational Psychology, 110*(7), 974–991. https://doi.org/10.1037/edu0000243

Intelligence Report. (2010). *Mississippi politician's obits skirt unpleasant truths.* Southern Poverty Law Center. https://www.splcenter.org/fighting-hate/intelligence-report/2010/mississippi-politician%E2%80%99s-obits-skirt-unpleasant-truths

Kendi, I. X. (2016). *Stamped from the beginning: The definitive history of racist ideas in America.* Nation Books.

Kunerth, J. (1990). Public education in the south: A story of race, money. *The Orlando Sentinel,* November 4.

Love, B. L. (2019). *We want to do more than survive: Abolitionist teaching and the pursuit of educational freedom.* Beacon Press.

McLaurin, C., Crosby, E., Bishop, J. M., & Civil Rights History Project, US. (2015) Charles McLaurin oral history interview conducted by Emilye Crosby in Indianola, Mississippi. *Library of Congress.* https://www.loc.gov/item/2016655412/

Moye, J. T. (2004). *Let the people decide: Black freedom and white resistance movements in Sunflower County, Mississippi, 1945–1986.* University of North Carolina Press.

Pagani, L., Tremblay, R., Vitaro, F., Boulerice, B., & McDuff, P. (2001). Effects of grade retention on academic performance and behavioral development. *Development and Psychopathology, 13*(2), 297–315.

Richburg, K. (1986). School chief quits to ease race crisis. *The Washington Post,* May 2.

Serwer, A. (2021). *The cruelty is the point.* Random House.

Sitton, C. (1964). Mississippi jails 106 court pickets. *The New York Times,* July 17.

Wallace-Wells, B. (2021). How a conservative activist invented the conflict over critical race theory. *The New Yorker.* https://www.newyorker.com/news/annals-of-inquiry/how-a-conservative-activist-invented-the-conflict-over-critical-race-theory

Chapter 11

Bryk, A. (2020). *Improvement in action.* Harvard Education Press.

Calkins, A., Guenther, W., Belfiore, G., & Lash, D. (2007). *The turnaround challenge.* Mass Insight Education.

Lester, P. (2018). *Evidence-based comprehensive school improvement.* Social Innovation Research Center.

Rich, M. J., & Stoker, R. P. (2010). Rethinking empowerment: Evidence from local empowerment zone programs. *Urban Affairs Review, 45*(6), 775–796. https://doi.org/10.1177/1078087410366530

Sun, M., Penner, E. K., & Loeb, S. (2017). Resource- and approach-driven multidimensional change: Three-year effects of school improvement grants. *American Educational Research Journal, 54*(4), 607–643. https://doi.org/10.3102/0002831217695790

Trujillo, T., Woulfin, S., & Jarrell, T. (2010). *An external evaluation of partners in school innovation: A final report on the findings.* UC Berkeley.

UCLA Center X. (2015). *Evaluation report to partners in school innovation.* UCLA Center X Northeast Region.

Index

A SAGE Publishing Company

Helping educators make the greatest impact

CORWIN HAS ONE MISSION: to enhance education through intentional professional learning.

We build long-term relationships with our authors, educators, clients, and associations who partner with us to develop and continuously improve the best evidence-based practices that establish and support lifelong learning.

SUPPORTING
educators to grow as change agents

partners
IN SCHOOL INNOVATION

If you're a teacher, instructional coach, or leader working for educational equity, you are not alone! We engage with educators in some of the country's most challenged neighborhoods who understand the joys and struggles of transforming schools into lively, loving, learning communities.

Many of these educators are already gathering in a virtual community of practice to support each other in growing as leaders of change. Together, we work on the technical and relational skills, as well as the values and mindsets, needed to transform schools into more vibrant places to teach and learn. The community includes educators at all career stages, and we welcome those who show up as a crew of one or a team of hundreds. Please visit our website to learn more.

www.partnersinschools.org

EQDN22773

CORWIN